AUSONIUS

II

AUSONIUS

WITH AN ENGLISH TRANSLATION BY
HUGH G. EVELYN WHITE, M.A.
SOMETIME SCHOLAR OF WADHAM COLLEGE, OXFORD

IN TWO VOLUMES

II

WITH THE *EUCHARISTICUS* OF
PAULINUS PELLÆUS

CAMBRIDGE, MASSACHUSETTS
HARVARD UNIVERSITY PRESS
LONDON
WILLIAM HEINEMANN LTD
MCMLXXXV

American ISBN 0-674-99127-3
British ISBN 0 434 99115 5

First printed 1921
Reprinted 1949, 1961, 1967, 1985

Printed in Great Britain

CONTENTS

AUSONIUS

OPUSCULA

D. MAGNI AUSONII

OPUSCULA

LIBER XVIII

EPISTULARUM

I.—SYMMACHUS AUSONIO

MERUM mihi gaudium eruditionis tuae scripta tri-
buerunt, quae Capuae locatus accepi. erat quippe in
his oblita Tulliano melle festivitas et sermonis mei
non tam vera, quam blanda laudatio. quid igitur
magis mirer, sententiae incertus addubito, ornamenta
oris an pectoris tui. quippe ita facundia antistas ce-
teris, ut sit formido rescribere; ita benigne nostra
conprobas, ut libeat non tacere. si plura de te prae-
dicem, videbor mutuum scabere et magis imitator tui
esse adloquii quam probator. simul quod ipse nihil
ostentandi gratia facis, verendum est genuina in te
bona tamquam adfectata laudare. unum hoc tamen
a nobis indubitata veritate cognosce, neminem esse
mortalium quem prae te diligam; sic vadatum me
honorabili amore tenuisti.

AUSONIUS

BOOK XVIII

THE EPISTLES

I.—SYMMACHUS TO AUSONIUS

YOUR learned pages, which I received while stay-
ing at Capua, brought me sheer delight. For there
was in them a certain gaiety overlaid with honey
from Tully's hive, and some eulogy on my discourse
flattering rather than deserved. And so I am at a
loss to decide which to admire the more—the graces
of your diction or of your disposition. Indeed you
so far surpass all others in eloquence that I fear to
write in reply; you so generously approve my essays
that I am glad not to keep silence. If I say more
in your praise, I shall seem to be "scratching your
back" and to be copying more than complimenting
your address to me. Moreover, since you do nothing
consciously for the sake of display, I must beware
of praising your natural good qualities as though
they were studied. This one thing, however, I must
tell you as an absolute fact—that there is no man
alive whom I love more than you, so deeply pledged
in honest affection have you always held me.

Set in eo mihi verecundus nimio plus videre, quod libelli tui arguis proditorem. nam facilius est ardentes favillas ore comprimere quam luculenti operis servare secretum. cum semel a te profectum carmen est, ius omne posuisti: oratio publicata res libera est. an vereris aemuli venena lectoris, ne libellus tuus admorsu duri dentis uratur? tibi uni ad hoc locorum nihil gratia praestitit aut dempsit invidia. ingratis scaevo cuique proboque laudabilis es. proinde cassas dehinc seclude formidines et indulge stilo, ut saepe prodaris. certe aliquod didascalicum seu protrepticum nostro quoque nomini carmen adiudica. fac periculum silentii mei, quod etsi tibi exhibere opto, tamen spondere non audeo. novi ego, quae sit prurigo emuttiendi operis, quod probaris. nam quodam pacto societatem laudis adfectat, qui aliena bene dicta primus enuntiat. ea propter in comoediis summatim quidem gloriam scriptores tulerunt, Roscio tamen atque Ambivio ceterisque actoribus fama non defuit.

Ergo tali negotio expende otium tuum et novis voluminibus ieiunia nostra sustenta. quod si iactantiae fugax garrulum indicem pertimescis, praesta etiam tu silentium mihi, ut tuto simulem nostra esse, quae scripseris. vale.

---

[1] Q. Roscius Gallus, a freedman of Lanuvium, was raised to equestrian rank by Sulla and defended by Cicero in a speech still extant. His fame as a comic actor made his

THE EPISTLES

But in this I think you are excessively modest, that you complain of me for playing traitor to your book. For it is easier to hold hot coals in one's mouth than to keep the secret of a brilliant work. Once you have let a poem out of your hands, you have renounced all your rights : a speech delivered is common property. Or do you fear the venom of some jealous reader, and that your book may smart from the snap of his rude fangs ? You are the one man who up to now has owed nothing to partiality, lost nothing through jealousy. Involuntarily everyone, perverse or honest, finds you admirable. Therefore banish henceforth your groundless fears, and let your pen run on so that you may often be betrayed. At any rate assign some didactic or hortatory poem to my name also. Run the risk of my keeping silence ; and though I desire to give you proof of it, yet I dare not guarantee it. Well I know how I itch to give voice to your work when you are so popular. For somehow he secures a partnership in the glory who first pronounces another's neat phrases. That is why in comedy authors have won but slight renown, while Roscius, Ambivius,[1] and the other players have had no lack of fame.

So spend your leisure in such occupation and relieve my famine with fresh books. But if in your flight from vainglory you dread a chattering informer, do you also guarantee me your silence, that I may safely pretend that what you have written is mine ! Farewell.

name proverbial (*cp.* Horace, *Epist.* II. i. 82). Ambivius was intimately associated with Terence, in most of whose plays he acted.

5

AUSONIUS

Modo intellego, quam mellea res sit oratio; quam
delinifica et quam suada facundia. persuasisti mihi,
quod epistulae meae aput Capuam tibi redditae con-
cinnatio inhumana non esset; set hoc non diutius,
quam dum epistulam tuam legi, quae me blanditiis
inhiantem tuis velut suco nectaris delibuta perducit.
ubi enim chartulam pono et me ipsum interrogo,
tum absinthium meum resipit et circumlita melle
tuo pocula deprehendo. si vero, id quod saepe facio,
ad epistulam tuam redii, rursus inlicior: et rursum
ille suavissimus, ille floridus tui sermonis adflatus
deposita lectione vanescit et testimonii pondus pro-
hibet inesse dulcedini. hoc me velut aerius bratteae
fucus aut picta nebula non longius, quam dum vi-
detur, oblectat chamaeleontis bestiolae vice, quae de
subiectis sumit colorem. aliud sentio ex epistula
tua, aliud ex conscientia mea. et tu me audes fa-
cundissimorum hominum laude dignari? tu, inquam,
mihi ista, qui te ultra emendationem omnium pro-
tulisti? quisquamne ita nitet, ut conparatus tibi
non sordeat? quis ita Aesopi venustatem, quis so-
phisticas Isocratis conclusiones, quis ad enthyme-
mata Demosthenis aut opulentiam Tullianam aut
proprietatem nostri Maronis accedat? quis ita ad-
fectet singula, ut tu imples omnia? quid enim aliud

---

[1] A mode of administering bitter medicine. *cp.* Lucretius.

6

THE EPISTLES

II.—Ausonius to Symmachus

Now I understand how honey-sweet is the power of speech, how enchanting and persuasive a thing is eloquence! You have made me believe that my letter delivered to you at Capua was not a barbarous compilation; but this only for so long as I am actually reading your letter, which is so spread, as it were, with the syrop of your nectar as to over-persuade me while I hang agape over its allurements. For as soon as I lay down your page and question myself, back comes the taste of my own wormwood, and I realize that the cup is smeared round with your honey.[1] If indeed—as I often do—I return to your letter, I am enticed again: and then again that most soothing, that most fragrant perfume of your words dies away when I have done reading, and denies that sweetness carries weight as evidence. Like the flaunting glitter of tinsel or a tinted cloud, it delights me only for so long as I see it—like that little creature the chameleon, which takes its colour from whatever is beneath it. Your letter makes me feel one thing, my own conscience another. And do you venture to count me worthy of praise belonging to the most eloquent? Do you, I say, speak so of me—you who soar above all writers in faultlessness? What author is there so brilliant, but he appears unpolished by comparison with you? Who like you can approach the charm of Aesop, the logical deductions of Isocrates, the arguments of Demosthenes, the richness of Tully, or the felicity of our own Maro? Who can aspire to such success in any one of these, as you fully attain in them all? For what else are you but the concentrated

es, quam ex omni bonarum artium ingenio collecta perfectio?

Haec, domine mi fili Symmache, non vereor, ne in te blandius dicta videantur esse quam verius. et expertus es fidem meam mentis atque dictorum, dum in comitatu degimus ambo aevo dispari, ubi tu veteris militiae praemia tiro meruisti, ego tirocinium iam veteranus exercui. in comitatu tibi verus fui, nedum me peregre existimes conposita fabulari. in comitatu, inquam, qui frontes hominum aperit, mentes tegit, ibi me et parentem et amicum et, si quid utroque carius est, cariorem fuisse sensiti. set abeamus ab his: ne ista haec conmemoratio ad illam Sosiae formidinem videatur accedere.

Illud, quod paene praeterii, qua adfectatione addidisti, ut ad te didascalicum aliquod opusculum aut sermonem protrepticum mitterem? ego te docebo docendus adhuc, si essem id aetatis, ut discerem? aut ego te vegetum atque alacrem commonebo? eadem opera et Musas hortabor, ut canant, et maria, ut effluant, et auras, ut vigeant, et ignes, ut caleant, admonebo: et, si quid invitis quoque nobis natura fit, superfluus instigator agitabo. sat est unius erroris quod aliquid meorum me paenitente vulgatum est, quod bona fortuna in manus amicorum incidit. nam si contra id evenisset, nec tu mihi persuaderes placere me posse.

---

[1] *cp.* Cic. *Pro Planco,* vi. 16: tabella quae frontes aperit hominum, mentes tegit.

essence of every great mind in the realm of the liberal arts?

My lord, my son Symmachus, I do not fear that you may think I speak thus of you more smoothly than truly. Indeed, you have proved how truthful I am both in thought and word while the two of us, so ill-matched in years, lived at court, where you, a recruit, earned a veteran's pay, while I, already a veteran, went through my recruit's training. At court I was truthful with you: much less when I am away from it should you think I tell stories. At court, I repeat, which bares the face and veils the heart[1]—there you felt that I was a father and a friend and, if anything can be dearer than either, then something dearer still. But let us leave this matter, lest such a reminder seem too like the fear felt by Sosias.[2]

Now for that matter which I almost passed over. What mock humility of yours is this, that you add a request for me to send you some didactic work or hortatory discourse? Shall I teach you when I myself need teaching[3] were I of an age to learn? Shall I counsel you, whose mind is so alert and vigorous? As well exhort the Muses to sing and advise the waves to flow, the breezes to blow freely, fire to give heat, and where anything occurs naturally, whether we will or no, to urge it forward with superfluous zeal! Enough this one mistake that a work of mine has, to my regret, become public property; though by good fortune it has fallen into the hands of friends. For had it been otherwise, not even you would convince me that I can give satisfaction.

[2] Terence, *Andria* 43 f., nam istaec commemoratio Quasi exprobratio est inmemori benefici.
[3] Horace, *Epist.* I. xvii. 3, disce docendus adhuc.

Haec ad litteras tuas responsa sint : cetera, quae
noscere aves, conpendi faciam ; sic quoque iam longa
est epistula.   Iulianum tamen familiarem domus
vestrae, si quid de nobis percontandum arbitraris,
adlego ; simul admoneo, ut, cum causam adventus
eius agnoveris, iuves studium, quod ex parte fovisti.
vale.

III.—SYMMACHUS AUSONIO

ETSI plerumque vera est aput parentes praedi-
catio filiorum, nescio quo tamen pacto detrimentum
meriti sui patiatur, dum personarum spectare gratiam
iudicatur.   quaero igitur incertus animi, quae mihi
nunc potissimum super viro honorabili Thalassio
genero tuo verba sumenda sint.   si parce decora
morum eius adtingam, liventi similis existimabor :
si iuste persequar, ero proximus blandienti.   imitabor
igitur Sallustiani testimonii castigationem.   habes
virum dignum te et per te familia consulari, quem
fortuna honoris parti maiorem beneficiis suis rep-
perit, emendatio animi et sanctitas potioribus iam
paravit.   vale.

Let that be my answer to your letter: with the other matters which you desire to know, I will make short work: even so this letter is already long. However, I depute Julian, an intimate of your household, to answer any questions you care to ask concerning me: at the same time I urge that, when you learn his reason for coming, you aid him in a purpose which to some extent you have already favoured. Farewell.

III.—SYMMACHUS TO AUSONIUS

ALTHOUGH praise bestowed upon their children is generally accepted as gospel by parents, yet it is somehow discounted when it is considered to have an eye to the favour of the great. I am at a stand, therefore, and ask what words I shall choose especially at this time in speaking of that worshipful man, Thalassius, your son-in-law. If I touch sparingly upon the graces of his character, I shall be thought to show signs of jealousy: if I duly enlarge upon them, I shall be next door to a flatterer. I will therefore copy Sallust[1] in his rigid mode of giving evidence. You have as son-in-law a man worthy of you, and, through you, of a consular family—one whom Fortune in her bestowal of distinctions has found too great to need her benefits, whom a faultless nature and stainless character have already furnished with higher gifts. Farewell.

[1] *Jugurtha*, ix. 3: habes virum te dignum et avo suo Masinissa.

AUSONIUS

Tandem eluctati retinacula blanda morarum
　　Burdigalae molles liquimus inlecebras.
Santonicamque urbem vicino accessimus agro :
　　quod tibi si gratum est, optime Paule, proba.
cornipedes rapiant inposta petorrita mulae ;　　　　5
　　vel cisio triiugi, si placet, insilias,
vel celerem mannum vel ruptum terga veraedum
　　conscendas, propere dum modo iam venias ;
instantis revocant quia nos sollemnia Paschae
　　libera nec nobis [1] est mora desidiae.　　　　10
perfer in excursu vel teriuga milia epodon
　　vel falsas lites, quas schola vestra serit.
nobiscum invenies nullas, quia liquimus istic
　　nugarum veteres cum sale relliquias. [2]

V.—Ausonius Paulo

Ostrea nobilium cenis sumptuque nepotum
cognita diversoque maris deprensa profundo,
aut refugis nudata vadis aut scrupea subter
antra et muriceis scopulorum mersa lacunis,
quae viridis muscus, quae decolor alga recondit,　　5
quae testis concreta suis ceu saxa cohaerent,
quae mutata loco, pingui mox consita limo,
nutrit secretus conclusae uliginis umor,
enumerare iubes, vetus o mihi Paule sodalis,
adsuefacte meis ioculari carmine nugis.　　　　10

[1] vobis, _G_.
[2] _Z_ adds : Vale valere si voles me vel vola.

---

[1] The word is said to be a Celtic compound : _petor_ = four,
rit = wheel.　　　[2] A conveyance with two wheels.

THE EPISTLES

IV.—Ausonius to Axius Paulus the Rhetorician, Greeting

At last, having struggled free from delay's seductive toils, I have left Bordeaux's soft enticements and on a neighbouring farm dwell nigh the town of Saintes: if this pleases you, friend Paulus, give me proof of it. Let horn-hoofed mules whirl hither a harnessed four-wheeled car,[1] or, if you please, jump in a three-horse gig,[2] or mount a cob, or else a back-broken hack, if only you come quickly; for approaching Easter's rites summon me back, nor am I free to linger idly here. Bring over on your jaunt thrice a thousand lyrics or the feigned cases[3] which your pupils weave. With me you will find none, for I have left yonder the old remnants of my trifles together with my wit.

V.—Ausonius to Paulus

Of oysters famed through the lavish feasts of high-born prodigals, whether dredged from the depths of various seas or left bare by ebbing shallows, or sheltered beneath rugged caves and in jagged clefts amid the rocks, those which green moss, which stained seaweed hides, whose welded shells are firm-shut as the stones, which when removed[4] from their home and planted in rich ooze are fattened by the inward moisture of the packed slime;—of these you bid me tell all the kinds, Paulus, my old comrade, made used to my trifling by sportive

[3] *sc.* the declamations (in the form of imaginary lawsuits) composed as exercises in the rhetorical schools.
[4] *i.e.* transplanted to specially prepared beds for fattening: *cp.* Pliny, *N.H.* xxxii. 6.

adgrediar; quamvis curam non ista senilem
sollicitent frugique viro dignanda putentur.
nam mihi non Saliare epulum, non aura dapalis,
qualem Penelopae nebulonum mensa procorum
Alcinoique habuit nitidae cutis uncta iuventus.[1]   15
enumerabo tamen famam testesque secutus
pro studiis hominum semper diversa probantum.

   Set mihi prae cunctis lectissima, quae Medulorum
educat Oceanus, quae Burdigalensia nomen
usque ad Caesareas tulit admiratio mensas,   20
non laudata minus, nostri quam gloria vini.
haec inter cunctas palmam meruere priorem,
omnibus ex longo cedentibus: ista et opimi
visceris et nivei dulcique tenerrima suco
miscent aequoreum tenui sale tincta saporem.   25
proxima sint quamvis, sunt longe proxima multo
ex intervallo, quae Massiliensia, portum
quae Narbo ad Veneris nutrit; cultuque carentia
Hellespontiaci quae protegit aequor Abydi;
vel quae Baianis pendent fluitantia palis;   30
Santonico quae tecta salo; quae nota Genonis;
aut Eborae mixtus pelago quae protegit amnis,
ut multo iaceant algarum obducta recessu:
aspera quae testis et dulcia, farris opimi.

   Sunt et Aremorici qui laudent ostrea ponti,   35
et quae Pictonici legit accola litoris, et quae
mira Caledoniis nonnunquam detegit aestus.

---

[1] *cp.* Horace, *Epist.* I. ii. 28 f.

[1] The Salii, priests of Mars, were famous for their banquets.
[2] *cp.* Horace, *Epist.* I. ii. 28 f. : sponsi Penelopae nebu-
lones Alcinoique In cute curanda plus aequo operata iuventus.

verse. I will approach the task, albeit the theme
stir not an old man's zest nor be thought fit for the
notice of a frugal man. For I have no Salian fare,[1]
no repasts of savour such as had the banquets of
Penelope's wastrel suitors or of the sleek and scented
youth about Alcinoüs.[2] Yet will I tell o'er the tale,
following report and testimony according to the tastes
of men ever diverse in judgment.

[18] Howbeit, for me the choicest above all are those
bred by the Ocean of the Meduli,[3] which, named
after Bordeaux, high esteem hath raised even to
Caesar's board, no less renowned than are our famous
wines. These amongst all have won the pride of
place, the rest lagging far behind : these be of sub-
stance both full fat and snowy white, and with their
sweet juice most delicately mingle some flavour of
the sea touched with a fine taste of salt. Next,
though next at distance of long interval, are the
oysters of Marseilles, which Narbo feeds near Venus'
haven ; [4] and those which, untended, the Hellespon-
tine wave shelters at Abydos ; or those which cling
afloat to the piles of Baiae ; those washed by the
Santonic surge ; those known to the Genoni ; or
those harboured by Ebora's [5] stream where it joins
the sea, so that they lie covered with a deep bed of
weed : rough of shell are these, and sweet and rich
of meat.

[35] There are, too, such as praise the oysters of the
Armoric deep, and those which shoremen gather on
Pictonic coasts, and which the tide sometimes leaves
bare for the wondering Caledonian.[6] Add those

---

[3] The people of Médoc.   [4] Port Vendres.
[5] Ebora (or Libertas Iulia), on the Guadalquivir.
[6] *cp. Mosella.* 68 ff. The reference is no doubt to the
pearl-oysters of Britain, on which see Tacitus, *Agric.* xii.

accedunt, quae fama recens Byzantia subter
litora et insana generata Propontidis acta
Promoti celebrata ducis de nomine laudat.   40
    Haec tibi non vates, non historicus neque toto
orbe vagus conviva loquor, set tradita multis,
ut solitum, quotiens dextrae invitatio mensae
sollicitat lenem comi sermone Lyaeum.
haec non per vulgum mihi cognita perque popinas 45
aut parasitorum collegia Plautinorum,
set festos quia saepe dies partim ipse meorum
excolui inque vicem conviva vocatus adivi,
natalis si forte fuit sollemnis amico
coniugiove dapes aut sacra repotia patrum,   50
audivi meminique bonos laudare frequentes.

VI.—Invitatio ad Paulum

Si qua fides falsis umquam est adhibenda poetis
    nec plasma semper adlinunt,
Paule, Camenarum celeberrime Castaliarum
    alumne quondam, nunc pater,
aut avus, aut proavis antiquior, ut fuit olim   5
    Tartesiorum regulus :
intemerata tibi maneant promissa, memento.
    Phoebus iubet verum loqui :

---

¹ An officer of Theodosius I. who defeated the Gruthungi
on the Danube in 386, served against Maximus in 388, and
was consul in 389. He was assassinated c. 391 A.D.
    ² The meaning is : I have gained my knowledge partly at
feasts given by myself and partly at those to which I have
been invited.

which, reared below Byzantium's shores and the
vexed beaches of Propontis, late-born renown now
honours with distinction after the name of Promotus
the general.[1]

[41] These I tell thee, no bard, no historian, nor yet a
world-wandering gourmand, but things I have heard
from many, as wont is, whenever a challenge from
a table on the right provokes gentle Lyaeus with
friendly converse. These are known to me not from
common company nor from taverns, nor from the
guilds of Plautine parasites, but because I myself
have often celebrated festal days, sometimes with
gatherings of my friends,[2] or going in turn to ban-
quets as a bidden guest, when perchance a friend
observed a birthday or a marriage feast, or a
carouse[3] sanctioned by our fathers' custom : there
I have heard many a worthy man praise these, and
I remember them.

VI.—An Invitation to Paulus

If any trust is ever to be placed in the feigned
words of poets, and if they scrawl not ever fiction,
Paulus—once the most famous child of the Castalian
Camenae, now their father or grandfather or yet
more ancient than a great-grandfather, as was of old
the kinglet of Tartessus [4]—remember to keep your
promises inviolate. Phoebus bids us speak truth :

---

[3] *Repotia* were drinking bouts held on the day after any
festival.
[4] *sc.* Argantonius, king of Tartessus, who reigned eighty,
and lived one hundred and twenty years (Hdt. i. 163 : *cp.*
Cicero, *de Sen.* 69). But Silius Ital. (iii. 397) makes him live
three hundred years, and observes : "rex proavis fuit
humani ditissimus aevi."

etsi Pierias patitur lirare sorores,
    numquam ipse torquet αὔλακα.   10
te quoque ne pigeat consponsi foederis : et iam
    citus veni remo aut rota,
aequoris undosi qua multiplicata recursu
    Garumna pontum provocat,
aut iteratarum qua glarea trita viarum   15
    fert militarem ad Blaviam.
nos etenim primis sanctum post Pascha diebus
    avemus agrum visere.
Nam populi coetus et compita sordida rixis
    fastidientes cernimus   20
angustas fervere vias et congrege volgo
    nomen plateas perdere.
turbida congestis referitur vocibus echo :
    " Tene, feri, duc, da, cave ! "
sus lutulenta fugit, rabidus canis impete saevo   25
    et impares plaustro boves.
nec prodest penetrale domus et operta subire :
    per tecta clamores meant.
haec et quae possunt placidos offendere mores,
    cogunt relinqui moenia,   30
dulcia secreti repetantur ut otia ruris,
    nugis amoena seriis ;
tempora disponas ubi tu tua iusque tuum sit,
    ut nil agas vel quod voles.
ad quae si properas, tota cum merce tuarum   35
    veni Camenarum citus :
dactylicos, elegos, choriambum carmen, epodos,
    socci et coturni musicam

---

[1] *cp. Ordo Urb. Nob.* xx. 15, where however Ausonius
contradicts this reflexion on the " broadways " of Bordeaux.
    [2] Horace, *Epist.* ii. ii. 75 : hac rabiosa fugit canis, hac
lutulenta ruit sus.

although he suffers the Pierian sisters to swerve from the line, he himself never twists a furrow. You also must not regret your plighted bond; come quickly now by river or by road, either where Garonne, swelled with the flood-tide of the billowy deep, challenges the main, or where the beaten gravel of the relaid road leads to the garrison of Blaye. For in the first days after holy Easter I long to visit my estate.

[19] For I am weary at the sight of throngs of people, the vulgar brawls at the cross-roads, the narrow lanes a-swarm, and the broadways belying their name [1] for the rabble herded there. Confused Echo resounds with a babel of cries: "Hold!"—"Strike!"—"Lead!"—"Give!"—"Look out!" Here is a mucky sow in flight, there a mad dog in fell career,[2] there oxen too weak for the waggon. No use to steal into the inner chamber and the recesses of your home: the cries penetrate through the house.[3] These, and what else can shock the orderly, force me to leave the walled city and seek again the sweet peace of the retired country and the delights of trifling seriously; and there you may arrange your own hours and have the right to do nothing or else what you will. If you haste after these joys, come quickly with all the wares of your Camenae: [4] dactyls, elegiacs, choriambics, lyrics, comedy and tragedy—pack them all in

---

[3] Lucr. *de Rerum Nat.* i. 354: inter saepta meant voces et clausa domorum Transvolitant.

[4] Horace, *Od.* iv. xii. 21: ad quae si properas gaudia cum tua velox merce veni.

carpentis impone tuis: nam tota supellex
  vatum piorum chartea est.   40
nobiscum invenies κατ' ἐναντία, si libet uti
  non Poena [1] sed Graeca fide.

VII.—Rescriptum Paulo Suo

Versus meos utili et conscio sibi pudore celatos
carmine tuo et sermone praemissis dum putas elici,
repressisti. nam qui ipse facundus et musicus editi-
onis alienae prolectat audaciam, consilio, quo suadet,
exterret. tegat oportet auditor doctrinam suam, qui
volet ad dicendum sollicitare trepidantem, nec eme-
rita adversum tirunculos arma concutiat veterana
calliditas. sensit hoc Venus de pulchritudinis palma
diu ambiguo ampliata iudicio. pudenter enim ut
apud patrem velata certaverat nec deterrebat aemu-
las ornatus aequalis; at postquam in pastoris ex-
amen deducta est lis dearum, qualis emerserat mari
aut cum Marte convenerat, et consternavit arbitrum
et contendentium certamen oppressit. ergo nisi De-
lirus tuus in re tenui non tenuiter laboratus opuscula
mea, quae promi studueras, retardasset, iam dudum
ego ut palmes audacior in hibernas adhuc auras im-
probum germen egissem, periculum iudicii gravis

---

[1] _T_ (poema, _M:_ penna, _ed. princ._): προῖκα, _Peiper_ (after
Weil.).

---

[1] Plaut. _Asin._ 199: cetera quae volumus uti, Graeca mer-
camur fide—_i.e._ for cash down. The meaning is: I will
repay you, not with vague (Punic) promises, but poem for
poem.

your carriage, for the devout poet's baggage is all paper. With me you will find a *quid pro quo* if you please to trade on Greek,[1] not Punic, terms.

VII.—A Reply to his Friend Paulus

As for my verses, which a salutary and self-conscious sense of shame had sent into hiding, while you thought you were enticing them forth by sending forward your own poetry and prose, you have driven them back. For when one who is himself eloquent and a poet tries to lure an author to venture on publication, he frightens the other out of the purpose which he advocates. A listener ought to conceal his own skill if he wishes to induce a nervous orator to speak, and a practised veteran should not brandish in the face of mere recruits weapons he has wielded through a full term of service. Venus understood this in the matter of the prize for beauty so long withheld for lack of a decisive verdict. For it was modestly arrayed, when in the presence of her father, that she had contended, and her similar adornment did not discourage her rivals; but when the suit of the goddesses was brought down for a shepherd's decision, she appeared as when she had risen from the sea or had met with Mars, both overwhelming the judge and crushing her competitors' rivalry. And so, had not your *Crazy Man*, slight in theme though not in finish,[2] checked my poor little works which you were eager to have brought out to light, I should long since, like a too venturesome shoot, have put forth an impudent bud in the still wintry air, only to run

[1] *cp.* Virgil, *Georgics*, iv. 6.

inconsulta festinatione subiturus. denique pisonem,
quem tollenonem existimo proprie a philologis ap-
pellatum, adhibere, ut iubebas, recenti versuum
tuorum lectione non ausus, ea quae tibi iam cursim
fuerant recitata, transmisi. etenim hoc poposcisti
atque id ego malui, tu ut tua culpa ad eundem
lapidem bis offenderes, ego autem, quaecumque
fortuna esset, semel erubescerem.

Vide, mi Paule, quam ineptum lacessieris in verbis
rudem, in eloquendo hiulcum, a propositis discre-
pantem, in versibus concinnationis expertem, in ca-
villando nec natura venustum nec arte conditum,
diluti salis, fellis ignavi, nec de mimo planipedem
nec de comoediis histrionem. ac nisi haec a nobis
missa ipse lecturus esses, etiam de pronuntiatione
rideres. nunc commodiore fato sunt, quod, licet
apud nos genuina, aput te erunt adoptiva.

> Vinum[1] cum biiugo parabo plaustro
> primo tempore Santonos vehendum,
> ovum tu quoque[2] passeris marini,
> quod nunc promus ait procul relictum
> in fundo patriae Bigerritanae,

> *　　　*　　　*　　　*　　　*

[1] So *T*: virum, *Peiper* and other MSS.
[2] So *Z*: coque, *Scaliger*, *Peiper*.

---

[1] A beam working on a pivot, by which a cage full of
men was raised to the height of the enemy's walls in a siege.
Ausonius suggests that to send his complete collection
would be like employing such an engine—like our "heavy
artillery."

the risk of heavy censure for my ill-advised haste. In short, to bring into play, as you bade me, the "swipe" [1]—which, I fancy, is correctly termed by scholars a "swing-beam '—I did not dare after lately reading your verses; but I send you those pieces which have already been hurriedly recited to you. For indeed this you demand and I prefer; so that you, through your own fault, may stumble twice over the same stone, while I, whate'er befall, may blush but once.

See, my dear Paulus, what a sorry poet you have provoked!—in wording harsh, in utterance halting, wandering from his points, in versifying without elegance, in satire without natural grace or spice of art, watery in wit, sluggish in spleen, no true performer in mime,[2] no actor in comedy. And were not you yourself to read these pieces I send, you would laugh at my delivery also. As it is, theirs is a more kindly destiny, because though begotten by me they will be adopted by you.

So soon as I shall get wine carried to Saintes by two-horse cart, do you also get your cup of ostrich-shell which your steward says was left on your farm far away in your native Bigorre,[3]

*　　　*　　　*　　　*　　　*

[2] In mime neither slipper (as in comedy) nor buskin (as in tragedy) was worn.

[3] In the Dépt. des Hautes Pyrénées. The meaning of the verses is (apparently) that Ausonius is to get in a cart-load of wine, while Paulus is to come with a large cup made from an ostrich's ("sea sparrow's") shell to help to drink it up.

AUSONIUS

VIII.—ΑΥΣΟΝΙΟΣ ΠΑΥΛΩΙ

Ἑλλαδικῆς μέτοχον μούσης Latiaeque camenae
Ἄξιον Αὐσόνιος sermone adludo bilingui.
  Musae, quid facimus? τί κεναῖσιν ἐφ' ἐλπίσιν αὕτως
ludimus ἀφραδίῃσιν ἐν ἤματι γηράσκοντες;
Σαντονικοῖς κάμποισιν, ὅποι κρύος ἄξενόν ἐστιν,   5
erramus gelidοτρομεροὶ καὶ frigdopoetae,
Πιερίδων τενεροπλοκάμων θεράποντες inertes.
πάντα δ' ἔχει παγετός τε pedum καὶ κρουσμὸς ὀδόντων,
θαλπωρὴ quia nulla φοκοῦ χιονώδει χώρῃ,
et duplicant frigus ψυχρὰ carmina μητιόωντες.   10
ἀρχόμενος δ' ἄρα μηνὶ νέῳ Ιανοῦ τε calendaις
primitias Paulo nostrae πέμψωμεν ἀοιδῆς.
  Μνημοσύνης κρηδεμνοκόμου πολυcantica τέκνα,
ἐννέα verbosae κριννοστέφανοί τε puellae,
ἔνθ' ἄγε μοι πολυrisa ἔπη, σκουρώδεα μολπήν,   15
frontibus ὑμετέραις πτέρινον praeferte triumphum—
ὑμᾶς γὰρ καλέω σκαιὸς Διονυσοποιητής—
Παύλῳ ἐφαρμόσσαιτε μεμιγμενοβάρβαρον ᾠδήν.
οὐ γάρ μοι θέμις ἐστὶν in hac regione μένοντι
Ἄξιον ab nostris ἐπιδεύεα εἶνε καμήναις·   20
κεῖνος ἐμοὶ πάντων μέτοχος, qui seria nostra,
qui ioca παντοδαπῇ novit tractare παλαίστρῃ.
καὶ νῦν sepositus μοναχῷ ἐνὶ rure Κρεβέννου
ἀσταφύλῳ ἐνὶ χώρῳ habet θυμαλγέα λέσχην
οὔτε φίλοις ἑτάροις nec mensae accommodus ulli.   25
otia θελξινόοις aeger συμμέμφεται Μούσαις.

---

[1] No attempt can here be made to reproduce this macaronic verse.
[2] Ἄξιος is of course used in a double sense, as proper name and epithet.

24

THE EPISTLES

VIII.—Ausonius to Paulus [1]

To Axius, worthy [2] participant in Hellenic poësy and Roman song, I, Ausonius, send playful greeting in a medley of the two tongues.

[3] Muses, what do we? Wherefore with empty hopes do I sport idly, heedless of growing older day by day? O'er the Santonic plains, where frost accords chill welcome, I wander shivering with cold, a frigid bard indeed, a servant unemployed of the soft-tressed Pierides. Cold feet and chattering of teeth are each man's lot, because no hearth gives warmth in this snowy country, and men redouble all the cold with meditating their frigid verse. Yet even so, at the beginning of the new month and on the first of January let me send to Paulus the first-fruits of my song.

[13] Ye songful children of Mnemosyne with tresses coiffed, nine wordy maids with locks begarlanded, come now with chant ridiculous and macaronic [3] lay, wear wingèd triumph on your brows—for 'tis on you I call, a clumsy bottle-bard—compose for Paulus some mixed barbarian strain! For I may not, albeit tarrying in these parts, leave worthy Axius lacking my poësy. He shareth all with me, and knoweth all sorts of tricks for wrestling with my serious and my jesting verse. And now retired in the lonely country of Crebennus he hath his heart-vexing dwelling in a grapeless land, remote alike from his dear friends and from all dinner-tables. There, sick at heart, he chides the heart-soothing Muses for his loneliness.

[3] = Lat. *scurrilis*, from *scurra*, a dandy, fop, macaroni or buffoon.

Iam satis, ὦ φίλε Παῦλε, πόνου ἀπεπειρήθημεν
ἔν τε forῳ causaις τε καὶ ingrataισι καθέδραις,
ῥητορικοῖς λυνδοῖσι, καὶ ἔπλετο οὐδὲν ὄνειαρ·
ἀλλ' ἤδη κεῖνος μὲν ἅπας iuvenalios ἱδρὼς   30
ἐκκέχυται μελέων, τρομερὴ δὲ πάρεστι senectus
καὶ minus in sumptum δαπάνας levis arca ministrat.
οὐ γὰρ ἔχει ἀπάλαμνος ἀνὴρ κουαιστώδεα lucrον,
κλεινικὸς οὔτε γέρων χρυσέην ἐργάζετ' ἀμοιβήν.
aequanimus quod si fueris et πάντα vel αἰνεῖν   35
malueris, λήθη πόνου ἔσσεται ἠδὲ πενίης.
κεῖνο δὲ παγκάλλιστον, ut omnibus undique Musis
σὺν φιάλῃque οἴνῳque, ἐτεῶν συνοπάονι Μουσῶν,
θυμοῦ ἀκηχεμένου solacia blanda requiras.
hic erit et fructus Δημητέρος ἀγλαοκάρπου,   40
ἔνθα σύες θαλεροί, πολυχανδέα pocula ἔνθα,
κιρνᾶν εἴ κε θέλοις νέκταρ οὐίνοιο βόνοιο.
ambo igitur nostrae παραθέλξομεν otia vitae,
    dum res et aetas et sororum
        νήματα πορφύρεα πλέκηται.   45

IX.—ΑΥΣΟΝΙΟΣ ΠΑΥΛΩΙ

Ῥωμαίων ὕπατος ἀρεταλόγῳ ἠδὲ ποιητῇ,
    Αὐσόνιος Παύλῳ· σπεῦδε φίλους ἰδέειν.

X

AEQUOREAM liqui te propter, amice, Garumnam,
    te propter campos incolo Santonicos;
congressus igitur nostros pete. si tibi cura,
    quae mihi, conspectu iam potiere meo.

---

¹ = Lat. *quaestorius*, since official payments were made by
the quaestor.

[27] Enough experience have I had of toil ere now, friend Paulus, both as a pleader in the courts and in the thankless professorial chair at Schools of Rhetoric, and got therefrom no profit. But now has all that youthful energy oozed from these limbs, trembling old age is nigh, and my strong-box grown light furnishes means for outlay less readily. For the helpless draws no salary from the Exchequer,[1] and the bed-ridden dotard earns no golden fees. Yet if only thou wilt be of unruffled mind and rather see good in everything, thy toil and poverty will find oblivion. But this is the very best of all, from all the Muses everywhere – not without bowl and wine, comrade of the true Muses—to seek soothing consolation for a troubled heart. Here shalt thou find the fruit of Demeter, rich in crops, here fat swine, here capacious goblets if thou wouldst mix the nectar of good wine. So shall we twain cheer the blank hours of our life, so long as means and age allow and the Three Sisters spin their purple thread.[2]

IX.—Ausonius to Paulus

Ausonius, consul of the Romans, to Paulus, poet and declaimer:[3] haste to see thy friends.

X

For thee I left the flood of the Garonne, for thee I dwell amid the plains of Saintes; our meeting, therefore, be thy aim! If thou art eager as I, full soon wilt thou enjoy the sight of me. But make

---

[2] cp. Horace, Od. II. iii. 15 f. : dum res et aetas et sororum Fila trium patiuntur atra.

[3] Primarily one who vaunts his good qualities, and so by transitions a declaimer, a rhetorician.

sed tantum adpropera, quantum pote corpore et aevo;
    ut salvum videam, sat cito te video.   6
si post infaustas vigor integratus habenas
    et rediit membris iam sua mobilitas,
si riguam laetis recolis Pipleida Musis,
    iam vates et non flagrifer Automedon,   10
pelle soporiferi senium nubemque veterni
    atque alacri mediam carpe vigore viam.
sed cisium aut pigrum cautus conscende veraedum :
    non tibi sit raedae, non amor acris equi.
cantheris moneo male nota petorrita vites,   15
    ne celeres mulas ipse Metiscus agas.
sic tibi sint Musae faciles, meditatio prompta
    et memor, et liquidi mel fluat eloquii :
sic, qui venalis tam longa aetate Crebennus
    non habet emptorem, sit tibi pro pretio.   20
Attamen ut citius venias leviusque vehare,
    historiam, mimos, carmina linque domi.
grande onus in musis : tot saecula condita chartis,
    quae sua vix tolerant tempora, nostra gravant.
nobiscum invenies ἐπέων πολυμορφέα πληθύν,   25
    γραμματικῶν τε πλοκὰς καὶ λογοδαιδαλίην,
δάκτυλον ἡρῷον καὶ ἀοιδοπόλων χορίαμβον,
    σὺν Θαλίης κώμῳ σύρματα Τερψιχόρης,
σωταδικόν τε κίναιδον, ἰωνικὸν ἀμφοτέρωθεν,
    ῥυθμῶν Πινδαρικῶν ἔννομον εὐεπίην.   30

---

[1] A fountain in Pieria, sacred to the Muses.
[2] The charioteer of Achilles : cp Virgil, *Aen.* ii. 476 f.
[3] This is usually described as a four-wheeled car, but it was evidently somewhat dangerous.

such haste as thy strength and years permit; so that
I see thee safe, I see thee soon enough. If after
that unlucky drive thy powers are restored, and if
thy limbs have now regained their wonted pliancy,
if to the Muses' joy thou dost again frequent well-
watered Pimpla,[1] a bard once more and no scorching
Automedon,[2] banish the clouds of eld which haunt
a drowsy greybeard, briskly devour the intervening
road. But be heedful, mounting some chaise or slow
post-horse: let no dog-cart[3] tempt thee, no high-
mettled steed. I counsel thee avoid four-wheeled
cars[4] with their notorious geldings, drive no swift
mules thyself to play Metiscus.[5] So be the Muses
gracious to thee, thy conception ready, thy memory
sound, and free thy flow of melting honey: so may
Crebennus, so long for sale without a purchaser, be
thine for a reward.

[21] But that thou mayest come more quickly, travel-
ling the lighter, leave histories, mimes, and lyrics all
at home. Muses make heavy baggage: those books
stored with so many centuries, which scarce endure
their own ages, are crushed by ours. With me thou
wilt find a motley throng of epics, grammarians'
subtilties and niceties of speech, the heroic dactyl
and the lyrist's choriambus, Thaleia's comedy beside
Terpsichore's tragic train, Sotades'[6] wanton verse,
the Ionic of both kinds,[7] the ordered sweetness of

---

[4] See note on *Epist.* iv. 5. This too was a swift and
dangerous conveyance.

[5] The charioteer of Turnus struck down by Juturna: see
Virgil, *Aen.* xii. 469 f.

[6] Sotades of Crete, notorious for his wanton poems and for
Sotadic verse, which could be read backwards way.

[7] *i.e.* Ionic *a maiore* and *a minore*. But since Sotades
wrote in Ionic, another meaning was probably intended.

εἰλιπόδην σκάζοντα καὶ οὐ σκάζοντα τρίμετρον,
ὀκτὼ Θουκυδίδου. ἐννέα Ἡροδότου.
ῥητορικῶν θάημα, σοφῶν ἐρικυδέα φῦλα,
  πάντα μάλ' ὅσσ' ἐθέλεις, καὶ πλέον, εἴ κε θέλοις.
Hoc tibi de nostris ἀσπαστικὸν offero libris.   35
  vale; valere si voles me, iam veni.

XI.—AUSONIUS TETRADIO SAL.

O qui vetustos uberi facundia
  sales opimas, Tetradi,
cavesque, ne sit tristis et dulci carens
  amara concinnatio;
qui felle carmen atque melle temperans   5
  torpere musas non sinis
pariterque fucas, quaeque gustu ignava sunt,
  et quae sapore tristia;
rudes camenas qui Suessae praevenis
  aevoque cedis, non stilo: 10
cur me propinquum Santonorum moenibus
  declinas, ut Lucas boves
olim resumpto praeferoces proelio
  fugit iuventus Romula?
non ut tigris te, non leonis impetu,   15
  amore sed caro expeto.
videre alumni gestio vultus mei
  et indole optata frui.
invitus oli n devoravi absentiae
  necessitatem pristinae,   20
quondam docendi munere adstrictum gravi
  Iculisma cum te absconderet,

---

[1] The *scazon* was an iambic trimeter with a spondee or
trochee in the sixth foot, causing the verse to limp or drag.

Pindaric rhythms, the shambling scazon [1] and the unlimping trimeter, eight books of Thucydides, nine of Herodotus, a goodly show of orators, and the philosophers in glorious tribes—all that thou wouldst, and still more shouldst thou wish.

[35] This word of greeting I send thee from my books. Farewell; if thou wouldst have me fare well, fare hither now.

XI.—Ausonius to Tetradius,[2] Greeting

O thou, who with copious eloquence enrichest our ancient stores of wit, Tetradius, and takest heed that thy tart compositions be not gloomy and bereft of sweetness; who, blending gall and honey in thy verse, sufferest not thy Muses to grow dull, and flavourest alike what is insipid to the taste and what bitter to the palate; thou who outstrip'st the unpolished Muses of Suessa,[3] yielding in age to them but not in style; why dost thou shun me, neighbour to the walls of Saintes, as of old the Roman youth fled from the Lucanian oxen [4] who renewed the battle with exceeding fury? Not like a tiger, not with lion's spring, but in fond love I seek thee out. I yearn to see my pupil's countenance and to enjoy the longed-for fruits of his mind. Reluctant hitherto I have gulped down the necessity which parted us in bygone days when Iculisma [5] kept thee hidden, once fettered with the heavy chains of teaching,

---

[2] Otherwise unknown.

[3] Now Sessa, in Campania; the birthplace of Lucilius the satirist.

[4] "Lucanian Oxen" was the name given by the Romans to elephants as first seen in Lucania in the army of Pyrrhus.

[5] Now Angoulême.

et invidebam devio ac solo loco
   opus camenarum tegi.
at nunc—frequentes atque claros nec procul   25
   cum floreas inter viros
tibique nostras ventus auras deferat
   auresque sermo verberet—
cur me supino pectoris fastu tumens
   spernis poetam consulem,   30
tuique amantem teque mirantem ac tua
   desiderantem carmina
oblitus alto neglegis fastidio?
   plectendus exemplo tuo,
ni stabilis aevo pectoris nostri fides   35
   quamquam recusantes amet.
Vale.   valere si voles me, pervola
   cum scrinio et musis tuis.

XII.—Ausonius Probo Praefecto Praetorio S.

Oblata per antiquarios mora scio promissi mei
gratiam expectatione consumptam, Probe, vir op-
time ; in secundis tamen habeo non fefellisse. apo-
logos Titiani et Nepotis chronica quasi alios apologos
(nam et ipsa instar sunt fabularum) ad nobilitatem
tuam misi, gaudens atque etiam glorians fore ali-
quid, quod ad institutionem tuorum sedulitatis meae
studio conferatur.

Libello tamen apologorum antetuli paucos epodos,
studio in te observantiae meae impudentissimo,

---

[1] Sextus Petronius Probus, born c. 330 A.D., was proconsul
of Africa in 358, consul with Gratian in 371. Ammianus
Marcellinus (XXVII ii. 1), referring to his first appointment
as praetorian prefect, in 368, speaks of his immense wealth
but equivocal character as a friend. He died c. 398 A.D.

[2] Probably Julius Titianus, tutor of Maximinus, who was
raised to the consulate (cp. Gratiarum Act. vii.).

and I would grudge that in so remote and lonely a
spot the Muses' handiwork was concealed. But now
—seeing thou flourishest amid throngs of famous
men and not far hence, where the wind wafts to
thee my renown and talk of me rings in thine ears—
why, puffing out thy chest with proud disdain, dost
thou scorn me, a poet-consul, and to one who loves
thee, admires thee, longs to enjoy thy verse, for-
getfully show neglect and proud contempt? Thou
shouldst be punished after thine own example, did
not the loyalty of my heart, unmoved by time, love
even the reluctant.

[37] Farewell. If thou wilt my welfare, whirl here
forthwith with writing-case and all thy Muses.

XII.—Ausonius to Probus,[1] Praetorian Prefect, Greeting

After the delay caused by the copyists, I know
that the pleasure caused by my promise has been
outworn by hope deferred, most noble Probus; yet
I count it good fortune that I have not broken my
word. The *Fables* of Titianus[2] and the *Chronicles*
of Nepos[3]—as though they were further fables; for
they, too, are like fairy tales—I now send your ex-
cellency, glad, nay exultant, that there will be some-
thing which my devotion and pains can contribute
towards your children's education.

To the little book of Fables, however, I have, in
the zeal of my respect for you, taken the extreme
liberty of prefixing a few verses—few at least as I

[3] The friend and contemporary of Cicero and Catullus
(celebrated by the latter, i. 5). He died during the princi-
pate of Augustus: his *Chronicles* are not extant.

paucos quidem, ut ego loquax iudico; verum tu,
cum legeris, etiam nimium multos putabis. adiuro
benevolentiam tuam, verecundiae meae testem, eos
mihi subita persuasione fluxisse. nam quis hos diu
cogitaret? quod sane ipsi per se probabunt. fors
fuat, ut si mihi vita suppetet, aliquid rerum tuarum
quamvis incultus expoliam: quod tu etsi lectum non
probes, scriptum boni consules. cumque ego imi-
tatus sim vesaniam Choerili, tu ignoscas magnani-
mitate Alexandri.

Hi igitur, ut Plautus ait, interim erunt antelogium
fabularum, garruli et deceptores. qui compositi
ad honorificentiae obsequium, ad aurium convicium
concurrerunt. vale et me dilige.

> Perge, o libelle, Sirmium
> et dic ero meo ac tuo
> have atque salve plurimum.
> quis iste sit nobis erus,
> nescis, libelle? an, cum scias,   5
> libenter audis, quod iuvat?
> possem absolute dicere,
> sed dulcius circumloquar
> diuque fando perfruar.
> hunc dico, qui lingua potens   10
> minorem Atridam praeterit
> orando pauca et musica;
> qui grandines Ulixei
> et mel fluentem Nestora
> concinnat ore Tulli;   15
> qui solus exceptis tribus

---

[1] A poet who sang the praises of Alexander in bad verse
and was rewarded in good coin: *cp.* Horace, *Epist.* II. i. 232 f.,
Ars Poet. 357.

judge, who am a man of words; though you, when you have read them, will think them all too many. I solemnly assure your good-natured self, who can vouch for my honour, that I gave vent to them on a sudden impulse. For who would need to ponder long over these? This, indeed, the verses themselves will confirm. It may be that, if I live long enough, I will fashion out some work on your career, rude craftsman though I am: even should you not be satisfied with the reading of it, you will take the writing in good part. And since I have copied Choerilus in his madness, you must pardon me with the generosity of Alexander.[1]

These verses then (to use Plautus' word [2]) will serve meanwhile as "Foreword" to the *Fables,* wordy and treacherous though they are. Though put together to convey my dutiful compliments to you, they have rushed off with one accord to offend your ears.

Farewell, and give me your good regard.

Go forth, little book, to Sirmium, and to thy lord and mine bid hearty health and greeting. Thou knowest not, little book, who is that our lord? Or though thou knowest, dost thou love to hear what delights thee? I might tell thee outright, but for more pleasure I will talk in mazes and with speech drawn out get full enjoyment. Him I mean who, full eloquent, outstrips Atreus' younger son [3] in pleading with few but melodious words; who combines Ulysses' hail and Nestor's honeyed flow with Tully's utterance; who is the all-highest save the

[2] See Plautus, *Menaechmus*, Prol. 13 : hoc argumento ante-logium fuit.
[3] *cp.* Homer, *Iliad*, iii. 214, 222; i. 248 f. and *Proff.* xxi. 21 ff.

eris erorum primus est
praetorioque maximus.
dico hunc senati praesulem,
praefectum eundem et consulem   20
(nam consul aeternum cluet
collega Augusti consulis),
columen curulis Romulae
primum in secundis fascibus;
nam primus e cunctis erit   25
consul, secundus principi.

Generi hic superstes aureo
satorque prolis aureae
convincit Ascraeum senem,
non esse saeclum ferreum,   30
qui vincit aevi iniuriam
stirpis novator Anniae
paribusque comit infulis
Aniciorum stemmata.

Probum loquor: scis optime,   35
quem nemo fando dixerit,
qui non prius laudaverit.
perge, o libelle, et utere
felicitate intermina.

Quin et require, si sinet   40
tenore fari obnoxio:
"Age vera proles Romuli,
effare causam nominis.
utrumne mores hoc tui
nomen dedere, an nomen hoc   45
secuta morum regula?
an ille venturi sciens
mundi supremus arbiter,
qualem creavit moribus,
iussit vocari nomine?"   50

three Lords of Lords,[1] and supreme in the Prae-
torium. Him I mean, the Senate's chief, prefect
likewise and consul (for as consul he has endless
fame as colleague of an Emperor-consul), prop of
the Roman curule chair—first, though his authority
is second in degree; for first of all citizens shall he
be as consul, but second to the Prince.

[27] He, the survivor of the Golden Race, begetter
of a golden progeny, refutes the sage of Ascra,[2]
showing this is no Iron Age, since, conquering Time's
ravages, he renews the line of the Annii and has
equal right to deck with fillets the Anician family-
tree.[3]

[35] Of Probus speak I: thou knowest him full well
—whom none ever named in speech without first
praising him.[4] Go forth, my little book, there to
enjoy boundless good fortune.

[40] And ask withal, if he will suffer thee to address
him in humble tones: "Prithee, true son of Romulus,
declare the reason of thy name. Was it thy conduct
earned thee this name, or to this name hath thy rule
of conduct conformed? Or of his fore-knowledge
did the supreme Disposer of the world bid thee be
called by a name expressive of the nature with which
he created thee?"

[1] *i.e.* Valentinian, Valens, and Gratian.
[2] *sc.* Hesiod: see *W. and D.* 176.
[3] *Stemmata* could only be decorated with wreaths by
actual members of the family: Probus was such by mar-
riage with Anicia Fultonia Proba.
[4] *i.e.* they are compelled to call him "*probus*" = "upright":
see ll. 43 ff.

Nomen datum praeconiis
vitaeque testimonio.
libelle felix, quem sinu
vir tantus evolvet suo
nec occupari tempora   55
grato queretur otio,
quem melleae vocis modis
leni aut susurro impertiet,
cui nigellae luminum
vacare dignabunt corae,   60
quem mente et aure consciis,
quibusdam omissis, perleget:
   Quaecumque fortuna est tibi,
perge, o libelle, et utere
felicitate intermina.   65
dic me va'ere et vivere,
dic vivere ex voto pio,
sanctis precantem vocibus,
ut, quem curulis proxima
collegio nati dedit,   70
hunc rursus Augustus prior
suis perennet fascibus.
subnecte et illud leniter:
"Apologos en misit tibi
ab usque Rheni limite   75
Ausonius, nomen Italum,
praeceptor Augusti tui,
Aesopiam trimetriam,
quam vertit exili stilo
pedestre concinnans opus   80
fandi Titianus artifex;
ut hinc avi ac patris decus,
mixto resurgens sanguine,
Probiano itemque Anicio,

[51] The name was given in his praise and for a token of his life. Ah, happy little book, that such a man will unroll thee on his knee and not complain that thou takest up the hours of his welcome leisure; that he will vouchsafe thee the tones of his honeyed voice or his soft whispers; that for thee the dear dark pupils of his eyes will deign to find leisure; that with mind and ear in unison he will read thee through, some pages skipped.

[63] Whate'er thy fortune, go forth, little book, and enjoy thy boundless happiness. Say that I fare well and live, say that I live as I devoutly asked, praying with hallowed words that, as the last consul-ship made him colleague of the son, so again Augustus the sire[1] will renown him with partnership in his own honours. This also gently add: "Lo, from the very borders of the Rhine Ausonius, Italian of name,[2] tutor of thy belov'd Augustus, sends thee these Fables, by Aesop writ in trimeters, but ren-dered in simple style and adapted into prose by Ti-tianus, artist in words; that hereby he who is his father's and grandfather's pride, sprung from the mingled strains of the Probi and Anicii—as of old

---

[1] *sc.* Valentinian I.
[2] *Ausonius*=Italian, as in *Aen.* vii. 547.

ut quondam in Albae moenibus   85
supremus Aenea satus
Silvios Iulis miscuit,
sic iste, qui natus tui,
flos flosculorum Romuli,
nutricis inter lemmata   90
lallique somniferos modos
suescat peritus fabulis
simul et iocari et discere."
　　His adde votum, quod pio
concepimus rei deo: 95
" Ut genitor Augustus dedit
collegio nati Probum,
sic Gratianus hunc novum
stirpi futurae copulet."
rata sunt futura, quae loquor: 100
sic merita factorum iubent.
　　Set iam ut loquatur Iulius,
fandi modum invita accipe,
volucripes dimetria,
haveque dicto dic vale.   105

XIII.—Ad Ursulum Grammaticum Trevirorum cui
　　Strenas Kalendis Ianuariis ab Imperatore non
　　datas reddi fecit

Primus iucundi foret[1] hic tibi fructus honoris
　　Augustae faustum munus habere manus:
proximus ex longo gradus est quaestoris amici
　　curam pro strenis excubuisse tuis.

　　　[1] So MSS. (Z): fuat, Toll: fuit, Avantius, Peiper.

---

　　[1] Silvius, son of Aeneas by Lavinia, and half-brother and
successor of Iulus (cp. Virgil, Aen. vi. 760 ff.).
　　[2] sc. Julius Titianus, the translator of the Fables.

in Alba town the last scion of Aeneas' stock united the lines of Silvius[1] and Iulus—so he who is thy off-spring, flower of the flowerlets of Rome, amid nurse's tales and drowsy strains of lullaby, may become versed in fables, growing used to play and learn at the same time."

[94] Thereto add this prayer which I, though sinful, have addressed to the all-loving God : " Even as Augustus the sire hath made Probus colleague to his son, so may Gratian link this new Probus with his offspring which shall be." Fulfilled hereafter shall be the words I speak : the worth of Probus' deeds demands it so.

[102] But now, that Julius[2] may speak, though all unwilling make an end of words, swift-footed dimeter, and having said "hail," say now "fare-well!"

XIII.—To Ursulus, a Grammarian of Trèves, to whom he had caused to be paid the Bounty[3] which had not been given to him by the Emperor on the First of January

Fullest enjoyment of a sweet distinction for thee were this—to have an auspicious gift from Imperial hands : next—though far inferior in degree—that thy quaestor-friend took tireless pains to gain thy New

[3] *Strenae* were New Year's presents given for the sake of good omen, and such were regularly distributed by the Emperors : see Suetonius, *Aug.* 57, *Tib.* 34.

ergo interceptos regale nomisma Philippos   5
    accipe tot numero, quot duo Geryones;
quot terni biiuges demptoque triente Camenae
    quotque super terram sidera zodiaci;
quot commissa viris Romana Albanaque fata
    quotque doces horis quotque domi resides;   10
ostia quot pro parte aperit stridentia circus
    excepto, medium quod patet ad stadium;
quot pedibus gradiuntur apes et versus Homeri
    quotque horis pelagus profluit aut refluit;
protulit in scaenam quot dramata fabellarum,   15
    Arcadiae medio qui iacet in gremio,
vel quot iuncturas geometrica forma favorum
    conserit extremis omnibus et mediis;
quot telios primus numerus solusque probatur;
    quot par atque impar partibus aequiperat,   20
bis ternos et ter binos qui conserit unus,
    qui solus totidem congeminatus habet,
quot faciunt iuncti subterque supraque locati;
    qui numerant Hyadas Pleiadasque simul.

---

[1] cp. Horace *Epist.* II. i. 234: rettulit acceptos, regale nomisma, Philippos.

[2] *sc.* the Horatii and Curiatii, who fought for Rome and Alba respectively in the time of Tullus Hostilius: see Livy, i. 24.

[3] The teaching profession, therefore, enjoyed a six-hour day.

[4] The circus having twelve gates in all, a single half of it contained seven: one of these (the gate looking along the *spina*) has to be omitted from the count.

Year's bounty. Therefore of royal coinage, of *Phi-lippes d'or*[1] waylaid by me receive as many as two Geryons; as three pair of horses, or as the Muses less one-third their band, or as those stars of the Zodiac that are above the earth; as many as the heroes to whom were committed the destinies of Rome and Alba,[2] or as the hours wherein thou dost teach[3] or wherein thou dost rest at home; as many as the jarring gates which open on one half of the circus, except-ing that which looks along the axis of the course;[4] as many as the feet whereon bees and Homer's verses move, or as the hours of the tide's flow and ebb; as many as the dramatic plots put on the stage by him who rests in the midst of Arcadia's bosom,[5] or as the angles which the geometric figure of the honey-cell forms by the meeting of its extreme and intervening sides;[6] as many as that which is ap-proved the one and only perfect number;[7] as that which consists equally of odd and even numbers, which alone unites in itself twice three and thrice two—the only number which, if doubled, contains as many units as the numbers[8] above it and below when added contain, and as the joint total of the Hyades and Pleiades.[9]

---

[5] Terence, who is said to have died at Stymphalus in Arcadia.

[6] In plan the hexagonal honeycomb appears to have two perpendicular (or "middle") sides and two pair of con-verging (or "extreme") sides which connect the "middle" sides at top and bottom, thus: ⬡.

[7] *sc.* six, as the first compound of odd and even factor (2×3, or $1 + 2 + 3$).

[8] *sc.* 5 and 7.

[9] The Hyades are five, the Pleiades seven in number.

[Tot numero auratos pro strenis accipe nummos[1]] 25
   Ursule collega nobilis Harmonio,
Harmonio, quem Claranus, quem Scaurus et Asper,
   quem sibi conferret Varro priorque Crates
quique sacri lacerum collegit corpus Homeri
   quique notas spuriis versibus adposuit: 30
Cecropiae commune decus Latiaeque camenae,
   solus qui Chium miscet et Ammineum.

XIV.—Ausonius Theoni

Ausonius, cuius ferulam nunc sceptra verentur,
paganum Medulis iubeo salvere Theonem.
   Quid geris extremis positus telluris in oris,
cultor harenarum vates, cui litus arandum
oceani finem iuxta solemque cadentem,   5
vilis harundineis cohibet quem pergula tectis
et tinguit piceo lacrimosa colonica fumo?
quid rerum Musaeque gerunt et cantor Apollo—
Musae non Helicone satae nec fonte caballi,
set quae facundo de pectore Clementini   10
inspirant vacuos aliena mente poetas?
iure quidem: nam quis malit sua carmina dici,
qui te securo possit proscindere risu?

           [1] Suppl. *Translator.*

---

[1] See Martial, *Ep.* x. xxi. 1 f.
[2] See notes on *Praef.* i. 20.
[3] Crates of Mallus in Cilicia, founder of the Pergamene school of critics, and rival of Aristarchus.
[4] Zenodotus, to whom is here attributed the work with which Pisistratus is traditionally credited. On this subject see Pausanias, vii. xxvi. 6, and Monro, *Odyssey, XIII.-XXIV.* pp. 403 f.

THE EPISTLES

25 So many sovereigns take as thy New Year's
gift, Ursulus, famed as colleague of Harmonius—
Harmonius, whom Claranus,[1] whom Scaurus and
Asper,[2] whom Varro would rank as his equal, or
Crates[3] in earlier days, or he who gathered the
mangled limbs of sacred Homer;[4] or who placed
symbols to mark out spurious verses:[5] Harmonius,
glory alike of the Attic and the Latin Muse, who
alone dost mingle wine of Chios and Aminaea.[6]

XIV.—Ausonius to Theon

Ausonius, whose rod now overawes a sceptre, sends
greeting to rustic Theon at Médoc.

8 What dost thou, dwelling on earth's farthest
verge, poetic tiller of the sands, who must plough
the shore next Ocean's border and the setting sun,
whom a poor hovel, thatched with reeds, confines,
and a peasant's hut smothers with sooty smoke that
brings tears to the eyes? What can the Muses be
doing, and songster Apollo—Muses not sprung from
Helicon nor from the Horse's Spring,[7] but those which,
springing from Clementinus' eloquent breast, inspire
empty-headed bards with borrowed thoughts? And
rightly so: for who would rather have verses called
his when he can safely rend thee with his laughter?[8]

[5] Aristarchus of Samos, who in his edition of Homer
employed such critical marks.
[6] Aminaea in Picenum was famous for its wine, cp.
Virgil, Georg. ii. 97.
[7] i.e. Hippocrene.
[8] i.e. Clementinus rightly lets you claim his verses; for to
hear you recite them is worth the price, you do it so
ridiculously: cp. Martial, Ep. i. 38 f. The whole piece is a
burlesque remonstrance with Theon for not sending any of
his " trifles " (cp. xv. ad init.)

haec quoque ne nostrum possint urgere pudorem,
tu recita, et vere poterunt tua dicta videri.   15
  Quam tamen exerces Medulorum in litore vitam?
mercatusne agitas leviore nomismate captans,
insanis quod mox pretiis gravis auctio vendat—
albentis sevi globulos et pinguia cerae
pondera Naryciamque picem scissamque papyrum   20
fumantesque olidum, paganica lumina, taedas?
  An maiora gerens tota regione vagantes
persequeris fures, qui te postrema timentes
in partem praedamque vocent?   tu mitis et osor
sanguinis humani condonas crimina nummis   25
erroremque vocas pretiumque inponis abactis
bubus et in partem scelerum de iudice transis?
  An cum fratre vagos dumeta per avia cervos
circumdas maculis et multa indagine pinnae?
aut spumantis apri cursum clamoribus urges   30
subsidisque fero?   moneo tamen, usque recuses
stringere fulmineo venabula comminus hosti.
exemplum de fratre time, qui veste reducta
ostentat foedas prope turpia membra lacunas
perfossasque nates vicino podice nudat.   35
inde ostentator volitat, mirentur ut ipsum
Gedippa Ursinusque suus prolesque Iovini
taurinusque ipsum priscis heroibus aequans,
qualis in Olenio victor Calydonius apro
aut Erymantheo[1] pubes fuit Attica monstro.   40

[1] So *VZ*: Cromyoneo, *Peiper*.

---

[1] A conventional epithet (*cp.* Virgil, *Aen.* xii. 750),
Naryx being a city of the Ozolian Locrians.
[2] *i.e.* bunches of feathers tied on a cord to scare the prey
and prevent it from escaping through gaps. *cp.* Virgil,
Aen. xii. 750.
[3] Meleager.   [4] Theseus.

THE EPISTLE

These verses also, lest they may force my blushes, do thou recite: and truly they will easily seem thy very words.

[16] Yet what life dost thou pursue on the coasts of Médoc? Art busy trafficking, snapping up for a clipped coinage goods presently to be sold in dear salerooms at outrageous prices—as balls of sickly tallow, greasy lumps of wax, Narycian[1] pitch, torn paper, and rank-smoking torches, your country lights?

[22] Or art thou busy about greater matters, chasing the thieves who roam through all thy neighbourhood, until they fear the worst and invite thee to share their spoils? Dost thou through tenderness and hatred of bloodshed compound felonies for cash, call them mistakes, levy fines for cattle rieved, and leave the part of judge to share the crime?

[28] Or with thy brother amid impenetrable thickets dost thou surround the wandering harts with mesh and feathers[2] in wide circle? Or dost thou urge on with shouts the foaming boar's career and lay wait for the monster? Yet I warn thee ever to avoid wielding thy spear at close quarters with a bolt-like foe. Take warning from thy brother, who pulls back his clothes displaying ugly scars near his privy parts, and bares his breech to show how awkwardly 'twas pierced. Then to display his wounds he flits away to be admired by Gedippa, and his friend Ursinus, and Jovinus' young hopeful, and Taurinus who ranks him with ancient heroes such as was the Calydonian conqueror[3] of the boar in Olenus, or the Attic stripling[4] victorious o'er the Erymanthian[5] monster.

[5] Theseus, however, killed the wild sow of Crommyon: it was Hercules who slew the Erymanthian boar. But the slip is due to Ausonius himself, not to his copyists. Peiper's correction is therefore needless.

Set tu parce feris venatibus et fuge nota
crimina silvarum, ne sis Cinyreia proles
accedasque iterum Veneri plorandus Adonis.
sic certe crinem flavus niveusque lacertos
caesariem rutilam per candida colla refundis,   45
pectore sic tenero, plana sic iunceus alvo,
per teretes feminum gyros surasque nitentes
descendis, talos a vertice pulcher ad imos—
qualis floricoma quondam populator in Aetna
virgineas inter choreas Deoida raptam   50
sustulit emersus Stygiis fornacibus Orcus.

An, quia venatus ob tanta pericula vitas,
piscandi traheris studio?   nam tota supellex
Dumnitoni tales solita est ostendere gazas,
nodosas vestes animantum Nerinorum   55
et iacula et fundas et, nomina vilica, lina
colaque et insutos terrenis vermibus hamos.
his opibus confise tumes ?   domus omnis abunda
litoreis dives spoliis.   referuntur ab unda
corroco, letalis trygon mollesque platessae,   60
urentes thynni et male tecti spina elacati [1]
nec duraturi post bina trihoria corvi.

An te carminibus iuvat incestare canoras
Mnemosynes natas, aut tris aut octo sorores ?
et quoniam huc ventum, si vis agnoscere, quid sit 65

---

[1] *Turnebus*: ligari, ligati, or ligatri, *MSS.*: ligatri, *Peiper*.

---

[1] *cp.* Horace, *Epist.* II. ii. 4.   The caricature is clumsy,
for Theon (*cp.* xvi. 31), though rounded, was not slim.

[2] Probably hooks sewn on a long line (such as are used for
sea-fishing) and baited with earthworms.

[3] The nature of this fish is doubtful: Vinet identifies it
with that known at Bordeaux as *créac* (sturgeon); Corpet
equates it with the Spanish *corrujo* (a kind of turbot).

[41] But do thou give up the chase and shun the well-known tragedies of the woods, lest thou be as the son of Cinyras and become a second Adonis for Venus to mourn. Like him, assuredly, fair-haired and snowy-white of arms, thou dost let stream ruddy locks over a gleaming neck; like him soft of breast, like him slender as a reed with shapely body, dost thou pass lower into smoothly curving hips and shining ankles, beauteous from top to toe [1]—even such as of old the ravisher in flowery Aetna, who from amid maiden throngs carried off Deo's daughter —Orcus, arisen from his Stygian furnaces!

[52] Or, because thou avoidest the chase by reason of such great dangers, does zeal for fishing draw thee? For all the gear at Dumnitonus is wont to display such treasures as the knotty wraps of Nereus' creatures, casting-nets, drag-nets, lines with rustic names, wears, and stitched hooks for earthworms. [2] On this outfit dost thou proudly rely? The whole house is rich to overflowing with the spoils of the sea-shore. From the waves are brought home sturgeon, [3] the deadly sting-ray, soft tender plaice, bitter tunnies, [4] spindle-fish [5] ill-guarded by their spines, and grayling which will not keep above twice three hours.

[63] Or dost thou delight to outrage with thy verses the songful daughters of Mnemosyne, be they sisters three or eight? [6] And since we are come to this, if thou wouldst learn what is midway between learned

[4] *cp.* Matthew Arnold, *Scholar Gipsy*: "Tunnies steeped in brine."

[5] A species of tunny shaped like a spindle (ἠλακάτη).

[6] For three Muses *cp. Griphus*, 31 : the number eight is otherwise unknown and is perhaps dictated by metrical necessity.

inter doctrinam deridendasque camenas,
accipe congestas, mysteria frivola, nugas,
quas tamen explicitis nequeas deprendere chartis,
scillite decies nisi cor purgeris aceto
Anticyraeve bibas[1] Samii Lucumonis acumen.   70

    aut adsit interpres tuus,
    aenigmatum qui cognitor
    fuit meorum, cum tibi
    Cadmi nigellas filias,
    Melonis albam paginam   75
    notasque furvae sepiae
    Gnidiosque nodos prodidit.
    nunc adsit et certe, modo
    praesul creatus litteris,
    enucleabit protinus   80
    quod lusitantes scribimus.

    Notos fingo tibi, poeta, versus,
    quos scis hendecasyllabos vocari,
    set nescis modulis tribus moveri.
    istos conposuit Phalaecus olim,   85
    qui penthemimeren habent priorem
    et post semipedem duos iambos.
    sunt quos hexametri creant revulsi,
    ut penthemimeres prior locetur,

    [1] *Peiper* : Antichiramque bibas, *Z* : anticipesque vivum,
or anticipetque tuum, *V.*

---

    [1] For this mixture see Pliny, *N.H.* XXVI. viii. 48.
    [2] *i.e.* "until you drink hellebore at Anticyra and become
as wise as Pythagoras of Samos." *Lucumo* is probably an
Etruscan prince.
    [3] *i.e.* the letters (invented by Cadmus) written on papyrus
from Egypt (Melo = the Nile) with ink taken from the
cuttle-fish with a reed pen (for Cnidian knots *cp. Epist.*
XV. 20). Probably the riddle is a scribe's "conceit" An
analogous piece of wit was affected by Syriac scribes, as :

verse and verse ridiculous, take this trumped-up
rubbish, this trifling mystery, though with the sheet
unrolled thou wilt not be able to comprehend it un-
less thou dost purge thy wits ten times over with
vinegar seasoned with squills,[1] or at Anticyra drink
in the sagacity of the Samian nabob.[2]

[71] Or let thy interpreter come to thy aid, he who
read my riddles and revealed to thee the secret of
"Cadmus' little darky-girls, Melo's white page, the
marks of the swart cuttlefish, and the knots of
Cnidos."[3] Let him now come to thy help, and cer-
tainly once appointed literary dictator, he will worry
out forthwith what I write playfully.

[82] I am making up verses, Master Poet, well
known to thee, and which thou knowest are called
hendecasyllables, though thou knowest not that they
move to three measures. Those were composed by
Phalaecus[4] of old, in which a penthemimeris is fol-
lowed by a half-foot after two iambi. Others are so
formed from a mutilated hexameter that the pen-
themimeris is placed first, and then, what left after

"Lord, let not be withheld the reward of the five twins who
have laboured, and the two who have exerted themselves and
sowed seed in the field of animals with the feathers of birds,"
(*i.e.* the five pairs of fingers and the two hands which have
written on parchment with quills). See Wright, *Cat. of Syr.
MSS in the B.M.*, p. 107.

[4] A lyrist of uncertain date Ausonius represents him as
early, but some moderns regard him as an Alexandrine.
Ausonius means that there are three varieties of hendeca-
syllables :—

(1) $- - - \smile \smile - \smile - \smile - -$
(2) $- - - \smile \smile - \smile \smile - -$
(3) $- \smile - - - \smile \smile - \smile - -$

tum quod bucolice tome relinquit.   90
sunt et quos generat puella Sappho :
quos primus regit hippius secundus,
ut cludat choriambon antibacchus.
set iam non poteris, Theon, doceri,
nec fas est mihi regio magistro   95
plebeiam numeros docere pulpam.
    Verum protinus ede, quod requiro.
nil quaero, nisi quod libris tenetur
et quod non opicae tegunt papyri
quas si solveris, o poeta, nugas,   100
totam trado tibi simul Vacunam,
nec iam post metues ubique dictum :
" Hic est ille Theon poeta falsus,
bonorum mala carminum Laverna "

XV.—Ausonius Theoni cum ei triginta Ostrea
grandia quidem set tam pauca misisset

Expectaveram, ut rescriberes ad ea, quae dudum
ioculariter luseram de cessatione tua valde impia et
mea efflagitatione, cuius rei munus reciprocum quo-
niam in me colendo fastidisti, inventa inter tineas
epistula vetere, quam de ostreis et musculis adfec-
tata obscuritate condideram, quae adulescens temere
fuderam, iam senior retractavi. set in eundem modum
instaurata est satirica et ridicula concinnatio, saltem
ut nunc respondeas novissimae cantilenae, qui illam
noviciam silentio condemnasti.

---

[1] Vacuna is the goddess of leisure : *i.e.* Theon shall be
immune from further bantering.
[2] Patroness of gain, good or bad, and so the goddess of
thieves.

the bucolic caesura.   There are also those which
the girl Sappho brought forth, where first reigns
a second hippius, leaving an antibacchius to cap a
choriambus.

[94] But thou wilt no longer be able to learn, Theon,
and 'tis not lawful for me, a royal schoolmaster, to
teach prosody to common clay.

[97] But forthwith produce what I demand. I ask
for naught but what thy notebooks hold and
unsoiled sheets contain.   If thou, Sir Poet, wilt
pay me this trifle, all Vacuna[1] do I cede to thee
outright, and no more hereafter shalt thou dread the
universal cry: "This is that feigned poet, Theon,
the bad Laverna[2] of good poetry."

XV.—Ausonius to Theon, who had sent him thirty
    Oysters: he complains that though large
    they are so few

I have been looking for a reply from you to the
letter I wrote some time ago dealing playfully with
your positively unnatural neglect of me and my own
urgent demands; and since you have disdained to
do me the courtesy of sending a favour in return,
having found an old letter, half worm-eaten, which
I once composed in a style of deliberate obscurity
on oysters and mussels, now that I am older I have
revised that careless effusion of my youth.   But
though recast, this composition still retains the
same satirical and burlesque character, that now at
least you may send an answer to my ditty in its
newest guise, though by your silence you condemned
it when new born.

AUSONIUS

Ostrea Baianis certantia, quae Medulorum
dulcibus in stagnis reflui maris aestus opimat,
accepi, dilecte Theon, numerabile munus.
verum quot fuerint, subiecta monosticha signant:

Quot ter luctatus cum pollice computat index;　5
Geryones quot erant, decies si multiplicentur;
ter quot erant Phrygii numerata decennia belli,
aut iter ut solidi mensis tenet ignicomus Sol;
cornibus a primis quot habet vaga Cynthia noctes;
singula percurrit Titan quot signa diebus　　　　10
quotque annis sublimis agit sua saecula Phaenon;
quot numero annorum Vestalis virgo ministrat
Dardaniusque nepos regno quot protulit annos;
Priamidae quot erant, si bis deni retrahantur,
bisque viros numeres, qui fata Amphrysia servant;　15
quot genuit fetus Albana sub ilicibus sus
et quot sunt asses, ubi nonaginta trientes,
vel quot habet iunctos Vasatica raeda caballos.

Quod si figuras fabulis adumbratas
numerumque doctis involutum ambagibus　20
ignorat alto mens obesa viscere,
numerare saltim more vulgi ut noveris,
in se retortas explicabo summulas.

Ter denas puto quinquiesve senas,
vel bis quinque, dehinc decem decemque,　　25
vel senas quater et bis adde ternas;
septenis quater adde et unum et unum,　　　27

---

[1] i e. xxx.
[2] i.e. in which the sun passes from one Sign of the Zodiac
to another.
[3] A Vestal spent ten years in learning her duties, another
ten in performing them, and a final ten in instructing novices.
[4] Priam.

THE EPISTLES

Oysters rivalling those of Baiae, which the surge of the ebbing sea fattens in the lush marshes of Médoc, I have received, dear Theon—a gift not beyond reckoning. But what was their number, the following single lines declare.

[5] As many were they as the forefinger thrice crossed with the thumb[1] reckons up; as many as there were Geryons, if ten times multiplied; thrice as many as the decades told over in the Phrygian (Trojan) War, or as the journeys made by the flame-tressed Sun in a full month; as the nights which wandering Cynthia enjoys after she first shows her horns; as the days wherein Titan traverses each several Sign;[2] as the years in which Phaenon (Saturn) accomplishes his circuit aloft; as the tale of years in which a Vestal maid does service,[3] and as those o'er which the scion of Dardanus[4] prolonged his reign; as many as Priam's sons if twice ten are deducted, or, if you count them twice, as they who keep the Amphrysian Oracles;[5] as the young littered beneath the oaks by the Alban sow,[6] and as the unit when there are ninety thirds—or as many hacks as are harnessed to a car at Bazas.

[19] But if the figure shadowed forth in story, and the number wrapped up in this learned rigmarole baffles a mind smothered deep in fat—that you may know how to count in the common way at least, I will unfold the sum reduced to its factors.

[24] Thrice ten, methinks, or five times six, or two times five *plus* ten and ten, or four times six with twice three added; to seven times four add one and

---

[5] The Sibylline Oracles, kept by fifteen commissioners (see note on *Griphus*, 86 f.). Amphrysian is here a purely conventional epithet.

[6] See Virgil, *Aen.* iii. 390 f.

aut ter quattuor adde bis novenis ;   29
duc binas decies semelque denas ;   28
octonas quater, hinc duae recedant ;   30
binas ter decies, semel quaternas.
et sex adde novem vel octo septem,
aut septem geminis bis octo iunge,
aut—ne sim tibi pluribus molestus,
triginta numero fuere cunctae.   35

  Iunctus limicolis musculus ostreis
primo conposuit fercula prandio,
gratus deliciis nobilium cibus
et sumptu modicus pauperibus focis.
non hic navifrago quaeritur aequore,   40
ut crescat pretium grande periculis ;
set primore vado post refugum mare
algoso legitur litore concolor.
nam testae duplicis conditur in specu,
quae ferventis aquae fota vaporibus   45
carnem lacteoli visceris indicat.
  Set damnosa nimis panditur area.
fac campum replices, Musa, papyrium
nec iam fissipedis per calami vias
grassetur Gnidiae sulcus harundinis,   50
pingens aridulae subdita paginae
Cadmi filiolis atricoloribus.
aut cunctis pariter versibus oblinat
furvam lacticolor sphongia sepiam.
  Parcamus vitio Dumnitonae domus,   55
ne sit charta mihi carior ostreis.

XVI.—AUSONIUS THEONI

Ausonius salve caro mihi dico Theoni,
  versibus expediens, quod volo quodve queror.

one, or to thrice four add nine twice over; take ten times two and one time ten, four times eight with two subtracted, two thirteen times *plus* a single four. Add also six to nine and eight to seven, or with twin sevens twice join eight, or—not to bother you with more—thirty in number were they all.

³⁶ The mussel not without mud-haunting oysters, makes up a course for early luncheon—a food delightful to the taste of lords and cheap enough for poor folks' kitchens. 'Tis not sought on the ship-wrecking deep so that the price grows great to match the danger, but is picked up in the nearest shallows after the sea's ebb, matching in colour the weed-strewn shore. For it is hidden in the cavern of a double shell which, warmed by the steam of boiling water, reveals the milk-white substance within.

⁴⁷ But too careless of cost this broad sheet is spreading out. See that thou abridge, my Muse, thy acreage of paper, and no longer let the furrow of the Cnidian reed proceed along the paths of the cloven-footed pen painting the surface of my poor parched page with Cadmus' dark-hued little daughters. Or from all the lines alike let a milk-white sponge blot out the dusky sepia.

⁵⁵ Let us spare the shortcomings of the folk at Dumnitonus, lest paper cost me more than the value of the oysters.

XVI.—Ausonius to Theon

I, Ausonius, send greeting to my dear Theon, here setting out in verse my wishes and complaints.

Tertia fissipedes renovavit Luna iuvencas,
   ut fugitas nostram, dulcis amice, domum.
nonaginta dies sine te, carissime, traxi;   5
   huc adde aestivos : hoc mihi paene duplum est.
vis novies denos dicam deciesque novenos
   isse dies?   anni portio quarta abiit.
sexaginta horas super et duo milia centum
   te sine consumpsi, quo sine et hora gravis.   10
milia bis nongenta iubet demensio legum
   adnumerata reos per tot obire dies.
iam potui Romam pedes ire pedesque reverti,
   ex quo te dirimunt milia pauca mihi.
scirpea Dumnitoni tanti est habitatio vati?   15
   Pauliacos tanti non mihi villa foret.
an quia per tabulam dicto pangente notatam
   debita summa mihi est, ne repetamus, abes?
bis septem rutilos regale nomisma Philippos,
   nec tanti fuerint, perdere malo, Theon,   20
implicitum quam te nostris interne medullis
   defore tam longi temporis in spatio.
ergo aut praedictos iam nunc rescribe Darios
   et redime, ut mora sit libera desidiae,
aut alios a me totidem dabo, dum modo cari   25
   conspicer ora viri, pauperis usque licet.
Puppe citus propera sinuosaque lintea veli
   pande : Medullini te feret aura[1] noti

---

[1] So *Souclay* : ora, *Peiper*.

---

[1] Some late authors represent the chariot of the moon as
drawn by oxen.
[2] Roman law required the defendant to travel (if necessary)
twenty miles per day in order to appear in Court at the

[3] Thrice hath Luna renewed her cloven-footed heifers,[1] since thou, sweet friend, dost avoid my house. Ninety days without thee have I dragged out, my dearest comrade; add further, summer days: this makes them nearly twice as long for me. Wouldst have me say that nine times ten days or ten times nine are gone? A fourth part of the year is passed away. Sixty hours and two thousand and a hundred beside without thee have I spent—without whom even an hour hangs heavy. Miles twice nine hundred the laws' appointment bids men accused traverse to full reckoning in so many days.[2] By this time could I have gone afoot to Rome, and afoot returned, since the time when a few miles have parted thee from me. Has a thatched cot at Dumnitonus such charms for a bard? My villa Pauliacos[3] would not weigh so with me. Or because by bond drawn up hard and fast money is owed to me, dost thou keep from me lest I claim it back? Those twice seven gleaming *Philippes d'or* of royal mintage,[4] Theon, I had rather lose—they would not be worth so much—than that thou, who art so closely twined about my heart, shouldst desert me over this long stretch of time. So either send back now forthwith the aforesaid *louis* and buy back thy freedom slothfully to linger, or I will freely give as many more besides, provided I behold the face of one so dear, however poor he be.[5]

[27] Haste hither, sped by boat, and spread the bellying canvas of thy sail: the breath of the south wind from Médoc will waft thee reclining beneath

stated time; otherwise the case went against him by default (*Digest* ii. xi. 1).

  [3] Possibly Pauliac on the Garonne.
  [4] See note on *Epist.* xiii. 5.
  [5] Presumably, "however often I have to pay this sum."

expositum subter paradas lectoque iacentem,
    corporis ut tanti non moveatur onus.   30
unus Dumnitoni te litore perferet aestus
    Condatem ad portum, si modo deproperes
inque vicem veli, quotiens tua flamina cessant,
    remipedem iubeas protinus ire ratem.
invenies praesto subiuncta petorrita mulis :   35
    villa Lucani- mox potieris -aco.
rescisso disces conponere nomine versum :
    Lucili vatis sic imitator eris.

XVII.—<Ausonius Theoni>

Ausonius consul vatem resaluto Theonem.

Aurea mala, Theon, set plumbea carmina mittis ;
    unius massae quis putet has species ?
unum nomen utrisque, set est discrimen utrisque :
    poma ut mala voces, carmina verte mala.   5

    Vale beatis nomen a divis Theon,
    metoche set ista saepe currentem indicat.

XVIII.—Ausonius Hesperio S. D.

Qualis Picenae populator turdus olivae
    clunes opimat cereas
vel qui lucentes rapuit de vitibus uvas,
    pendetque nexus retibus,

---

[1] According to d'Anville this port, no longer existing, was
at Condat near Libourne in the Dordogne.

[2] Identified with Lugaignac in the canton of Brannes.
Ennius is more famous for his split nouns, as in "saxo
cere- comminuit -brum."

[3] *i.e.* "alter your verse—even if it means calling your

an awning and stretched upon a couch, that the bulk
of so great a body be not shaken. One tide will
bear thee from the shore of Dumnitonus right to the
harbour of Condate,[1] if only thou makest good haste,
and in place of sail, whene'er thy favouring breezes
die away, biddest the bark speed straight on pro-
pelled with oars. Thou shalt find ready a four-
wheeled car with team of mules : soon wilt thou
gain the Lucani- villa -acus.[2] Thou shalt learn to
make verse with such split nouns : thus shalt thou
be a copier of the bard Lucilius.

XVII.—Ausonius to Theon

I, Ausonius the Consul, return greeting to Theon
the Bard.

[2] Apples of gold thou sendest, Theon, but verse
of lead : who would think these species were of the
same substance ? Both have one name. but both
have differences: to call your apples quinces, alter
your quinsied verse.[3]

[6] Farewell, Theon, whose name is from the blessed
gods, but often as a participle it means one running.[4]

XVIII —Ausonius to Hesperius sends Greeting

Even as the thrush who, ravaging the olives of
Picenum,[5] fattens his waxen haunches,[6] or who has
torn the gleaming clusters from the vines and now
hangs entangled in the nets which in the evening

apples by another name." But the play on *mala . . . mala*
cannot adequately be reproduced.

[4] Theon might be either θεῶν or θέων.
[5] *cp.* Martial, *Epigr.* ix. lv. 1: Si mihi Picena turdus
palleret oliva.
[6] *id.* XIII. v. 1 : Cerea quae patulo lucet ficedula lumbo.

quae vespertinis fluitant nebulosa sub horis   5
    vel mane tenta roscido :
tales hibernis ad te de saepibus, ipsos
    capi volentes, misimus
bis denos ; tot enim crepero sub lucis eoae
    praeceps volatus intulit.   10
tum, quas vicinae suggessit praeda lacunae,
    anites maritas iunximus,
remipedes, lato populantes caerula rostro
    et crure rubras Punico,
iricolor vario pinxit quas pluma colore,   15
    collum columbis aemulas.
Defrudata meae non sunt haec fercula mensae :
    vescente te fruimur magis.
          Vale bene, ut valeam.

XIX.—Ausonius ad Patrem de Suscepto Filio

Credideram nil posse meis adfectibus addi,
    quo, venerande pater, diligerere magis.
accessit (grates superis medioque nepoti,
    bina dedit nostris qui iuga nominibus)   4
accessit titulus, tua quo reverentia crescat,   9
    quo doceam natum, quid sit amare patrem.   10
ipse nepos te fecit avum : mihi filius idem   5
    et tibi ego : hoc nato nos sumus ambo patres.
nec iam sola mihi pietas mea suadet amorem :
    nomine te gemini iam genitoris amo.   8
quippe tibi aequatus videor, quia parvulus isto   11
    nomine honoratum me quoque nobilitat :

---

[1] It was customary for a father to take up (*suscipere*) a
newborn son as a sign that he acknowledged it and would

hour float loose like clouds, or in the morn are taut with dew—such are the birds I send thee from our wintry hedges, themselves glad to be caught, twice ten in all; for so many in the twilight of early dawn flew headlong into the net. Thereto I add full-grown ducks which a raid on the neighbouring meres supplies, web-footed birds whose broad beaks ravage the blue waters, with legs of crimson-red and plumage rich as the rainbow dight with various colours, with necks that rival doves.

[17] I have not cheated my own table to send these dainties: that thou shouldst eat them causes me more enjoyment.

[19] Fare thee well, that so I may fare well.

XIX.—AUSONIUS TO HIS FATHER ON THE ACKNOWLEDGMENT [1] OF HIS SON

I HAD believed that nought could be added to the sum of my affection whereby, mine honoured father, my love might be increased. Added (thanks to the gods above and to thy grandson, their instrument, who has laid upon our names a two-fold yoke), added is a title whereby my reverence for thee is increased, whereby I may teach my son what 'tis to love a father. This grandson himself hath made thee a grandfather: to me he too is son, and to thee am I: his birth makes us both fathers. No longer doth natural affection alone inspire me with love for thee: as doubly a father I love thee now. For I seem made thy peer, because a little boy ennobles me too with the distinction of that name; not because our

rear it. For the circumstances in which this fulsome piece was written see *Introduction*, p. xv.

non aetas quia nostra eadem : nam subparis aevi
    sum tibi ego et possum fratris habere vicem,
nec tantum nostris spatium interponitur annis,   15
    quanta solent alios tempora dividere.
vidi ego natales fratrum distare tot annis,
    quot nostros : aevum nomina non onerant.
pulchra iuventa tibi senium sic iungit, ut aevum
    quod prius est maneat, quod modo ut incipiat.   20
et placuisse reor geminis aetatibus, ut se
    non festinato tempore utraque daret,
leniter haec flueret, haec non properata veniret,
    maturam frugem flore manente ferens.
annos me nescire tuos, pater optime, testor   25
    totque putare tuos, quot reor esse meos.
nesciat hos natus, numeret properantior heres,
    testamenta magis quam pia vota fovens
exemploque docens pravo iuvenescere natos,
    ut nolint patres se quoque habere senes.   30
verum ego primaevo genitus genitore fatebor
    subparis haec aevi tempora grata mihi.
debeo quod natus, suadet pia cura nepotis
    addendum patri, quo veneremur avum.
tu quoque, mi genitor, geminata vocabula gaude,   35
    nati primaevi nomine factus avus.
exiguum, quod avus : faveant pia numina divum
    deque nepote suo fiat avus proavus.
largius et poterunt producere fata senectam :
    set rata vota reor, quae moderata, magis.   40

age is the same, since I somewhat approach thee in age and can pass as thy brother, nor does so great a span divide our years as the seasons which part others. I have seen brothers whose birthdays were separated by as many years as ours : names add no weight to years. Fair youth so blends with old age in thee, that thy earlier time of life lingers, while thy present but begins. And, methinks, these two ages have agreed each to present itself without hurrying on their seasons, this gently gliding onwards, that approaching without haste, bringing ripe fruit while yet the flower remains. I vow, my dearest father, that I know not thy years, and account thine as many as I deem my own. Let no son know these, let the too hasty heir reckon them up, his heart set more on inheritance than loving wishes, teaching his sons to grow up after such bad pattern as to hope they too have no long-lived father. But I, born when my sire was in his earliest youth, will avow that I delight that our times of life are so nearly matched. What I owe as a son, my dear love for thy grandson moves me, his father, to increase, the more to honour thee as a grandsire. Thou too, my sire, rejoice in thy doubled title now that thy son in early youth hath made thee grandfather. A small thing 'tis to be a grandfather : may the kind powers be propitious, and by his own grandson may the grandfather be made great-grandfather. Even further the Fates will have power to prolong thine age : but those prayers, methinks, are rather answered which are moderate.

AUSONIUS

XX.—Pater ad Filium cum temporibus tyrannicis
ipse Treveris remansisset et Filius ad Patriam
profectus esset. Hoc incohatum neque in-
pletum sic de Liturariis scriptum

*   *   *   *   *

Debeo et hanc nostris, fili dulcissime, curis
historiam : quan quam titulo non digna sereno
anxia maestarum fuerit querimonia rerum.
  Iam super egeliaae stagnantia terga Mosellae
protulerat te, nate, ratis maestique parentis   5
oscula et amplexus discreverat invidus amnis.
solus ego et quamvis coetu celebratus amico
solus eram profugaeque dabam pia vota carinae
solus adhuc te, nate, videns ; celerisque remulci
culpabam properos adverso flumine cursus.   10
quis fuit ille dies ? non annus longior ille est,
Attica quem docti collegit cura Metonis.
desertus vacuis solisque exerceor oris.
nunc ego pubentes salicum deverbero frondes,
gramineos nunc frango toros viridesque per ulvas   15
lubrica substratis vestigia libro lapillis.
sic lux prima abiit, sic altera meta diei,
sic geminas alterna rotat vertigo tenebras,
sic alias : totusque mihi sic annus abibit,
restituant donec tua me tibi fata parentem.   20
hac ego condicione licet vel morte paciscar,
dum decores suprema patris tu, nate, superstes.

---

[1] i e. Ausonius to Hesperius.
[2] i.e. in 383 A.D. when Maximus seized the Empire of the
West : see *Introduction*, pp. xi f., xx.
[3] On the importance of this editorial note see *Introduction*,
p. xxxvi.

XX.—The Father to his Son,[1] when in the days of usurpation [2] he himself remained at Trèves and his Son set out for his native place. This Poem, begun but never finished, has been copied as it stands from the rough draft [3]

* * * * *

This narrative also I owe to my cares for thee, my dearest son; although this troubled plaint for my gloomy fortunes scarce deserves so mild a term.

[4] Already o'er the sluggish surface of chill Moselle the bark had borne thee forward, O my son, and from the kisses and embraces of thy weeping sire the envious stream had parted thee. Alone! though compassed with a throng of friends, I was alone and offered yearning prayers for that fleeting craft; alone, though still I saw you, my child, and grudged the hasty speed of the swift oarage plying against the stream. What day was that? No longer is that year which Attic Meton [4] worked out with such patient skill. Forlorn I pace the empty, lonely shores. Now I strike down the sprouting willow-shoots, now I crush beds of turf and o'er green sedge I poise my slippery footsteps on the pebbles strewn beneath. So the first day passed away, so the second reached its bourne, so the two nights which wheeled revolving after each, so others: and the whole year for me will so pass by until thy destiny gives back me, thy sire, to thee. With this condition I may bargain even for death, that thou, my son, payest thy father the last tributes, surviving him.

[4] Meton of Athens (flor. c. 432 B.C.) discovered the Lunar Cycle in which 235 lunar months = 19 solar years. By *annus* Aus. seems to mean the Cycle, not the Lunar Year.

AUSONIUS

XXI.—Genethliacos ad Ausonium Nepotem

Ausonius Avus Ausonio Nepoti

Carmina prima tibi cum iam puerilibus annis
traderet adsidui permulcens cura magistri
inbueretque novas aures sensusque sequaces,
ut respondendas docili quoque murmure voces
emendata rudi perferret lingua palato,   5
addidimus nil triste senes, ne cura monendi
laederet aut dulces gustus vitiaret amaris.
at modo, cum motu vigeas iam puberis aevi
fortiaque a teneris possis secernere et ipse
admonitor morumque tibi fandique videri,   10
accipe non praecepta equidem, set vota precantis
et gratantis avi festum ad sollemne nepotis.

. . . .

adnuit, ut reducem fatorum ab fine senectam
sospes agam festumque diem dubitataque cernam
sidera, deposito prope conclamatus in aevo.   15
hoc, mellite nepos, duplicato faenore partum
natali accedente tuo, munusque salutis
plenius hoc nostrae, quod iam tibi puberis aevi
crescit honos iuvenemque senex iam cerno nepotem.

Sexta tibi haec primo remeat trieteris ab anno, 20
Septembres notis referens natalibus idus.

68

THE EPISTLES

Ausonius the Grandfather to Ausonius his Grandson

WHILE thy persistent master with coaxing pains
was committing to thee, still of boyish years, thy
earliest poems,[1] and was training thy prentice ear
and the faculties it guides, so that thy tongue, cor-
rected of the unskilled palate's faults, might produce
the words to be repeated with an obedient murmur,[2]
I, an old man, added naught severe lest anxious
admonition might gall, or mar the sweet first-taste
with bitterness.   But now, when thou dost feel the
stir and pulse of youth, and canst distinguish between
the manly and the feeble and show thyself thine
own councillor in behaviour as in speech, accept, not
indeed precepts, but prayers of thy grandfather who
entreats while rejoicing at the high festival of his
grandson's birthday.   .   .   .   .   .   .
(I thank Heaven which) has consented that, re-
covered, I may spend my old age brought back from
the Fates' borderland,[3] and behold this happy day
and the stars I scarce hoped to see, I who was well-
nigh mourned as one dead.   This, my sweet grand-
son, is a gift doubly profitable, in that thy birthday
now occurs, and the prize of my own safety is by
this the richer that the glory of thy ripening age
now waxes, and that I, now old, behold my grandson
attain to youth.

[20] Now comes round for thee the sixth period of
three years since thou wert born, bringing back the

---

[3] Apparently Ausonius had just recovered from some
serious illness of which he had well-nigh died.

Idus alma dies, geniis quoque culta deorum.
Sextiles Hecate Latonia vindicat idus,
Mercurius Maias, superorum adiunctus honori.
Octobres olim genitus Maro dedicat idus : 25
    Idus saepe colas bis senis mensibus omnes,
Ausonii quicumque mei celebraveris idus.
        Vale nepos dulcissime.

XXII.—Liber Protrepticus ad Nepotem

Ausonius Hesperio Filio

Libellum, quem ad nepotulum meum, sororis tuae
filium, instar protreptici luseram, venturus ipse prae-
misi legendum. hoc enim malui quam ipse recitare,
esset ut tibi censura liberior, quae duabus causis
impediri solet: quod aures nostras audita velocius
quam lecta praetereunt et quod sinceritas iudicandi
praesentia recitantis oneratur. nunc tibi utrumque
integrum est, quia et legenti libera mora est et
iudicaturo non obstat nostri verecundia.

Set heus tu, fili dulcissime, habeo quod admo-
neam. si qua tibi in his versiculis videbuntur (nam
vereor, ut multa sint) fucatius concinnata quam ve-
rius et plus coloris quam suci habere, ipse sciens

---

[1] Ll. 23 ff. are in imitation of Martial xii. lxvii. :—
    Maiae Mercurium creastis Idus ;
    Augustis redit Idibus Diana ;

Ides of September. The Ides is an auspicious day, observed too by the genii of gods. In Sextilis Hecate, Leto's daughter, claims the Ides; in May, Mercury, who was raised to the ranks of the gods. October's Ides are hallowed by the birth of Maro long ago.

[26] Oft mayest thou observe each Ides of all the twice six months, whoso shalt celebrate the Ides of my Ausonius.[1]

[28] Farewell my sweetest grandson.

XXII.—A Book of Exhortation to his Grandson

Ausonius to his Son Hesperius

Being about to come myself, I send on ahead a booklet which I have amused myself by writing in the form of an exhortation to my little grandson, your sister's son. For this I prefer to reciting it myself, in order that you may feel less restraint in your criticism—a faculty which is usually hampered by two circumstances: first that what is heard passes over our ears more quickly than what is read; and second the presence of the reciter handicaps the frankness of the critic. As it is, you have nothing to fear on either score, because both as you read you are free to linger, and as you come to criticize your feelings for me do not stand in your way.

But look you, my dearest son, I have a caution to add. If any passages in these verses shall appear to you (and I fear that there are many such) to be composed with more brilliance than truth, and have more colour than vigour, know that I deliberately

> Octobres Maro consecravit Idus.
> Idus saepe colas et has et illas,
> Qui magni celebras Maronis Idus.

fluere permisi, venustula ut essent magis, quam
forticula, instar virginum,

> quas matres student
demissis umeris esse, vincto pectore, ut graciles
sient.

nosti cetera.

Superest igitur, ut dicas : quid moraris iudicatio-
nem meam de eo, quod ipse pronuntias esse men-
dosum ? dicam scilicet me huiusmodi versibus foris
erubescere, set intra nos minus verecundari ; namque
ego haec annis illius magis quam meis scripsi aut
fortasse et meis: δὶς παῖδες οἱ γέροντες. ad summam
valeat austeritas tua : mihi cum infante [ratio est].

Vale, fili dulcissime.

Ad Nepotem Ausonium

Sunt etiam musis sua ludicra : mixta camenis
otia sunt, mellite nepos ; nec semper acerbi
exercet pueros vox imperiosa magistri,
set requie studiique vices rata tempora servant.
et satis est puero memori legisse libenter,   5
et cessare licet.   Graio schola nomine dicta est,
iusta laboriferis tribuantur ut otia musis.
quo magis alternum certus succedere ludum
disce libens : longum delinitura laborem
intervalla damus.   studium puerile fatiscit,   10
laeta nisi austeris varientur, festa profestis.
disce libens, tetrici nec praeceptoris habenas

---

[1] Terence, *Eun.* 313.

allow them to run on smoothly, so that these little
bits may be attractive rather than forceful, like those
marriageable daughters—

> " whom their mothers seek to make
> Low-shouldered and tight-laced, to seem more trim "[1]

—you know the rest.

It only remains, then, for you to say: " Why do
you wait for my criticism on what you yourself pro-
claim to be a faulty piece of work?"   My answer,
of course, will be that I blush for verses of this sort
in public, but am less ashamed of them when be-
tween you and me; for I write them to suit his
years rather than my own—or perhaps to suit mine
also: old men are twice children!   In short, good-
bye to your strictures: I have to do with a child.

Farewell, my darling son.

To Ausonius my Grandson

The Muses also have their own sports: hours of
ease find place among the Camenae, my honey-
sweet grandson; nor does the sour schoolmaster's
domineering voice always harass boys, but spells of
rest and study keep each their appointed times.
As for an attentive boy to have read his lessons
willingly is enough, so to rest is lawful.   " School"
has been called by that Greek name, that the labo-
rious Muses may be allowed due share of leisure.
Wherefore the more, assured that play follows work
in turn, learn willingly: to beguile the weariness of
long toil we grant spells of leisure.   Boyish zeal
flags unless serious work is interspersed with merri-
ment, and workaday with holiday.   Learn readily,
and loathe not, my grandson, the control of your

detestere, nepos. numquam horrida forma magistri.
ille licet tristis senio nec voce serenus
aspera contractae minitetur iurgia frontis,   15
numquam inmanis erit, placida suetudine vultus
qui [1] semel inbuerit. rugas nutricis amabit,
qui refugit matrem. pappos aviasque trementes
anteferunt patribus seri, nova cura, nepotes.
sic neque Peliaden terrebat Chiron Achillem   20
Thessalico permixtus equo nec pinifer Atlans
Amphitryoniadem puerum, set blandus uterque
mitibus adloquiis teneros mulcebat alumnos.
tu quoque ne metuas, quamvis schola verbere multo
increpet et truculenta senex gerat ora magister :   25
degeneres animos timor arguit. at tibi consta
intrepidus, nec te clamor plagaeque sonantes,
nec matutinis agitet formido sub horis.
quod sceptrum vibrat ferulae, quod multa supellex
virgea, quod fallax scuticam praetexit aluta,   30
quod fervent trepido subsellia vestra tumultu,
pompa loci et vani fucatur scaena timoris.
haec olim genitorque tuus genetrixque secuti
securam placido mihi permulsere senectam.
tu senium, quodcumque superlabentibus annis   35
fata dabunt, qui nomen avi geris, indole prima,
prime nepos, vel re vel spe mihi porge fruendum.
nunc ego te puerum, mox in iuvenalibus annis
iamque virum cernam, si fors ita iusserit ; aut si

----

[1] *MSS.*: cui, *Peiper.*

grim teacher. A master's looks need never cause a
shudder. Though he be grim with age and, ungentle
of voice, threaten harsh outbursts with frowning
brows, never will he seem savage to one who has
tutored his face to habitual calm. A child will love
its nurse's wrinkles, who shrinks from its mother;
grandchildren when they come at last, a new anxiety,
prefer doddering grandsires and granddams to their
parents. So Thessalian Chiron did not affright Achilles,
Peleus' son, though he was quite half a horse, nor
pine-bearing Atlas scare Amphitryo's youthful son,
but both coaxingly used to soothe their young pupils
with gentle words. You also be not afraid, though
the school resound with many a stroke and the old
master wear a lowering face: "fear proves a spirit
degenerate." [1] But to yourself be true, mocking at
fear, and let no outcry, nor sound of stripes, nor
dread, make you quake as the morning hours come
on. That he brandishes the cane for sceptre, that he
has a full outfit of birches, that he has a tawse
artfully hidden in innocent washleather, that scared
confusion sets your benches abuzz, is but the outward
show of the place and painted scenery to cause idle
fears. Your father and mother went through all
this in their day, and have lived to soothe my peace-
ful and serene old age. To that old age, for what-
ever space the Fates shall grant in the still coming
years, do you, who bear your grandfather's name,
my first-born grandson, with your first-born powers,
afford the joy that springs from achievement or
from promise. Now I see you a boy, soon shall I
see you in years of youth, and by and by a man, if
Chance so bid; or if this be grudged, yet will I

---

[1] Virgil, *Aen.* iv. 13.

invidia est, sperabo tamen, nec vota fatiscent,   40
ut patris utque mei non inmemor ardua semper
praemia musarum cupias facundus et olim
hac grad are via, qua nos praecessimus et cui
proconsul genitor, praefectus avunculus instant.

Perlege, quodcumque est memorabile. prima
  monebo.   45
conditor Iliados et amabilis orsa Menandri
evolvenda tibi : tu flexu et acumine vocis
innumeros numeros doctis accentibus effer
adfectusque inpone legens.   distinctio sensum
auget et ignavis dant intervalla vigorem.   50

Ecquando ista meae contingent dona senectae?
quando oblita mihi tot carmina totque per aevum
conexa historiae, soccos aulaeaque regum
et melicos lyricosque modos profando novabis
obductosque seni facies puerascere sensus ?   55
te praeeunte, nepos, modulata poemata Flacci
altisonumque iterum fas est didicisse Maronem.
tu quoque, qui Latium lecto sermone, Terenti,
comis et adstricto percurris pulpita socco,

---

[1] Thessalius (the father) was proconsul of Africa (378–
379 A.D.); Hesperius (the uncle) prefect of Italy, Illyricum
and Africa (377–380).

[2] i.e. the loose measures of Comedy : cp. the epitaph of
Plautus ap. Au us Gellius, i. 24 :—

  Scena est deserta.   Dein Risus, Ludu', Jocusque
  Et numeri innumeri simul omnes collacrumarunt.

[3] For the general sense of this passage compare the obser-
vation of the Comte de Tressan on the Abbé Le Sage (quoted
in Sir Walter Scott's *Life of Le Sage*) : "He possessed the

76

hope—nor shall my prayers grow weary—that, not
unmindful of your father and myself, you may ever
strive to win through eloquence the hard-won prizes
of the Muses, and some day tread this path wherein
I have gone before and your father, the proconsul,
and your uncle the prefect [1] now press on.

[45] Read thoroughly whatever is worth remember-
ing: I will give you some first hints. You must open
the pages of the *Iliad's* creator, study the works
of lovable Menander: with modulation and with
stress of voice bring out "measureless measures" [2]
with a scholar's accent, and infuse expression as you
read. Punctuation enforces the meaning, and pauses
give strength even to dull passages. [3]

[51] Ah, when shall these gifts reward mine old age?
When shall those many poems by me forgot, those
many links in the chain of history through the ages,
those comedies, royal tragedies, and strains melic
and lyric [4] by thine [5] utterance be recalled? When
wilt thou make an old man's clouded faculties grow
youthful? With thee for guide, my grandson, once
more may I dare to learn Flaccus' rhythmic strains
and Maro's sonorous lines. Do thou, too, Terence,
who with thy choice speech [6] adornest Latium, and
with well-fitting sock [7] trippest o'er our stage, compel

uncommon art of that variation of tone and of employing
those brief pauses, which, without being actual declamation,
impress on the hearers the sentiments and beauties of the
author."

[4] *i.e.* adapted for the flute or the lyre.

[5] The style being here elevated, a change to the second
person singular may be permitted.

[6] *cp.* Cicero quoted in Suetonius, *Life of Terence* : tu quo-
que qui solus lecto sermone, Terenti. . . .

[7] *cp.* Milton, *L'Allegro* : "If Jonson's learned sock be on."

ad nova vix memorem diverbia coge senectam.   60
iam facinus, Catilina, tuum Lepidique tumultum,
ab Lepido et Catulo iam res et tempora Romae
orsus bis senos seriem conecto per annos.
iam lego civili mixtum mavorte duellum,
movit quod socio Sertorius exul Hibero.[1]   65
    Nec rudis haec avus admoneo, set mille docendo
ingenia expertus. multos lactantibus annis
ipse alui gremioque fovens et murmura solvens
eripui tenerum blandis nutricibus aevum.
mox pueros molli monitu et formidine leni   70
pellexi, ut mites peterent per acerba profectus,
carpturi dulcem fructum radicis amarae.
idem vesticipes motu iam puberis aevi
ad mores artesque bonas fandique vigorem
produxi, quamquam imperium cervice negarent   75
ferre nec insertis praeberent ora lupatis.
ardua temperies, dura experientia, rarus
eventus, longo rerum spectatus ab usu,
ut regat indocilem mitis censura iuventam.
quae tolerata mihi, donec iam aerumna iuvaret   80
leniretque usu bona consuetudo laborem,
donec ad Augustae pia munera disciplinae
accirer varioque accingerer auctus honore,
aurea cum parere mihi palatia iussum.
absistat Nemesis, ferat et fortuna iocantem: 85

---

[1] *sc.* 78 B.C. Ausonius here adapts a fragment from
Sallust's *Histories* (frag. 1).

my scarce-remembering age to new delight in thy
dialogues. Now, Catiline, thy monstrous plot, now
Lepidus' sedition, now from the year of Lepidus
and Catulus [1] the fortunes and vicissitudes of Rome
do I commence and trace their sequence through
twice six years. Now read I of that war, not free
from civil strife,[2] which banished Sertorius stirred
up with the aid of his Iberian allies.

[66] And not without skill do I, thy grandfather,
counsel thee thus, but from the experience gained
in training a thousand minds. Many from their in-
fant years have I myself brought up, and, cherishing
them in my bosom and hushing their complaints,
have stolen their tender years from their fond nurses.
Presently, as boys, with mild warnings and gentle
threats I lured them to seek through sourness for
ripe success and pluck sweet fruit sprung from a
bitter root. I, too, when they assumed manhood's
garb and reached their vigorous prime, led them on
towards good living and sound learning and forceful
speaking, even though they refused to bear the yoke
of command upon their necks and submitted not
their mouths to the jagged bits thrust upon them.
Hard the control, rough the experience, scanty the
result when viewed after long practice, to govern
headstrong youth with mild correction! These toils
did I endure until—when now my pains were be-
coming pleasant and kindly Custom was lightening
my toil through use—until, invoked to the sacred
task of an Emperor's instruction, I am exalted and
compassed about with honours manifold, what time
the golden Palace was bidden to obey me. Let
Nemesis hold aloof, and may Fortune bear with my

[2] Sertorius was joined by a number of Marian refugees,
particularly by Perpenna who assassinated him in 72 B.C.

praesedi imperio, dum praetextatus in ostro
et sceptro et solio praefert sibi iura magistri
maioresque putat nostros Augustus honores.
quos mox sublimi maturus protulit auctu,
quaestor ut Augustis, patri natoque, crearer,   90
ut praefecturam duplicem sellamque curulem,
ut trabeam pictamque togam, mea praemia, consul
induerem fastisque meis praelatus haberer.

His ego quaesivi meritum quam grande nepoti
consul avus lumenque tuae praeluceo vitae.   95
quamvis et patrio iamdudum nomine clarus,
posses ornatus, posses oneratus haberi ;
accessit tamen ex nobis honor inclitus.   hunc tu
effice, ne sit onus, per te ut conixus in altum
conscendas speresque tuos te consule fasces.   100

XXIII.—Ausonius Pontio Paulino filio cum ille
    misisset Poematium versibus plurimis de Re-
    gibus ex Tranquillo collectis

Condiderat iam Solis equos Tartesia Calpe
stridebatque freto Titan iam segnis Hibero :

---

[1] Gratian.   [2] See *Introduction*, p. xi.
[3] *i.e.* he was exalted above his colleague, in that the year
was designated "Consule Ausonio."
[4] The characteristic play on *ornatus . . . oneratus* cannot
well be reproduced
[5] Paulinus, born at Bordeaux (?) in 353 or 354 A.D., had
been a pupil of Ausonius. He practised in the courts and
quickly rose to high honours, becoming consul in 378. He

light speaking: I held sway o'er the Empire, while
a schoolboy[1] endowed with purple, sceptre, throne,
submitted himself to a tutor's laws, and Augustus
held my dignity above his own. That dignity in
due time, when grown to manhood, he advanced to
dizzy heights, so that I was created Quaestor by
the Augusti, father and son; so that a two-fold
prefecture[2] and curule chair were mine; so that,
for my reward, as consul was I invested with the
purple robe and the embroidered toga, and was held
pre-eminent in the annals of my year.[3]

[94] Thus have I gained all possible advantage for
my grandchild, thy consul-grandfather, and shine
forth the beacon of thy life. Even though, long
since distinguished even through thy father's fame,
thou mightst seem graced, mightst seem laden;[4]
yet from me thou hast gained signal renown besides.
This render thou no load, but by thine own efforts
struggle to climb on high and hope for thine own
insignia, thine own consulate.

XXIII.—AUSONIUS TO PONTIUS PAULINUS,[5] HIS SON,
WHEN THE LATTER HAD SENT HIM A POEM ON
THE KINGS, OF GREAT LENGTH AND BASED ON
TRANQUILLUS

Now had Tartesian Calpe hidden the Sun's coursers
and Titan, now feeble, plunged hissing[6] 'neath the

married a Spanish wife, Therasia (the "Tanaquil" of sub-
sequent letters); but in 389 or 390 retired from the world to
Barcelona, where he was baptized and ordained priest in 393.
In 394 he left for Nola, where he dwelt as an ascetic near
the tomb of St. Felix. About 409 A.D. he was consecrated
bishop of Nola, and died in 431 A.D.
[6] cp. Juvenal Sat. xiv. 279 f.: sed longe Calpe relicta
Audiet Herculeo stridentem gurgite solem.

iam succedentes quatiebat Luna iuvencas,
vinceret ut tenebras radiis velut aemula fratris;
iam volucres hominumque genus superabile curis   5
mulcebant placidi tranquilla oblivia somni;
transierant Idus, medius suprema December
tempora venturo properabat iungere Iano;
et nonas decimas ab se Nox longa Kalendas
iugiter acciri celebranda ad festa iubebat.   10

Nescis, puto, quid velim tot versibus dicere. medius fidius neque ego bene intellego: tamen suspicor. iam prima nox erat ante diem nonum decimum kal. Ian., cum redditae sunt mihi litterae tuae oppido quam litteratae. his longe iucundissimum poema subdideras, quod de tribus Suetonii libris, quos ille de regibus dedit, in epitomen coegisti tanta elegantia, solus ut mihi videare adsecutus, quod contra rerum naturam est, brevitas ut obscura non esset. in his versibus ego ista collegi:

Europamque Asiamque duo vel maxima terrae
membra, quibus Libyam dubie Sallustius addit
Europae adiunctam, possit cum tertia dici,
regnatas multis, quos fama oblitterat et quos
barbara Romanae non tradunt nomina linguae—   5
Illibanum Numidamque Avelim Parthumque Vononem
et Caranum, Pellaea dedit qui nomina regum,

---

[1] *i.e.* Dec. 14th.
[2] For the opening of the letter down to this point *cp.* Seneca, *Apocolocyntosis*, 2.
[3] This work is no longer extant.
[4] The first two kings are unknown: for Vonones see Tac.

Iberian wave; now was Luna lashing on her advancing heifers to vanquish darkness with her beams as though vying with her brother; now birds and human kind, so vulnerable by care, were wooing peaceful sleep and calm forgetfulness; the Ides were passed, and mid-December was hastening to link his last days with approaching Janus; and long Night was bidding the nineteenth day of the Calends[1] be summoned forthwith to celebrate the feast.

You do not know, I expect, what I wish to say in all these verses. So help me Heaven! even I do not clearly understand: yet I have a glimmering. It was early in the night preceding the nineteenth day of the Calends of January[2] when your wonderfully lettered letter was delivered me. Together with this you sent an extremely delightful poem wherein you have condensed the three books of Suetonius, which he devotes to the Kings,[3] so gracefully that I regard you as having alone achieved what is contrary to the ordinary course of things— conciseness without obscurity. Amongst these verses I have picked out the following :—

"Europe and Asia, Earth's two greatest members, whereto uncertainly Sallust adds Libya as appanage of Europe, whereas it might be called a third part of the globe, have been ruled by many kings whom Fame blots from her page, and whom their uncouth names perpetuate not in Roman speech —Illibanus, Numidian Avelis, Vonones the Parthian, Caranus who founded the dynasty of Pella,[4] and he

Ann. ii. 1, 58, 68. Caranus, a Heraclid, was the reputed successor of Macedon, son of Deucalion, and ancestor of the Macedonian kings. For Nechepsos see Julius Firmicus, *Math.* viii. 5, and for Sesostris, Herodotus ii. 104 ff.

quique magos docuit mysteria vana Nechepsos
et qui regnavit sine nomine moxque Sesostris . . .

Haec tu quam perite et concinne, quam modulate
et dulciter, ita iuxta naturam Romanorum accentuum
enuntiasti, ut tamen veris et primigenis vocibus sua
fastiga non perirent.   iam quid de eloquentia dicam?
liquido adiurare possum nullum tibi ad poeticam fa-
cundiam Romanae iuventutis aequari: certe ita mihi
videri.   si erro, pater sum, fer me et noli exigere
iudicium obstante pietate.   verum ego cum pie dili-
gam, sincere et severe iudico.   adfice me, oro, tali
numere frequenter, quo et oblector et honoror.   ac-
cessit tibi ad artem poeticam mellea adulatio.   quid
enim aliud agunt:

Audax Icario qui fecit nomina ponto
et qui Chalcidicas moderate enavit ad arces,

nisi ut tu vegetam et sublimem alacritatem tuam
temeritatem voces, me vero, et consultum et quem
filius debeat imitari, salutari prudentia praeditum
dicas? quod equidem contra est.   nam tu summa
sic adpetis, ut non decidas: senectus mea satis
habet, si consistat.

Hacc ad te breviter et illico vesperis illius secuto
mane dictavi; ita enim tabellarius tuus, ut epistulam

---

[1] *cp.* Virgil, *Aen.* vi. 16.

who taught the wizards unavailing mysteries, Nechepsos, or reigned and left no name, and afterwards Sesostris . . ."

How skilfully and neatly, how harmoniously and sweetly have you delivered these names, conforming at once to the character of our Roman accent, yet not allowing the true and original sounds to lose their proper stress! And then what shall I say of your gift for expression? I can absolutely take my oath that for fluency in verse none of our Roman youths is your equal: at any rate, that is my opinion. If I am wrong, I am your father, bear with me and do not force from me a verdict which my natural feelings reject. But in fact, while I love fondly, I criticise frankly and strictly. Bestow on me, I beg, such favours constantly, thereby both delighting and complimenting me. Your skill in poetry has the additional attraction of delicious flattery. For what else do these lines mean?—

" He who through rashness gave his name to the
    Icarian Sea
  And he who, prudent, winged his way to the
    Chalcidian hold," [1]

save that you call your own lively and soaring vigour rashness, but affirm that I, being both wary and one whom a son ought to imitate, am endowed with a wholesome cautiousness? [2] But indeed the reverse is true. For you fly high in such wise that you do not fall: my old age is content to stay still.

I make this brief pronouncement out of hand on the morning next after the evening mentioned: for your messenger is only waiting long enough to take

[2] *i.e.* Paulinus compares himself to Icarus and Ausonius to Daedalus.

referret, instabat. nam si mihi otium fuerit, oblec-
tabile negotium erit ad te prolixius delirare, te ut
eliciam, mihi ut satisfaciam. vale.

XXIV.—Ausonius Paulino Sal. Pl. D.

Paulino Ausonius.   metrum sic suasit, ut esses
  tu prior et nomen praegrederere meum,
quamquam et fastorum titulo prior et tua Romae
  praecessit nostrum sella curulis ebur,
et, quae iamdudum tibi palma poetica pollet,   5
  lemnisco ornata est, quo mea palma caret.
longaevae tantum superamus honore senectae.
  quid refert?   cornix non ideo ante cycnum;
nec quia mille annos vivit Gangeticus ales,
  vincit centum oculos, regie pavo, tuos.   10
cedimus ingenio, quantum praecedimus aevo;
  adsurgit Musae nostra Camena tuae.
Vive, vale et totidem venturos consere ianos,
  quot tuus aut noster conseruere patres.

XXV.—Ausonius Paulino Suo Sal. Pl. D.

Quanto me adfecit beneficio non delata equidem,
sed suscepta mea querimonia, Pauline fili! veritus
displicuisse oleum, quod miseras, munus iterasti, ad-
dito etiam Barcinonensis muriae condimento cumu-

---

[1] The *lemniscus* was a streamer attached to a victor's
crown, as a mark of extraordinary distinction.
[2] The Phoenix: *cp. Griphus* 16.

back a reply. For if I have spare time, it will be a delightful occupation to maunder on at greater length to you, partly to draw you out, and partly to please myself. Farewell.

XXIV.—Ausonius to Paulinus sends hearty Greeting

To Paulinus, Ausonius. Metre so bids, placing you before me and setting your name in front of mine. And yet before mine comes your name in our annals, and at Rome your curule chair of ivory has precedence of mine, and in poetry your palm is long since decked with ribbons[1] which my palm lacks. 'Tis in the glory of prolonged old age alone I have the advantage—what matters that? The crow is not therein above the swan, nor, because he lives a thousand years, does the bird of Ganges[2] surpass the kingly peacock with his hundred eyes. I am beneath you in genius as far as I am above you in age; my homely Muse rises in deference to yours.

[13] Live, keep well, and in the time to come link New Year to New Year as oft as did your father or mine.

XXV.—Ausonius to his dear Paulinus sends hearty Greeting

What kind treatment of me, that my complaint is dealt with without even being delivered, my son Paulinus! Fearing that the oil you sent had not given satisfaction, you repeat the gift and, by the addition of some Barcelona sauce called *muria*,[3] in-

---

[3] = ἁλμυρίς: a sauce prepared by pickling the intestines of tunnies or scombers in brine.

latius praestitisti. scis autem me id nomen muriae, quod in usu vulgi est, nec solere nec posse dicere, cum scientissimi veterum et Graeca vocabula fastidientes Latinum in gari appellatione non habeant. sed ego, quocumque nomine liquor iste sociorum vocatur,

> Iam patinas implebo meas, ut parcior ille
> maiorum mensis applaria sucus inundet.

Quid autem tam amabile tamque hospitale, quam quod tu, ut me participes, delicias tuas in ipsa primitiarum novitate defrudas ? o melle dulcior, o Gratiarum venustate festivior, o ab omnibus patrio stringende complexu ! sed haec atque alia huius modi documenta liberalis animi aliquis fortasse et aliquando, quamvis rarus : illud de epistularum tuarum eruditione, de poematis iucunditate, de inventione et concinnatione iuro omnia nulli umquam imitabile futurum, etsi fateatur imitandum. de quo opusculo, ut iubes, faciam. exquisitim universa limabo et quamvis per te manus summa contigerit, caelum superfluae expolitionis adhibebo, magis ut tibi pare021, quam ut perfectis aliquid adiciam.

Interea tamen, ne sine corollario poetico tabellarius tuus rediret, paucis iambicis praeludendum

---

[1] = γάρον, a variety of *muria* prepared from the γάρος, or scomber.

[2] *cp.* Pliny, *N.H.* xxxi. 94 : aliud etiamnum liquoris exquisiti genus, quod *garon* vocavere, intestinis piscium . . .

crease its measure. But you know that I am neither
accustomed nor able to pronounce that name *muria*
which is popularly used, though the most learned of
the ancients, even while disdaining to use Greek
terms, have no Latin name by which to call *garum*.[1]
But by whatever name that " Liquor of the Allies " [2]
is called,

> " I'll flood my plate : this juice, too little used
>   By our forefathers, must overflow the spoon."

But what could be more friendly or more generous
than that you, to give me a share, should cheat
yourself of your own dainties just when freshly
coming into season? O friend sweeter than honey,
O more delightsome than the Graces' charms, O
worthy to be clasped by everyone in a fatherly
embrace! However, these and other tokens of a
generous nature some other, perchance, some day,
though but rarely, may reveal : as for your talent
shown in the scholarliness of your letter, in the
sweetness of your poem, in imagination and in apt
composition, I swear by everything that it will never
be imitable by any man, however much he admit
that it deserves imitation. As for the work itself,
I will do as you bid. I will work over the whole
minutely, and although it has received the highest
finish at your hands, I will apply my chisel to give a
superfinish however needless, but rather to obey you
than to add aught to what is perfect.

Meanwhile, however, that your messenger may
not return without a douceur of verse, I think I
must make a preliminary gambol in a few iambics

sale maceratis ut sit illa putrescentium sanies . . . Sociorum
id appellatur.

putavi, dum illud, quod a me heroico metro desideras, incohatur. isti tamen, ita te et Hesperium salvos habeam, quod spatio lucubratiunculae unius effusi, quamquam hoc ipsi de se probabunt, tamen nihil diligentiae ulterioris habuerunt. vale.

    Iambe Parthis et Cydonum spiculis,
iambe pinnis alitum velocior,
Padi ruentis impetu torrentior,
magna sonorae grandinis vi densior,
flammis corusci fulminis vibratior,   5
iam nunc per auras Persei talaribus
petasoque ditis Arcados vectus vola.
si vera fama est Hippocrene, quam pedis
pulsu citatam cornipes fudit fremens,
tu, fonte in ipso procreatus Pegasi,   10
primus novorum metra iunxisti pedum
sanctisque Musis concinentibus novem
caedem in draconis concitasti Delium.
    Fer hanc salutem praepes et volucripes
Paulini ad usque moenia, Hebromagum loquor, 15
et protinus, iam si resumptis viribus
alacri refecti corporis motu viget,
salvere iussum mox reposce mutuum.
nihil moreris iamque, dum loquor, redi,
imitatus illum stirpis auctorem tuae,   20
triplici furentem qui Chimaeram incendio
supervolavit tutus igne proximo.
dic "te valere," dic: "salvere te iubet
amicus et vicinus et fautor tuus,

---

[1] Mercury (born in Arcadia) was god of messengers: the *petasus*, with which he is represented, was worn by travellers and in later art is represented as winged.

[2] The first verse ever invented was believed to be the iambic ἰὴ παιάν, ἰὴ παιάν, ἰὴ παιάν—a strain with which

while the work in heroic strains which you want of me is beginning. But—so may I have you and Hesperius safe!—since they are dashed off in a single evening (though this they in themselves will guarantee), have had no further pains bestowed upon them. Farewell.

Iambus than Parthian or Cydonian dart, Iambus than wings of birds more fleet, than rushing Padus' current more impetuous, than the downpour of rattling hail more searching, than lightning's dazzling flash more darting, even now speed through the air borne by Perseus' winged sandals and with the cap of the Arcadian god.[1] If 'tis truly told that Hippocrene gushed forth at the hoof-beat of the impatient courser, thou, begotten in the very fount of Pegasus, wast first to link new rhythmic feet and, while the nine holy Muses sang in harmony, didst urge the lord of Delos to slaughter of the dragon.[2]

[14]Bear this my greeting, fleetfoot, winged-foot, even to the town where Paulinus dwells, I mean Hebromagus, and straightaway, if, his strength now regained, brisk vigour nerves his refreshed frame, bid him " hail," then demand of him a return. Tarry not at all, and return now ere I cease to speak, after the example of that author of thy source,[3] who o'er Chimaera with her triple blast of raging flame flew safe from the fire so near. Say " hail to thee," say " greetings to thee sends thy friend and neighbour

Apollo was encouraged in his struggle with the dragon for the possession of Delphi (see 1. 13). See Terentianus Maurus, 1558 ff., a passage which is almost paraphrased here.

[3] *i.e.* Hippocrene, which burst forth at the hoof-beat of Pegasus (auctor); *cp.* 11. 8 ff.

honoris auctor, altor ingenii tui." 25
dic et magister, dic parens, dic omnia
blanda atque sancta caritatis nomina.
haveque dicto dic vale, actutum et redi.

Quod si rogabit, quid super scriptis novis
maturus aevi nec rudis diiudicem : 30
nescire dices, sed paratum iam fore
heroicorum versuum plenum essedum.
cui subiugabo de molarum ambagibus,
qui machinali saxa volvunt pondere,
tripedes caballos terga ruptos verbere, 35
his ut vehantur tres sodales nuntii.
fors et rogabit, quos sodales dixeris
simul venire? dic : "Trinodem dactylum
vidi paratum crucianti cantherio :
spondeus illi lentipes ibat comes, 40
paribus moratur qui locis cursum meum,
mihique similis, semper adversus tamen,
nec par, nec impar, qui trochaeus dicitur."

Haec fare cursim nec moratus pervola,
aliquid reportans interim munusculi 45
de largitate musici promptarii.

XXVI.—Ausonius Paulino suo Sal. Pl. D.

Multas et frequentes mihi gratiae tuae causas et
occasio subinde nata concinnat et naturae tuae faci-
litas benigna conciliat, Pauline fili. nam quia nihil

---

[1] Paulinus owed his consulship to the influence of Ausonius.

and thy patron, the source of thine honours,[1] the
fosterer of thy intellect." Say also "master," say
"father," say every caressing name of hallowed
affection. And having said "Hail," say "Farewell"
and instantly return.

[29] But if he ask what judgment my ripe and not
unskilful age pronounces on his latest writings, say
thou knowest not, but that soon there will be ready
a waggon full of heroic verses. Thereto I will yoke
a pair of three-legged screws, back-broken with the
lash, taken from the labyrinths of the mill, where
by the heavy crank they turn the millstones, that
by these may travel three jovial messengers. Per-
chance, too, he will ask who are these jovial fellows
whom thou dost say are coming in a troop? Then
say: "I saw three-jointed Dactyl ready on a heart-
breaking hack;[2] slow-footed Spondee was tramping
in his company—he who at equal intervals checks
my career—and one much like me but always facing
about, neither equal to me nor unequal, who is called
Trochee."

[44] Thus speak: then in haste fly hither straight
without delay, bringing back meanwhile some little
gift from the abundance of that storehouse of poetry.

XXVI.—Ausonius to his friend Paulinus sends
hearty Greeting

Many and various are the causes I have for grati-
tude to you, which both circumstance, arising from
time to time, happily introduces, and the ready
generosity of your nature voluntarily invites, my
son Paulinus. For in that you deny me nothing

[2] cp. Plautus, Captivi, 814: qui advehuntur quadrupedanti
crucianti cantherio.

poscente me abnuis, magis acuis procaciam quam
retundis: ut nunc quoque in causa Philonis procu-
ratoris quondam mei experiere, qui apud Hebro-
magum conditis mercibus, quas per agros diversos
coemit, concesso ab hominibus tuis usus hospitio,
inmature periclitatur expelli. quod nisi indulseris
rogante me, ut et mora habitandi ad commodum
suum utatur et nauso aliave qua navi usque ad op-
pidum praebita frugis aliquantum nostrae advehi
possit, Lucaniacus ut inopia liberetur mature: tota
illa familia hominis litterati non ad Tullii frumen-
tariam, sed ad Curculionem Plauti pertinebit.

Hoc quo facilius impetrarem, aut quo maiorem
verereris molestiam, si negares, concinnatam iambis
signatamque ad te epistulam misi, ne subornatum
diceres tabellarium, si ad te sine signi fide veniret.
signavi autem, non, ut Plautus ait,

> Per ceram et linum [1] litterasque interpretes;

sed per poeticum characterem: magis notam inustam,
quam signum impressum iudicares.

> Philon, meis qui vilicatus praediis,
>   ut ipse vult, ἐπίτροπος,
> (nam gloriosum Graeculus nomen putat,
>   quod sermo fucat Dorius)

[1] So Plautus, *Pseud.* 42: lignum, *MSS.* and *Peiper.*

---

[1] Or Eburomagus, the modern Bram, near the foot of the
eastern Pyrenees.   [2] A.'s estate.

when I demand, you whet my effrontery rather than
blunt it; as now again you will realize in the matter
of Philo, formerly my bailiff, who, after storing at
Hebromagus[1] goods which he has bought up on
various estates, is in danger of being driven in-
conveniently from the shelter which your people
afforded him. And unless you kindly grant this my
request—namely that he be permitted to stay on
there as suits his purpose, and that a barge or some
sort of vessel be furnished him, that a little of my
corn may be transported as far as the town, thereby
delivering Lucaniacus[2] from famine betimes—a lite-
rary man's whole household there will be reduced,
not to Cicero's *Speech on the Corn Supply*,[3] but to the
Weevil of Plautus.

That I may the more easily obtain this boon, or
that you may fear greater bother if you refuse, I
send you a letter composed in iambics, and duly
sealed, that you may not say the messenger has
been tampered with, should he come to you without
the guarantee of a seal. Yet I have sealed it, not,
as Plautus says—

"With wax and thread and signs significant,"[4]

but with a poetic stamp: this you may regard more
as a brand burnt in than a seal impressed.[5]

Philo, who is bailiff of my estate, or as he him-
self wishes, the administrator (for your Greekling
thinks that a fine-sounding name which shows the

---

[3] *i.e.* the third speech against Verres, dealing with the
Sicilian corn supplies   [4] *Pseudolus*, 42.
[5] *i.e.* "my style is like the brand of a hot iron, not super-
ficial like the impression of a seal."

suis querellis adserit nostras preces,   5
    quas ipse lentus prosequor.
videbis ipsum, qualis adstet comminus,
    imago fortunae suae,
canus, comosus, hispidus, trux, atribux,
    Terentianus Phormio,   10
horrens capillis ut marinus asperis
    echinus aut versus mei.
hic saepe falsus messibus vegrandibus
    nomen perosus vilici,
semente sera sive multum praecoqua   15
    et siderali inscitia
caelum lacessens seque culpae subtrahens
    reos peregit caelites.
non cultor instans, non arator gnaruris,
    promusque quam condus magis,   20
terram infidelem nec feracem criminans
    negotiari maluit
mercator quo <libet> foro venalium,
    mutator ad Graecam fidem,
sapiensque supra Graeciae septem viros   25
    octavus accessit sophos.
et nunc paravit [1] triticum casco sale
    novusque pollet emporus ;
adit inquilinos, rura, vicos, oppida
    soli et sali commercio ;   30
acatis, phaselis, lintribus, stlattis, rate
    Tarnim et Garumnam permeat

[1] *Z* : parabit, *Peiper.*

---

[1] *cp.* Cic. *Pro Caecina,* x. 27 : nec minus niger, nec minus
confidens quam ille Terentianus est Phormio.

[2] Hor. *Epod* v. 27 f. : horret capillis ut marinus asperis
echinus aut Laurens aper.

gilt of the classic tongue), unites with his complaints
my prayers, which reluctantly I myself dispatch.
You shall see the man himself as he stands close by
me, the very image of his class, grey, bushy-haired,
unkempt, blustering, bullying, Terence's Phormio,[1]
with stiff hair bristling like a sea-urchin[2] or my lines.
This fellow, when light harvests had oft belied his
promises, came to hate the name of bailiff; and,
after sowing late or much too early through igno-
rance of the stars,[3] made accusation against the
powers above, carping at heaven and shifting the
blame from himself. No diligent husbandman, no
experienced ploughman, a spender rather than a
getter,[4] abusing the land as treacherous and un-
fruitful, he preferred to do business as a dealer in
any sale-market, bartering for "Greek credit,"[5] and,
wiser than the Seven Worthies of Greece, has joined
them as an eighth sage. And now he has provided
grain at the price of old salt,[6] and blossoms out
as a new trader; he visits tenants, country parts,
villages and townships, travelling by land and sea;
by bark, skiff, schooner, galley, he traverses the
windings of the Tarn and the Garonne, and by

[3] *i.e.* of those which mark the time for sowing. See
Hesiod, *W. and D.* 384, 615 f.
[4] *cp.* Plaut. *Pseud.* 608 : condus promus procurator peni.
[5] See *Epist.* vi. 42 (note).
[6] *i.e.* by bartering salt for grain.

ac lucra damnis, damna mutans fraudibus
  se ditat et me pauperat.
Is nunc ad usque vectus Hebromagum tuam   35
  sedem locavit mercibus,
ut inde nauso devehat[ur triticum [1]]
  nostros in usus, ut refert.
hunc ergo paucis ne graveris hospitem
  [cura diebus ut meet,[2]]   40
adactus ut mox navis auxilio tuae
  ad usque portus oppidi
iam iam Perusina, iam Saguntina fame
  Lucaniacum liberet.
Hoc si impetratum munus abs te accepero,   45
  prior colere quam Ceres :
Triptolemon olim, sive Epimenidem vocant,
  aut viliconum Buzygem,
tuo locabo postferendos numini,
  nam munus hoc fiet tuum.   50

XXVII.—Ad eundem cum ille ad alia magis
responderet neque se venturum polliceretur

Discutimus, Pauline, iugum, quod nota fovebat
temperies, leve quod positu et venerabile iunctis
tractabat paribus Concordia mitis habenis ;
quod per tam longam seriem volventibus annis
fabula non umquam, numquam querimonia movit, 5
nulla querella loco pepulit, non ira nec error

       [1] Suppl. *Schenkl.*   [2] Suppl. *Translator.*

---

   [1] *i.e.* where there is a profit he represents it (in his
accounts) as a loss ; and where there is really loss he
fraudulently enlarges it.
   [2] Perusia, held by L. Antonius, was reduced through
famine by Octavian (41–40 B.C.) ; Saguntum was similarly
taken by Hannibal (219 B.C.).

changing profits into losses and losses into frauds,[1] he makes himself rich and me poor.

[35] He now has sailed right up to your villa Hebromagus and made it the depôt for his goods, that thence by barge grain may be carried down for my service, as he avers. This guest, then, lest you be burdened, speed on his way in a few days, that, transported forthwith by the help of your vessel as far as the township's harbour, he may deliver Lucaniacus from famine by now, by now Perusian, by now Saguntine.[2]

[45] If I receive this boon I ask of you, you shall be worshipped above Ceres: old Triptolemus or, as some call him, Epimenides, or Buzyges,[3] the bailiff's patron, will I arrange to make inferior to your godhead, for this corn will become your gift.

XXVII.—To the same Paulinus, when he replied to everything else without promising to come

We are shaking off a yoke, Paulinus, which its tried equableness once made easy, a yoke lightly laid and worthy the respect of those it joined, which mild Concord used to guide with even reins; which through so long a line of rolling years never an idle tale, never a peevish complaint has stirred, nor quarrel thrust from its place, nor anger, nor misapprehension, nor Suspicion which, lending too ready

---

[3] According to Hesychius, an Attic hero who first yoked oxen to the plough: he was also known as Epimenides. Triptolemus was otherwise believed to have made this invention.

nec quae conpositis male suadae credula causis
concinnat veri similes suspicio culpas ;
tam placidum, tam mite iugum, quod utrique parentes
ad senium nostri traxere ab origine vitae   10
inpositumque piis heredibus usque manere
optarunt, dum longa dies dissolveret aevum.
et mansit, dum laeta fides nec cura laborat
officii servare vices, set sponte feruntur
incustoditum sibi continuantia cursum.   15

Hoc tam mite iugum docili cervice subirent
Martis equi stabuloque feri Diomedis abacti
et qui mutatis ignoti Solis habenis
fulmineum Phaethonta Pado mersere iugales.
discutitur, Pauline, tamen : nec culpa duorum   20
ista, set unius tantum tua.   namque ego semper
contenta cervice feram.   consorte laborum
destituor, nec tam promptum gestata duobus
unum deficiente pari perferre sodalem.
non animus viresque labant, sed iniqua ferendo   25
condicio est oneri, cum pondus utrumque relicto
ingruit acceduntque alienae pondera librae.
sic pars aegra hominis trahit ad contagia sanum
corpus et exigui quamvis discrimine membri
tota per innumeros artus conpago vacillat.   30
obruar usque tamen, veteris ne desit amici
me durante fides memorique ut fixa sub aevo
restituant profugum, solacia cassa, sodalem.

Inpie, Pirithoo disiungere Thesea posses
Euryalumque suo socium secernere Niso ;   35

ears to Persuasion's trumped-up pretexts, forms from them grievances to look like truth; so gentle, so easy a yoke which both our fathers drew on into old age from the beginning of their life, which, laid upon their duteous heirs, they would have had remain throughout till length of days broke up our lives. And remain it did, while there was joyous trust and no laborious care to maintain exchange of good offices, but they flowed freely, keeping unbroken their unguarded course.

[16] This yoke so mild Mars' horses would endure with obedient neck, and those wild steeds stolen from the stable of Diomedes, and even that team which, when another than the Sun held their reins, plunged lightning-blasted Phaëthon in the Padus. Yet it is being shaken off, Paulinus; and that, not through the fault of both, but of one alone—of thee. For my neck will ever bear it gladly. It is the partner of my toil deserts me, and 'tis not so easy for one, when his fellow fails, to carry on alone that which the two bare as comrades. Heart and strength fail not, but unfair is the condition of carrying a burden, when both loads are laid on the partner left and the weight of another's charge is added. So one ailing member in a man involves the sound body in infection, and the peril even of a tiny limb makes the whole knitted frame totter in all its countless joints. Yet let me even be crushed if only loyalty to my old friend fail not while I endure, and memory deep-planted in the years bring back—vain consolation!—my errant comrade.

[34] Ah, heartless! From Peirithous thou couldst part Theseus and separate Euryalus from the company of his dear Nisus; urged to flight by thee,

te suadente fugam Pylades liquisset Oresten
nec custodisset Siculus vadimonia Damon.
quantum oblectamen populi, quae vota bonorum
sperato fraudata bono! gratantia cuncti
verba loquebantur: iam nomina nostra parabant   40
inserere antiquis aevi melioris amicis.
cedebat Pylades, Phrygii quoque gloria Nisi
iam minor et promissa obiens vadimonia Damon.
nos documenta magis felicia, qualia magnus
Scipio longaevique dedit sapientia Laeli: 45
nos studiis animisque isdem miracula cunctis,
hoc maiora, pares fuimus quod dispare in aevo.
ocius illa iugi fatalis solvere lora
Pellaeum potuisse ducem reor, abdita opertis
principiis et utroque caput celantia nodo.   50

    Grande aliquod verbum nimirum diximus, ut se
inferret nimiis vindex Rhamnusia votis;
Arsacidae ut quondam regis non laeta triumphis
grandia verba premens ultrix dea Medica belli
sistere Cecropidum in terris monumenta paranti   55
obstitit et Graio iam iam figenda tropaeo
ultro etiam victis Nemesis stetit Attica Persis.

    Quae tibi Romulidas proceres vexare libido est?
in Medos Arabasque tuos per nubila et atrum
perge chaos: Romana procul tibi nomina sunto.   60

---

[1] cp. *Epigr.* xlii. Pausanias (I. xxxiii. 2) relates that the
Persians, making sure of victory, brought with them to Mara-
thon a block of Parian marble to be erected there as a
trophy (*Graio iam iam figenda tropaeo*). After the rout of the

Pylades would have left Orestes, and Sicilian Damon
would not have kept his bond! What general de-
light, what good men's prayers have thus been
cheated of their looked-for gain! They all were
speaking words of congratulation: already they were
about to enter our names in the lists of friends be-
longing to nobler days of old. Pylades was giving
place, Phrygian Nisus also now was growing less
famed, and Damon who met his promised bail. We
showed less tragic tokens of friendship, even as
great Scipio and Laelius, long-lived in wisdom: we,
with pursuits and hearts the same, were marvellous
to all, the more for this that we were equals though
unequal-aged. Sooner, methinks, could the Pellaean
war-lord have loosed the lashings of that fate-fraught
yoke, although their beginning was concealed from
view and their end hidden by a double knot.

[51] Some presumptuous word we surely spoke, that
the vengeful queen of Rhamnus thus made onslaught
on our excessive hopes; as in old days when, angered
at the vaunting of Arsaces' royal son, the avenging
goddess, crushing his presumptuous boasts, with-
stood his purpose to set up in the land of Cecrops'
sons a memorial of the Median arms, and just when
she was to be raised to support a trophy of Greek
arms, deliberately took her stand as Attic Nemesis
to mark the Persian rout.[1]

[58] What caprice of thine is this to harass nobles
of the seed of Romulus? Against Medes and Arabs,
thy natural foes, advance through clouds and chaos
black: from men of Roman name keep thou afar.

Persians this was wrought by Phidias (others say Agora-
critus) into a statue of Nemesis and set up at Rhamnus
(see l. 52).

illic quaere alios oppugnatura sodales,
livor ubi iste tuus ferrugineumque venenum
opportuna tuis inimicat pectora fucis.
Paulinum Ausoniumque, viros, quos sacra Quirini
purpura et auratus trabeae velavit amictus,   65
non decet insidiis peregrinae cedere divae.

    Quid queror eoique insector crimina monstri?
occidui me ripa Tagi, me Punica laedit
Barcino, me bimaris iuga ninguida Pyrenaei.
[laedis et ipse tuos qui deseris ultro, relictis[1]]
moenibus et patrio forsan quoque vestis et oris   70
[more, interque novos qui nunc versaris amicos[1]]
quemque suo longe dirimat provincia tractu
trans montes solemque alium, trans flumina et urbes
et quod terrarum caelique extenditur inter
Emeritensis Anae lataeque fluenta Garumnae.

    Quod si intervalli spatium tolerabile limes   75
poneret exiguus (quamvis longa omnia credant,
qui simul esse volunt), faceret tamen ipsa propinquos
cura locos, mediis iungens distantia verbis;
Santonus ut sibi Burdigalam, mox iungit Aginnum
illa sibi et populos Aquitanica rura colentes;   80
utque duplex Arelas Alpinae tecta Viennae,
Narbonemque pari spatio sibi conserit, et mox
quinquiplicem socias tibi, Martie Narbo, Tolosam.
hoc mihi si spatium vicinis moenibus esset,

                [1] Suppl. *Translator.*

There rather seek thou friendships to assail, where
that jealousy of thine and rankling venom estranges
hearts well fitted for thy deceits.   For Paulinus and
Ausonius, men whom the sacred purple of Quirinus
and the golden tissue of the consul's robe have
enwrapped, to yield to the stratagems of a foreign
goddess is not seemly.

[67] Wherefore do I complain and cry out on the
ravage of an eastern monster ? 'Tis western Tagus'
shores, 'tis Punic Barcelona that does me hurt, 'tis
the Pyrenees whose snowy crests join sea to sea,
thou thyself also dost me hurt, thou who abandonest
thy friends without a cause, deserting thy town and,
perchance, the native fashion of thy dress and speech,
thou who now dwellest among new friends, whom
the extent of a wide province parts from me beyond
mountains 'neath an alien sun, beyond rivers and
cities and all the land and sky which lie outspread
betwixt Merida by Ana's streams and the wide flood
of the Garonne.

[75] If only the division were narrow and interposed
a separating space not too formidable (albeit they
think every place far off who seek to be together),
even so affection's self would make the places near,
spanning the interval with a bridge of words ; even
as Saintes keeps touch with Bordeaux, and she again
with Agen and the folk who till the country parts
of Aquitaine ; and as two-fold Arles[1] links to her-
self at equal distances the roofs of Alpine Vienne
and Narbonne ; and then thou, Martian[2] Narbonne,
alliest with thee five-fold Toulouse.[3] If such the
distance severing our neighbouring towns, then

---

[1] cp. *Ordo Urb. Nob.* x. 1.
[2] *id.* 2 ; xix. 1.   [3] *id.* xviii. 7 ff.

tunc ego te ut nostris aptum conplecterer ulnis   85
adflaretque tuas aures nostrae aura loquellae.
    Nunc tibi trans Alpes et marmoream Pyrenen
Caesarea est Augusta domus, Tyrrhenica propter
Tarraco et ostrifero super addita Barcino ponto:
me iuga Burdigala,[1] trino me flumina coetu   90
secernunt turbis popularibus otiaque inter
vitiferi exercent colles laetumque colonis
uber agri, tum prata virentia, tum nemus umbris
mobilibus celebrique frequens ecclesia vico
totque mea in Novaro sibi proxima praedia pago,   95
dispositis totum vicibus variata per annum,
egelidae ut tepeant hiemes rabidosque per aestus
adspirent tenues frigus subtile Aquilones.
te sine set nullus grata vice provenit annus.
ver pluvium sine flore fugit, Canis aestifer ardet,   100
nulla autumnales variat Pomona sapores
effusaque hiemem contristat Aquarius unda.
agnoscisne tuam, Ponti dulcissime, culpam?
nam mihi certa fides nec conmutabilis umquam
Paulini illius veteris reverentia durat   105
quaeque meoque tuoque fuit concordia patri.
si tendi facilis cuiquam fuit arcus Ulixei
aut praeter dominum vibrabilis ornus Achilli,
nos quoque tam longo Rhamnusia foedere solvet.

       [1] *P* : Burdigalae, *Peiper*.

---

  [1] Originally Salduba, it was renamed in honour of Augustus in 25 B.C.

would I clasp thee, ready to my embrace, and the air of my complaint would be breathed into thy ears.

[87] Now for thee beyond the Alps and stony Pyrenees, Saragossa is thy home,[1] Tyrrhenian Tarragona[2] is near by, and Barcelona built above the oyster-bearing sea: me hills, me rivers in triple array[3] part from Bordeaux and from the common throng, and in my leisure the vine-clad hills engage me, the rich glebe with its blithe peasantry, now the green meads, now the copse with its dancing shades, the church[4] thronged with crowding villagers, and all those my domains hard by each other in Novarus village, which enjoy such change at the various seasons throughout the year, that the chill winters are warm for them and in the furious summer heats soft north winds breathe over them a gentle coolness. Yet without thee the year advances, bringing no grateful change. The rainy Spring flits by lacking its flower, the heat-bringing Dog-Star parches, Pomona brings not variety of sweet autumn fruits, and with outpoured water Aquarius makes gloomy all the winter. Dost thou perceive thy fault, my dearest Pontius? For my loyalty remains steadfast and, never to be changed, my regard for the Paulinus of old days endures, even as the harmony betwixt my sire and thine. If Ulysses' bow was easy to be strung by any man, or if Achilles' spear could be wielded save by its lord, then shall the queen of Rhamnus loose us from so long a bond.

[2] Tarragona was not an Etrurian foundation, but looks out over the Etruscan Sea.

[3] The Garonne, the Durane, and the Charente.

[4] Or assembly.

Set cur tam maesto sero tristia carmina versu   110
et non in meliora animus se vota propinquat?
sit procul iste metus.   certa est fiducia nobis,
si genitor natusque dei pia verba volentum
accipiat, nostro reddi te posse precatu,
ne sparsam raptamque domum lacerataque centum
per dominos veteris Paulini regna fleamus   116
teque vagum toto quam longa Hispania tractu,
inmemorem veterum peregrinis fidere amicis.

Adcurre, o nostrum decus, o mea maxima cura,
votis ominibusque bonis precibusque vocatus,   120
adpropera, dum tu iuvenis, dum nostra senectus
servat inexhaustum tibi gratificata vigorem.
ecquando iste meas inpellet nuntius aures?
"Ecce tuus Paulinus adest: iam ninguida linquit
oppida Hiberorum, Tarbellica iam tenet arva,   125
Hebromagi iam tecta subit, iam praedia fratris
vicina ingreditur, iam labitur amne secundo
iamque in conspectu est: iam prora obvertitur amni:
ingressusque sui celebrata per ostia portus
totum occursantis populi praevertitur agmen   130
et sua praeteriens iam iam tua limina pulsat."

Credimus an, qui amant, ipsi sibi somnia fingunt?

[110] But why weave I such sad refrain in mournful verse, why does my heart not turn to nobler prayers? Far be that fear! Sure is my confidence that, if the Father and the Son of God accept the reverent words of those who seek, thou canst be restored at my prayer, that I may weep not for a home scattered and ravaged, for the realm rent in pieces between a hundred owners, once Paulinus's, and for thee, that, wandering with a range as wide as the extent of Spain, unmindful of old friends thou dost trust in strangers.

[119] O hasten hither, my pride, my chiefest care, summoned with vows, good omens, and with prayers speed thee hither, while thou art young and while my old age to win thy favour preserves its vigour unconsumed. Ah, when shall this news break on my ears? "Lo, thy Paulinus is at hand: now he leaves the snowy towns of Spain, now reaches the fields of Tarbellae, now approaches the homesteads of Hebromagus, now enters his brother's domains hard by, now glides down stream, and now is in sight: now the prow is being swung out into the stream:[1] now he has passed the thronged entrance of his home-port, outstrips the whole host of folk who hurry to meet him, and passing his own doors now, even now beats at thine."

"Do I believe, or do those who love feign dreams for their own selves."[2]

[1] *cp.* Virgil, *Aen.* vi. 3: obvertunt pelago proras. The prow was swung outwards, the stern brought in to land for mooring.　[2] Virgil, *Ecl.* viii. 108.

AUSONIUS

XXVIII.—Ad eundem Pontium Paulinum Epistula
subinde scripta

Proxima quae nostrae fuerat querimonia chartae,
credideram quod te, Pauline, inflectere posset
eliceretque tuam blanda obiurgatio vocem.
set tu, iuratis velut alta silentia sacris
devotus teneas, perstas in lege tacendi.   5
non licet? anne pudet, si quis tibi iure paterno
vivat amicus adhuc maneasque obnoxius heres?
ignavos agitet talis timor, at tibi nullus
sit metus et morem missae acceptaeque salutis
audacter retine. vel si tibi proditor instat   10
aut quaesitoris gravior censura timetur,
occurre ingenio, quo saepe occulta teguntur.
Thraeicii quondam quam saeva licentia regis
fecerat elinguem, per licia texta querellas
edidit et tacitis mandavit crimina telis.   15
et pudibunda suos malo commisit amores
virgo nec erubuit tacituro conscia pomo.
depressis scrobibus vitium regale minister
credidit idque diu texit fidissima tellus:
inspirata dehinc vento cantavit harundo.   20
lacte incide notas: arescens charta tenebit
semper inaspicuas; prodentur scripta favillis.
vel Lacedaemoniam scytalen imitare, libelli
segmina Pergamei tereti circumdata ligno

---

[1] The allusion is probably to the rule of silence on which
monks at this period laid great stress.

[2] Therasia, Paulinus' wife is meant: *cp.* l. 31 (below).

[3] For the story of Philomela and Tereus see Ovid, *Metam.*
vi. 574 ff.

THE EPISTLES

XXVIII.—To the same Pontius Paulinus: a Letter
WRITTEN JUST AFTER THE PRECEDING

I HOPED that the complaint which filled my latest
letter might be able to move thee, Paulinus, and
that my caressing reproof might lure thee to reply.
But thou, as if after swearing by holy things thou
wast vowed to keep deep silence, abidest obstinately
by the rule of speechlessness.[1] Is it not allowed? Or
art thou ashamed to have a friend still alive who claims
a father's rights, whilst thou remainest the dependent
heir? Let cowards quake with such dread, but have
thou no fear, and boldly keep the custom of giving
and returning greeting. Or if an informer is beside
thee, and if 'tis an inquisitor's[2] too stern rebuke is
feared, baffle it with a device whereby secrets are
oft concealed. She whom the brutal outrage of the
Thracian king had robbed of her tongue, revealed
her sorrows by means of woven threads and com-
mitted the story of her wrongs to the silent loom.[3]
Also a shamefast maid entrusted the tale of her love
to an apple,[4] and blushed not to share her secret
with fruit which could never speak. To deep-dug
pits a servant revealed his royal lord's deformity,[5]
and long the earth hid the secret most faithfully:
thereafter the reed, breathed on by the wind, sang
the story. Trace letters with milk: the paper as it
dries will keep them ever invisible; yet with ashes
the writing is brought to light.[6] Or imitate the
Spartan *scytale*, writing on strips of parchment wound

---

[4] Cydippe: see Ovid, *Heroïdes*, xx. 9 f.
[5] Midas: for the story see Ovid, *Metam* xi. 180 ff.
[6] If a paper written as prescribed is sprinkled with ashes,
which are then shaken off, the writing shows up faintly in
grey.

perpetuo inscribens versu, qui deinde solutus,   25
non respondentes sparso dabit ordine formas,
donec consimilis ligni replicetur in orbem.

Innumeras possum celandi ostendere formas
et clandestinas veterum reserare loquellas :
si prodi, Pauline, times nostraeque vereris   30
crimen amicitiae ; Tanaquil tua nesciat istud.
tu contemne alios nec dedignare parentem
adfari verbis.   ego sum tuus altor et ille
praeceptor, primus veterum largitor honorum,
primus in Aonidum qui te collegia duxi.   35

XXIX. — Cum Pontius Paulinus iunior quartis
    iam litteris non respondisset sic ad eum
    scriptum est

Quarta tibi haec notos detexit epistula questus,
Pauline, et blando residem sermone lacessit.
officium set nulla pium mihi pagina reddit,
fausta salutigeris adscribens orsa libellis.
unde istam meruit non felix charta repulsam,   5
spernit tam longo cessatio quam tua fastu ?
hostis ab hoste tamen per barbara verba salutem
accipit et Salve mediis intervenit armis.
respondent et saxa homini et percussus ab antris
sermo redit, redit et nemorum vocalis imago ;   10

---

[1] See Aulus Gellius, XVII ix. 6 ff.
[2] i.e. for enciphering and deciphering.
[3] cp. Juvenal, vi. 566.   Tanaquil (wife of the elder Tarquin) the typical domineering woman, represents Therasia, the wife of Paulinus.

about a rounded stick in continuous lines, which, afterwards unrolled, will show characters incoherent because sequence is lost, until they are rolled again about just such another stick.[1]

[28] I can show thee countless codes of the ancients for concealing and unlocking secret messages[2]; if thou, Paulinus, fearest to be betrayed and dread'st the charge of my friendship, let thy Tanaquil[3] know naught of it. Do thou scorn others, but disdain not to address thy father. I am thy nourisher, thy old tutor, the first to lavish on thee the honours of old time,[4] the first to introduce thee into the guild of the Aonides.

XXIX.—WHEN PONTIUS PAULINUS THE YOUNGER DID NOT REPLY TO THE FOUR LETTERS ALREADY SENT, THE FOLLOWING WAS WRITTEN TO HIM

THIS is the fourth letter in which I have laid bare to thee, Paulinus, my familiar complaint, and with caressing words sought to stir thee from thy lethargy. But never a page comes to repay my loving attentions, no propitious words writ at the head of sheets which bring me greeting.[5] How has my luckless letter, for which your long neglect shows such disdain, deserved this rebuff? Yet foe from foe receives greeting[6] in savage speech and "hail" comes between opposed arms. Even rocks make answer to mankind and speech beating back from caves returns, returns too the vocal mimicry of the woods; cliffs by

---

[4] The reference may be either to the consulship which Ausonius procured for Paulinus in 378 A.D., or to the glories of ancient literature.

[5] *i.e.* no letter with the formula, *salutem dat plurimam.*

[6] As pugilists shake hands on entering the ring.

litorei clamant scopuli, dant murmura rivi,
Hyblaeis apibus saepes depasta susurrat.
est et harundineis modulatio musica ripis
cumque suis loquitur tremulum coma pinea ventis.
incubuit foliis quotiens levis eurus acutis,   15
Dindyma Gargarico respondent cantica luco.
nil mutum natura dedit.   non aeris ales
quadrupedesve silent, habet et sua sibila serpens,
et pecus aequoreum tenui vice vocis anhelat.
cymbala dant flictu sonitum, dant pulpita saltu   20
icta pedum, tentis reboant cava tympana tergis ;
Isiacos agitant Mareotica sistra tumultus
nec Dodonaei cessat tinnitus aeni,
in numerum quotiens radiis ferientibus ictae
respondent dociles modulato verbere pelves.   25
      Tu velut Oebaliis habites taciturnus Amyclis
aut tua Sigalion Aegyptius oscula signet,
obnixum, Pauline, taces.   agnosco pudorem,
quod vitium fovet ipsa suum cessatio iugis,
dumque pudet tacuisse diu, placet officiorum   30
non servare vices ; et amant longa otia culpam.
quis prohibet Salve atque Vale brevitate parata
scribere felicesque notas mandare libellis ?
non ego, longinquos ut texat pagina versus,
postulo multiplicique oneret sermone tabellas.   35

---

¹ *cp.* Virgil, *Ecl.* i. 54 ff. : saepes Hyblaeis apibus florem
depasta salicti, etc.
² Dindymus, near Pessinus, was famed for the noisy rites
of Cybele held there   Gargara is a part of Mount Ida.
³ *i.e.* Egyptian   The *sistrum* was a rattle consisting of
rings strung on the cross-bars of a metal frame, and was used
for ritual purposes.

the sea-shore cry out, streams utter their murmurs, the hedges, whereon bees of Hybla feed,[1] are ever whispering. Reed-grown banks also have their tuneful harmonies, and the pine's foliage in trembling accents talks with its beloved winds. So oft as the light eastern breeze leans on the shrill-voiced leaves, strains of Dindymus respond to the grove of Gargara.[2] Nature made nothing dumb. Birds of the air and four-footed beasts are not mute, even the serpent has its own hissing note, and the herds of the deep sigh with faint semblance of a voice. Cymbals give sound at a clash, stages at beat of bounding feet, the taut skins of hollow drums give back a booming ; Mareotic [3] sistra raise rattling din in Isis' honour nor does Dodona's brazen tinkling cease as oft as the lavers at the clappers' measured stroke obediently reply with rhythmic beat.[4]

[26] Thou, as though thou wert a mute citizen of Oebalian Amyclae,[5] or Egyptian Sigalion [6] were sealing thy lips, stubbornly keepest silence, Paulinus. I recognise shame in thee, for continued negligence cherishes her own defect, and in shame for long silence thou dost resolve not to maintain interchange of courtesies ; and lengthened idleness loves its own fault. Who forbids you to write " hail " and " farewell " with studied brevity, and to commit to paper these words of greeting ? I do not demand that thy page should weave a long drawn out web of verse and burden thy letter with a

---

[4] The Oracle at Dodona was surrounded by a circle of brazen pans hung in trees which were either struck by a priest, or clashed together in the wind.

[5] See *Professores*, xv. 6 and note.

[6] *i.e.* Harpocrates (Heru-pa-khrat), who is represented in Egyptian art with his finger upon his lips.

una fuit tantum, qua respondere Lacones
littera, et irato regi placuere negantes.
est etenim comis brevitas : sic fama renatum
Pythagoram docuisse refert.   cum multa loquaces
ambiguis sererent verbis, contra omnia solum   40
Est, respondebat, vel Non.   o certa loquendi
regula! nam brevius nihil est et plenius istis,
quae firmata probant aut infirmata relidunt.
nemo silens placuit, multi brevitate loquendi.

   Verum ego quo stulte dudum spatiosa locutus   45
provehor ?   ut diversa sibi vicinaque culpa est!
multa loquens et cuncta silens non ambo placemus.
nec possum reticere, iugum quod libera numquam
fert pietas nec amat blandis postponere verum.
vertisti, Pauline, tuos dulcissime mores ?   50
Vasconis hoc saltus et ninguida Pyrenaei
hospitia et nostri facit hoc oblivio caeli ?
inprecer ex merito quid non tibi, Hiberia tellus!
te populent Poeni, te perfidus Hannibal urat,
te belli sedem repetat Sertorius exul.   55
ergo meum patriaeque decus columenque senati
Birbilis aut haerens scopulis Calagorris habebit,
aut quae deiectis iuga per scruposa ruinis
arida torrentem Sicorim despectat Hilerda ?
hic trabeam, Pauline, tuam Latiamque curulem   60
constituis, patriosque istic sepelibis honores ?

   Quis tamen iste tibi tam longa silentia suasit

---

   [1] When Philip asked leave to visit their city, the Spartans
replied *o* (= *oὐ*).   See *Technopaegn.* xiii. 5 and note.

multitude of words. 'Twas but one letter wherewith
the Spartans made reply and, though refusing,
pleased the angry king.[1]   For indeed terseness is
courteous ; so, report says, taught reborn Pythagoras.[2]
While babblers would be stringing indecisive words,
in all cases he would answer only " Yes " or " No."
O stable rule of speech ! For nothing is shorter and
more adequate than these, which approve the valid
or reject the invalid.   None pleased by silence ;
many by brief reply.

[45] But I, whither with foolish amplitude of speech
have I been long careering ?   How distant from
itself and yet how near is error ! I with long speech,
thou with utter silence, we both displease.   Yet can
I not keep silence, for free affection never bears
yoke, nor loves to screen truth with glozing words.
Hast thou, dearest Paulinus, changed thy nature ?
Do Biscayan glades and sojourns in the snowy
Pyrenees and doth forgetfulness of our clime work
thus ?   What curse shall I not righteously call down
on thee, O land of Spain ?   May Carthaginians
ravage thee, may faithless Hannibal waste thee with
fire, may banished Sertorius again seek in thee the
seat of war !   Shall then Birbilis or Calagorris cling-
ing to its crags, or parched Ilerda [3] whose ruins,
littered over rugged hills, look down on brawling
Sicoris, possess him who is mine and his country's
pride, the mainstay of the Senate ?   Here dost thou,
Paulinus, establish thy robe consular and Roman
curule chair, and wilt thou bury there thy native
honours ?

[62] But who is that unhallowed wretch who has

---

[2] Pythagoras claimed to be a reincarnation of Euphorbus.
[3] The places named are Baubola, Calahorra, and Lerida.

impius? ut nullos hic vocem vertat in usus,
gaudia non illum vegetent, non dulcia vatum
carmina, non blandae modulatio flexa querellae,   65
non fera, non illum pecudes, non mulceat ales,
non quae pastorum nemoralibus abdita lucis
solatur nostras Echo resecuta loquellas.
tristis, egens deserta colat tacitusque pererret
Alpinis conexa iugis, ceu dicitur olim   70
mentis inops coetus hominum et vestigia vitans
avia perlustrasse vagus loca Bellerophontes.

    Haec precor, hanc vocem, Boeotia numina Musae,
accipite et Latiis vatem revocate camenis.

XXX.—Ausonio Paulinus

Continuata meae durare silentia linguae
te numquam tacito memoras placitamque latebris
desidiam exprobras neglectaeque insuper addis
crimen amicitiae formidatamque iugalem
obicis et durum iacis in mea viscera versum.   5
parce, precor, lacerare tuum, nec amara paternis
admiscere velis, ceu melle absinthia, verbis.

    Cura mihi semper fuit et manet officiis te
omnibus excolere, adfectu observare fideli.
non umquam tenui saltim tua gratia naevo   10
conmaculata mihi est; ipso te laedere vultu
semper et incauta timui violare figura;
cumque tua accessi, venerans mea cautius ora

---

[1] See Homer Z 201 f.
[2] On Paulinus see *Introduction*, and *Epist.* xxiii. (note).

urged you to so long silence? May he turn no
sound to any advantage, may no joys enliven him,
no sweet poets' lays, no melting harmonies of se-
ductive elegy, may no cry of beast nor low of cattle
nor song of bird cheer him, nor yet Echo, who
hidden in shepherds' bosky groves consoles us while
repeating our complaints. Sad, needy let him dwell
in waste places and in silence roam the borders of
Alpine hills, even as, 'tis said, in days of old Beller-
ophon, distraught, avoided the company of men and
wandered straying through untrodden places.[1]

[73] This is my prayer, this cry, Boeotian Muses
divine, receive ye and with Latin strains call back
your bard!

XXX.—PAULINUS [2] TO AUSONIUS

THOU tellest me that my tongue keeps unbroken
silence while thou art never dumb, and reproachest
me with choosing idleness in secret retreats, and
withal addest the charge of neglected friendship and
tauntest me with terror of my spouse, launching
a cruel line against my very heart.[3] Cease, I prithee,
to wound thy friend, and seek not to mingle bitter-
ness—as wormwood with honey—with a father's
words.

[8] My care has been and still endures, to honour
thee with every friendly token, to compass thee
with faithful affection. No blemish, however slight,
has ever marred my devotion towards thee; even by
a look I have ever feared to hurt thee and to wrong
thee with an unguarded aspect; and when I have
approached thee, out of respect I have the more

---

[3] *i.e.* against Therasia herself.

conposui et laeto formavi lumine frontem,
ne qua vel a tacito contractam pectore nubem   15
duceret in sanctum suspicio falsa parentem.
hoc mea te domus exemplo coluitque colitque
inque tuum tantus nobis consensus amorem est,
quantus et in Christum conexa mente colendum.

 Quis tua, quaeso, tuis obduxit pectora livor?   20
quo rumore pium facilis tibi fama per aures
inrupit pepulitque animum contraque vetustam
experta pietate fidem nova vulnera movit,
laederet ut natis placidum male suada parentem?

 Set mihi non fictae mens conscia simplicitatis   25
nec patris inculti pietas rea respuit omne
inmeritum et falso perstringi crimine non fert,
inmunis vero: gravius violatur iniquo
vulnere, tam tenera offensae, quam libera culpae.

 Discussisse iugum quereris me, quo tibi doctis   30
iunctus eram studiis. hoc nec gestasse quidem me
adsero. namque pares subeunt iuga: nemo valentes
copulat infirmis neque sunt concordia frena,
si sit conpulsis mensura iugalibus inpar.
si vitulum tauro vel equum committis onagro;   35
si confers fulicas cycnis et aedona parrae,
castaneis corulos; aequas viburna cupressis;
me conpone tibi: vix Tullius et Maro tecum
sustineant aequale iugum. si iungar amore,

heedfully ordered my looks and given my features a bright and cheerful cast, that no ungrounded suspicion might bring down a cloud upon thee, my revered father, even though arising from an unspoken thought. After like pattern my household has honoured and honours thee, and in love for thee we are as agreed together as our hearts are linked together in worship of Christ.

[20] What rancour, I beg of thee, against thy friends is crept over thy heart? With what idle tale has nimble Slander forced her way into thy ears, smitten thy fond heart, and aimed late blows against the tried affection of ancient faith, so as to harm a son by cozening a sire from his peace?

[25] But my heart is conscious of no feigned sincerity, my devotion, guiltless of neglect towards my father, hurls back with scorn every undeserved taunt, and brooks not to be scarred with a false charge because in truth innocent: as easy hurt as it is free from fault, it is the more sorely injured by an unjust blow.

[30] Thou dost complain that I have shaken off the yoke [1] wherewith I was joined with thee in the pursuit of letters. This I declare that I have never even borne. For only equals share one yoke: no one links the powerful with the weak, and no team works with one will, if the forced yoke-fellows are of unequal measure. If thou dost match calves with bulls or horses with wild-asses; if thou comparest moorhens with swans, and nightingales with owls, hazels with chestnuts, or rankest wayside shrubs with cypresses;—then place me beside thee: Tully and Maro scarce could uphold a like yoke with thee. If I be yoked in love, in that alone will

---

[1] In reply to *Epist.* xxvii. 1 f.

hoc tantum tibi me iactare audebo iugalem,   40
quo modicus sociis magno contendit habenis.
dulcis amicitia aeterno mihi foedere tecum
et paribus semper redamandi legibus aequat.
hoc nostra cervice iugum non scaeva resolvit
fabula, non terris absentia longa diremit,   45
nec perimet, toto licet abstrahar orbe vel aevo.
numquam animo divisus agam : prius ipsa recedet
corpore vita meo, quam vester pectore vultus.

Ego te per omne quod datum mortalibus
    et destinatum saeculum est,   50
claudente donec continebor corpore,
    discernar orbe quamlibet,
nec orbe longe nec remotum lumine
    tenebo fibris insitum :
videbo corde, mente conplectar pia   55
    ubique praesentem mihi.
et cum solutus corporali carcere
    terraque provolavero,
quo me locarit axe communis pater,
    illic quoque animo te geram ;   60
neque finis idem, qui meo me corpore
    et amore laxabit tuo.
mens quippe, lapsis quae superstes artubus
    de stirpe durat caeliti,
sensus necesse est simul et adfectus suos   65
    teneat aeque ut vitam suam,
et ut mori, sic oblivisci non capit,
    perenne vivax et memor.

    Vale domine illustris.

I dare boast myself thy yoke-fellow wherein the humble vies with the great in even career. Sweet friendship makes us peers through the eternal bond betwixt me and thee and through the equal laws of endless mutual love. This yoke no malicious tale has unloosed from my neck, no long absence from my land has broken it nor ever shall destroy it, though I should be removed from thee by the whole span of space and time. Never shall I live separate from thee in soul: sooner shall life itself depart from my frame than thy face from my heart.

49 Through all the length of time given to mortals and ordained, so long as I shall be confined in this halting frame, though I be held a world apart, thee neither parted by a world nor severed from my sight I will keep implanted in my inmost being: in heart I shall see thee, in loving thought embrace thee, having thee with me everywhere. And when, released from the prison of the body, I shall have flown forth from the earth, in whatever clime our general Father shall place me, there also will I bear thee in my heart; nor shall the selfsame end which severs me from my body, unloose me from love of thee. For the soul, which, surviving the body's ruin, endures in virtue of heavenly birth, must needs keep both its own faculties and affections no less than its own life, and so admits forgetfulness no more than death, remaining ever living, ever mindful.

69 Farewell, illustrious master.

XXXI.—Ausonio Paulinus

Quarta redit duris haec iam messoribus aestas,
  et totiens cano bruma gelu riguit,
ex quo nulla tuo mihi littera venit ab ore,
  nulla tua vidi scripta notata manu,
ante salutifero felix quam charta libello   5
  dona negata diu multiplicata daret.
trina etenim vario florebat epistula textu,
  set numerosa triplex pagina carmen erat.
dulcia multimodis quaedam subamara querellis,
  anxia censurae miscuerat pietas.   10
sed mihi mite patris plus quam censoris acerbum
  sedit, et e blandis aspera penso animo.
ista suo regerenda loco tamen et graviore
  vindicis heroi sunt agitanda sono.
interea levior paucis praecurret iambus   15
  discreto referens mutua verba pede.
Nunc elegi salvere iubent dictaque salute,
  ut fecere aliis orsa gradumque, silent.

Ausonio Paulinus

Quid abdicatas in meam curam, pater,
  redire Musas praecipis?   20
negant Camenis nec patent Apollini
  dicata Christo pectora.
fuit ista quondam non ope, sed studio pari
  tecum mihi concordia,

THE EPISTLES

XXXI.—Paulinus to Ausonius

'Tis the fourth summer now returns for hardy reapers, and as oft has winter grown stark with hoary rime, since any syllable from thy lips reached me, since I saw any letter penned by thy hand— ere thy page, auspicious with its message of greeting, bestowed manifold the gift so long denied. For indeed 'twas a triple letter enriched with various flowers of composition, but the melodious sheets were a three-fold poem. Things sweet, though somewhat soured with manifold complaints, troubled affection had mingled with criticism. But with me the father's gentleness rather than the critic's bitterness finds a resting place, and in my heart I draw from the kindly words what may weigh against the harsh. But these charges must be refuted in their proper place and canvassed in the sterner tones of the avenging heroic measure. Meanwhile, though briefly, lighter iambus shall hurry on ahead, in separate metre [1] paying back his debt of words.

17 Now my elegiacs bid thee " hail " and having hailed thee, since they have made for others a beginning and a step, cease to speak.

Paulinus to Ausonius

Why dost thou bid the deposed Muses return to my affection, my father ? Hearts consecrate to Christ give refusal to the Camenae, are closed to Apollo. Once was there this accord betwixt me and thee, equals in zeal but not in power—to call forth

---

[1] *i.e.* as distinct from the hexameters of ll. 103 ff. : the double sense of *pede* cannot well be reproduced. The debt of words is the obligation to reply to the strictures of Ausonius.

ciere surdum Delphica Phoebum specu,   25
    vocare Musas numina,
fandique munus munere indultum dei
    petere e nemoribus aut iugis.
nunc alia mentem vis agit, maior deus,
    aliosque mores postulat   30
sibi reposcens ab homine [1] munus suum,
    vivamus ut vitae patri.
vacare vanis, otio aut negotio,
    et fabulosis litteris
vetat ; suis ut pareamus legibus   35
    lucemque cernamus suam,
quam vis sophorum callida arsque rhetorum et
    figmenta vatum nubilant,
qui corda falsis atque vanis imbuunt
    tantumque linguas instruunt,   40
nihil adferentes, ut salutem conferant,
    quod veritatem detegat.
quid enim tenere vel bonum aut verum queant,
    qui non tenent summae caput,
veri bonique fomitem et fontem deum,   45
    quem nemo nisi in Christo videt ?
Hic veritatis lumen est, vitae via,
    vis, mens, manus, virtus patris,
sol aequitatis, fons bonorum, flos dei,
    natus deo, mundi sator,   50
mortalitatis vita nostrae et mors necis.
    magister hic virtutium,
deusque nobis atque pro nobis homo,
    nos induendus induit,
aeterna iungens homines inter et deum   55
    in utrumque se commercia.
hic ergo nostris ut suum praecordiis
    vibraverit caelo iubar,

                 [1] *MSS.* : nomine, *Peiper.*

deaf Apollo from his Delphic cave, to invoke the Muses
as divine, to seek from groves or hills the gift of utter-
ance by the god's gift bestowed. Now 'tis another
force governs my heart, a greater God, who demands
another mode of life, claiming for himself from man
the gift he gave, that we may live for the Father of
life. To spend time on empty things, whether in
pastime or pursuit, and on literature full of idle tales,
he forbids; that we may obey his laws and behold
his light which sophists' cunning skill, the art of
rhetoric, and poets' feignings overcloud. For these
steep our hearts in things false and vain, and train
our tongues alone imparting naught which can
reveal the truth. For what good thing or true can
they hold who hold not the head of all, God, the
enkindler and source of the good and true, whom
no man seeth save in Christ.

⁴⁷ He is the light of truth, the path of life, the
strength, mind, hand, and power of the Father, the
sun of righteousness, the fount of blessings, the
flower of God, born of God, creator of the world,
life of our mortality and death of Death. He, the
Lord of Virtues, to us God and for us Man, puts on
our nature as we must put on his, linking God with
man in perpetual intercourse, himself of each par-
taking. He, then, when he has launched his beams
from heaven upon our hearts, wipes off the sorry

abstergit aegrum corporis pigri situm
    habitumque mentis innovat :   60
exhaurit omne, quod iuvabat antea,
    castae voluptatis vice,
totusque nostra iure domini vindicat
    et corda et ora et tempora.
se cogitari, intellegi, credi, legi,   65
    se vult timeri et diligi.
aestus inanes, quos movet vitae labor
    praesentis aevi tramite,
abolet futura cum deo vitae fides.
    quae, quas videmur spernere,   70
non ut profanas abicit aut viles opes,
    set ut magis caras monet
caelo reponi creditas Christo deo,
    qui plura promisit datis,
contempta praesens vel mage deposita sibi   75
    multo ut rependat faenore.
sine fraude custos, aucta creditoribus
    bonus reddet debitor
multaque spretam largior pecuniam
    restituet usura deus.   80
Huic vacantem vel studentem et deditum,
    in hoc reponentem omnia
ne quaeso segnem neve perversum putes
    nec crimineris impium.
pietas abesse Christiano qui potest ?   85
    namque argumentum mutuum est
pietatis, esse Christianum, et impii,
    non esse Christo subditum.
hanc cum tenere discimus, possum tibi
    non exhibere, id est patri,   90
cui cuncta sancta iura, cara nomina
    debere me voluit deus?

filth of our dull bodies and renews the disposition of our hearts: he draws forth all which aforetime used to please, giving unsullied pleasure in return, and absolutely with a master's right claims both our hearts and lips and time. He seeks himself to engross our thoughts, our minds, belief and choice, himself to be feared and loved. Those aimless surges, which the toils of life stir up in the course of this present span of time, are brought to naught by faith in a life to come with God. This casts not away the riches, which we are thought to scorn, as unhallowed or little worth, but, as more dear, bids them be laid up in Heaven in trust with Christ our God, who has promised more than he receives, to pay back with large usury those things now despised or rather laid up in his keeping. A faithful guardian, an unfailing debtor, he will repay with increase wealth entrusted to him, and of his bounty God with abundant interest will restore the money we have spurned.

[81] To Him given up, whether waiting or serving, in Him laying up my all, think me not, I beseech thee, slothful nor wayward, nor charge me with want of filial piety. How can piety be wanting in a Christian? For "piety" has the acquired meaning to be a Christian, and "the impious" one not subject to Christ. When I am learning to hold fast this, can I fail to show it toward thee, that is, towards my father, to whom God has willed that I should owe all sacred duties and names of affection? To thee I owe

tibi disciplinas, dignitatem, litteras,
   linguae, togae, famae decus
provectus, altus, institutus debeo,   95
   patrone, praeceptor, pater.
Sed cur remotus tamdiu degam, arguis
   pioque motu irasceris.
conducit istud aut necesse est aut placet:
   veniale, quidquid horum, erit.   100
ignosce amanti, si geram quod expedit;
   gratare, si vivam, ut libet.

Ausonio Paulinus

Defore me patriis tota trieteride terris
atque alium legisse vagis erroribus orbem,
culta prius vestrae oblitum consortia vitae,   105
increpitas sanctis mota pietate querellis.
amplector patrio venerandos pectore motus
et mihi gratandas salvis adfectibus iras.
set reditum inde meum, genitor, te poscere mallem,
unde dari possit.   revocandum me tibi credam, 110
cum steriles fundas non ad divina precatus,
Castalidis supplex averso numine Musis?
non his numinibus tibi me patriaeque reduces.
surda vocas et nulla rogas (levis hoc feret aura,
quod datur in nihilum) sine numine nomina Musas. 115
inrita ventosae rapiunt haec vota procellae,
quae non missa deo vacuis in nubibus haerent
nec penetrant superi stellantem regis in aulam

training, honours, learning, my pride of eloquence, of civil rank, of reputation, being by thee advanced, fostered, and instructed, my patron, tutor, father.

97 But why do I live so long retired, thou askest reproachfully, and art stirred with a loving anger. It is expedient, or 'tis necessary, or 'tis my pleasure : whichever of these it be, it will be pardonable. Forgive me, as I love thee, if I do what is convenient; be thankful if I live as pleases me.

PAULINUS TO AUSONIUS

That I shall be absent from my native land full three years' space, and that I have traversed another world in aimless wanderings, forgetful of that fellowship in thy life, once cherished—thou dost reproach me with complaints hallowed by the love whence they spring. I welcome with reverence due the emotions of a father's heart and the anger which claims my gratitude leaving affection unimpaired. Yet for my return, my father, I would rather thou should'st ask it there where it can be granted. Shall I believe that thou canst call me back to thee while thou pourest forth barren prayers to beings not divine, suppliant to the Castalian Muses while God turns from thee ? Not through such deities wilt thou bring me back to thee and to my country. Thou call'st the deaf, implorest things of naught— a light breeze will bear away what is addressed to a nothing—the Muses, who are names but non-entities. The stormy winds whirl away ineffectual such prayers as these, which, not addressed to God, catch in the empty clouds nor make their way into the starry court of the King of Heaven.

Si tibi cura mei reditus, illum adspice et ora,
qui tonitru summi quatit ignea culmina caeli,   120
qui trifido igne micat nec inania murmura miscet
quique satis caelo soles largitur et imbres,
qui super omne, quod est, vel in omni totus ubique,
omnibus infuso rebus regit omnia Christo:
quo mentes tenet atque movet, quo tempora nostra 125
et loca disponit.   quod si contraria votis
constituat nostri, prece deflectendus in illa est,
quae volumus.

            Quid me accusas? si displicet actus
quem gero agente deo, prius est: fiat reus auctor,
cui placet aut formare meos aut vertere sensus.   130
nam mea si reputes, quae pristina, quae tibi nota,
sponte fatebor eum modo me non esse, sub illo
tempore qui fuerim, quo non perversus habebar
et perversus eram falsi caligine cernens,
stulta dei sapiens et mortis pabula vivens.   135
quo magis ignosci mihi fas, quia promptius ex hoc
agnosci datur a summo genitore novari,
quod non more meo geritur: non, arbitror, istic
confessus dicar mutatae in prava notandum
errorem mentis, quoniam sim sponte professus   140
me non mente mea vitam mutasse priorem.
mens nova mi, fateor, mens non mea: non mea quondam,
set mea nunc auctore deo, qui, si quid in actu
ingeniove meo sua dignum ad munia vidit,

---

[1] *cp.* 1 *Cor.* iii. 19.

[119] If thou carest for my return, look towards him and pray to him who with his thunder shakes the fiery heights of highest Heaven, who shoots forth his triple flash of flame, nor mingles it with idle sounds, who on the crops graciously bestows sunshine and rains from heaven, who being above all that is, or wholly in all things everywhere, reigns over all through Christ who permeates all things: through whom he occupies and sways our minds, through whom he orders our times and places. But if he ordains things opposed to our hopes, by prayer he may be turned aside to that which we desire.

[128] Why blamest thou me? If thou mislikest the course which I pursue under God's influence, there is an earlier step: let the Author be accused, who is pleased either to shape or change my feelings. For if thou thinkest my nature is as of old and as 'twas known to thee, I will avow of myself that now I am not the man I was about that time when I was not thought wayward though wayward I was, seeing with the darkness of error, wise in what with God is foolishness,[1] and living on the food of death. Wherefore thou art the more bound to pardon me, because by this the more readily 'tis permitted thee to recognize that this change is from the most high Father—that 'tis not in accordance with my nature: by this I shall not, methinks, be held to have admitted a lamentable distraction of a mind changed for the worse, since I have openly avowed that not my own mind has caused me to change my former life. I have a new mind, I confess—a mind not my own: not mine aforetime, though mine now through God's influence—and if in my deeds or thoughts he sees anything worthy for his gifts, to

gratia prima tibi, tibi gloria debita cedit, 145
cuius praeceptis partum est, quod Christus amaret.

Quare gratandum magis est tibi, quam queritandum,
quod tuus ille, tuis studiis et moribus ortus,
Paulinus, cui te non infitiare parentem,
nec modo, cum credis perversum, sic mea verti 150
consilia, ut sim promeritus Christi fore, dum sum
Ausonii. feret ille tuae sua praemia laudi
deque tua primum tibi deferet arbore fructum.

Unde, precor, meliora putes nec maxima perdas
praemia detestando tuis bona fontibus orta. 155
non etenim mihi mens vaga, sed neque participantum
vita fugax hominum, Lyciae qua scribis in antris
Pegaseum vixisse equitem, licet avia multi
numine agente colant, clari velut ante sophorum
pro studiis musisque suis : ut nunc quoque, castis 160
qui Christum sumpsere animis, agitare frequentant,
non inopes animi neque de feritate legentes
desertis habitare locis ; sed in ardua versi
sidera spectantesque deum verique profunda
perspicere intenti de vanis libera curis 165
otia amant strepitumque fori rerumque tumultus
cunctaque divinis inimica negotia donis,
et Christi imperiis et amore salutis, abhorrent
speque fideque deum sponsa mercede sequuntur,
quam referet certus non desperantibus auctor, 170
si modo non vincant vacuis praesentia rebus,

---

[1] *cp. Epist.* **xxix.** 70 ff.

thee chief gratitude, to thee the glory falls due,
since thy instruction has produced what Christ could
love.

147 Wherefore thou shouldst give thanks rather than
complain because I—that son of thine, offspring of
thy learning and thy character, Paulinus, whose
parentage thou dost not deny, even now when thou
believest me wayward—have so changed my prin-
ciples that I have gained grace to become the child
of Christ while I am the child of Ausonius. He will
confer his rewards upon thy merit and from this tree
of thine proffer the first fruit to thee.

154 And so, I pray thee, think nobler thoughts and
lose not the highest rewards by execrating good
things which have their source from thee. For
indeed my mind does not wander, nor even does
my life flee from intercourse with men—even as
thou writest that Pegasus' rider lived in Lycian
caves [1]—albeit many dwell in pathless places through
God's leading, just as before them men famous
among the sages did for the sake of their learning
and their inspiration. Even so in these days also,
they who with pure hearts have adopted Christ
are wont to live—not as beside themselves, nor out
of savagery choosing to dwell in desert places; but
because—turning their faces to the stars on high,
contemplating God, and intent to scan the deep
wells of truth—they love repose void of empty cares,
and shun the din of public life, the bustle of affairs,
and all concerns hostile to the gifts of Heaven both
by Christ's command and in desire for salvation. By
hope and faith these follow God for the pledged
reward which he, whose promise cannot fail, will
bestow on such as persevere, if only this present life

quaeque videt spernat, quae non videt ut mereatur
secreta ignitus penetrans caelestia sensus.
namque caduca patent nostris, aeterna negantur
visibus; et nunc spe sequimur, quod mente videmus, 175
spernentes varias, rerum spectacula, formas
et male corporeos bona sollicitantia visus.
attamen haec sedisse illis sententia visa est,
tota quibus iam lux patuit verique bonique,
venturi aeternum saecli et praesentis inane.   180

    At mihi, non eadem cui gloria, cur eadem sit
fama? fides voti par est, sed amoena colenti,
nunc etiam et blanda posito locupletis in acta
litoris, unde haec iam tam festinata locorum
invidia est? utinam iustus me carpere livor   185
incipiat: Christi sub nomine probra placebunt.
non patitur tenerum mens numine firma pudorem,
et laus hic contempta redit mihi iudice Christo.

    Ne me igitur, venerande parens, his ut male versum
increpites studiis neque me vel coniuge carpas   190
vel mentis vitio: non anxia Bellerophontis
mens est nec Tanaquil mihi, sed Lucretia coniunx.
nec mihi nunc patrii est, ut visa, oblivio caeli,
qui summum suspecto patrem, quem qui colit unum,
hic vere memor est caeli.   crede ergo, pater, nos 195
nec caeli inmemores nec vivere mentis egentes,
humanisque agitare locis.   studia ipsa piorum

---

[1] There is an inept play on the two-fold meaning of *coelum*
= heavens (clime) and Heaven.

with its vain interests does not prevail, and the fiery perceptions, penetrating to Heaven's secret places, scorn what they see to gain what they see not. For things perishable are open to our sight, the eternal are denied ; and now in hope we pursue what with the mind we see, scorning the various shapes, the images of things, and the attractions which provoke our natural sight. And yet such resolve has been found to lodge in those to whom already is revealed the light of the good and true, the eternity of the world to come and the emptiness of that which is.

181 But I, who have not the same cause for boasting, why do I bear the same reproach? My surety of hope is no less ; but since I dwell in pleasant places, and even now abide upon the agreeable shores of a prosperous coast, whence this so premature carping at my abode? I would that jealousy with good grounds may begin to pluck at me : bearing the name of Christ I shall welcome taunts. A mind strengthened by power divine feels no weak shame, and the praise I here despise is restored to me when Christ is judge.

189 Do not, then, chide me, my honoured father, as though I had turned to these pursuits perversely, and do not twit me with my wife or with defect of mind: mine is not the perturbed mind of Bellerophon, nor is my wife a Tanaquil but a Lucretia. Nor am I now forgetful, as thou thinkest, of the heavens 'neath which my fathers dwelt, seeing that I look up to the all-highest Father, and that whoso worships Him alone he is truly mindful of Heaven.[1] Believe then, father, that I am not unmindful of the heavens and do not live distraught in mind, but dwell in a civilized place : pursuits themselves bear witness to the

testantur mores hominum; nec enim impia summum
gens poterit novisse deum: sint multa locorum,
multa hominum studiis inculta, expertia legum,   200
quae regio agresti ritu caret? aut quid in istis
improbitas aliena nocet? quod tu mihi vastos
Vasconiae saltus et ninguida Pyrenaei
obicis hospitia, in primo quasi limine fixus
Hispanae regionis agam nec sit locus usquam   205
rure vel urbe mihi, summum qua dives in orbem
usque patet mersos spectans Hispania soles.
sed fuerit fortuna iugis habitasse latronum,
num lare barbarico rigui mutatus in ipsos,
inter quos habui, socia feritate colonos?   210
non recipit mens pura malum neque levibus haerent
inspersae fibris maculae: si Vascone saltu
quisquis agit purus sceleris vitam, integer aeque
nulla ab inhumano morum contagia ducit
hospite.   sed mihi cur sit ab illo nomine crimen,   215
qui diversa colo, ut colui, loca iuncta superbis
urbibus et laetis hominum celeberrima cultis?
ac si Vasconicis mihi vita fuisset in oris,
cur non more meo potius formata ferinos
poneret, in nostros migrans, gens barbara ritus?   220
   Nam quod in eversis habitacula ponis Hibera
urbibus et deserta tuo legis oppida versu
montanamque mihi Calagorrim et Birbilim acutis
pendentem scopulis collemque iacentis Hilerdae

---

[1] *i.e.* if they are just as wicked as others, that is no special
objection against them.

character of righteous men ; for an unrighteous race will not be able to know the most high God: granted that much of the country, much of the folk is unimproved and ignorant of laws, yet what tract is without its rustic worship? Or what offence in them is wickedness common to other parts?[1] And yet thou dost taunt me with the woodlands of Vasconia and snowy lodgings in the Pyrenees, as though I live tied down at the very frontier of the whole realm of Spain and have no place of my own anywhere in country or in town, where wealthy Spain outstretched along the world's boundary watches the suns dip down into the sea. But suppose it had been my lot to dwell amid the hills of brigands, have I become a block in a savage's hut, changed into the very serfs amid whom I lived, partaking of their wildness? A pure heart admits no evil, even as filth spattered upon smooth bristles does not stick: if one without stain of wickedness spends his life in a Vasconian glade, his character, unblemished as before, draws no infection from his host's barbarity. But why am I charged on that account when I dwell, as I have dwelt, in a far different country bordering on splendid cities and thickly covered with man's prosperous tillage ? And if my life had been led on the borders of Vasconia, why should not the savage folk rather have been moulded after my mode of life, laying aside their barbarous customs to come over to our own ?

[221] For whereas thou dost fix my Spanish dwelling-place in ruined cities, traversing in thy verse desolate towns, and castest in my teeth mountain Calahorra, Bambola hanging from its jagged crags, and Lerida prostrate on its hill-side—as though, an exile from

exprobras, velut his habitem laris exul et urbis   225
extra hominum tecta atque vias ;—an credis Hiberae
has telluris opes, Hispani nescius orbis,
quo gravis ille poli sub pondere constitit Atlans,
ultima nunc eius mons portio metaque terrae,
discludit bimarem celso qui vertice Calpen ?   230
Birbilis huic tantum, Calagorris, Hilerda notantur,
Caesarea est Augusta cui, Barcinus amoena
et capite insigni despectans Tarraco pontum ?

   Quid numerem egregias terris et moenibus urbes,
quas geminum felix Hispania tendit in aequor,   235
qua Betis Oceanum Tyrrhenumque auget Hiberus,
lataque distantis pelagi divortia conplet,
orbe suo finem ponens in limite mundi ?
anne tibi, o domine inlustris, si scribere sit mens,
qua regione habites, placeat reticere nitentem   240
Burdigalam et piceos malis describere Boios ?
cumque Maroialicis tua prodigis otia thermis
inter et umbrosos donas tibi vivere lucos,
laeta locis et mira colens habitacula tectis :
nigrantesne casas et texta mapalia culmo   245
dignaque pellitis habitas deserta Bigerris ?
quique superba tuae contemnis moenia Romae
consul, arenosas non dedignare Vasatas ?
vel quia Pictonicis tibi fertile rus viret arvis,
Raraunum Ausonias heu devenisse curules   250

---

[1] The Guadalquivir, " the Great River."
[2] The Ebro.
[3] The modern Bourbonnais of the Dép. de l'Allier.

home and city, I were dwelling in these far from the
dwellings and highways of men; dost thou believe
these are the resources of the Iberian land, ignorant
of the Spanish world where laden Atlas took his
stand beneath the load of Heaven, he whose moun-
tain, now the furthest fragment and boundary of the
earth, shuts out with its lofty peak Calpe that lies
betwixt two seas?   Are only Bambola, Calahorra,
Lerida, placed to the credit of this land which has its
Saragossa, pleasant Barcelona, and Tarragona looking
from majestic heights down to the sea?

[234] What need for me to tell over the cities,
distinguished for their territories and walls which
prosperous Spain thrusts forth between two seas;
where Betis [1] swells the Atlantic, Hiberus [2] theTuscan
sea—Spain whose compass occupies the wide inter-
vening tract which parts main from main, setting its
bounds at the extreme verge of the world?   If thou,
O famous master, wert minded to describe the
region where thou dwellest, wouldst thou be content
to leave unnamed cheerful Bordeaux preferring to
write of the pitchy Boii [3]?   And when thou bestowest
thy leisure on the hot springs of Maroialum [4] and
permittest thyself to live amid shady groves, dwelling
amid cheerful scenery and habitations marvellously
built, dost thou inhabit murky hovels and cabins of
twisted straw amid a wilderness fit for the skin-clad
natives of Bigorre?   Dost thou, a consul, scorn the
proud walls of thine own Rome while not disdaining
Bazas amid its sand hills?   Or because the fertile
country and green fields of Poiteau are about thee,
shall I lament that the Ausonian consulate—alas! —
has sunk to the level of Raraunum, [5] and that the

[4] Probably Baguères de Bigorre.
[5] Now Rom or Raum.

conquerar, et trabeam veteri sordescere fano;
quae tamen augusta Latiaris in urbe Quirini
Caesareas inter parili titulo palmatas
fulget inadtrito longum venerabilis auro,
florentem retinens meriti vivacis honorem.   255
aut cum Lucani retineris culmine fundi,
aemula Romuleis habitans fastigia tectis,
materiam praebente loco, qui proxima signat,
in Condatino diceris degere vico?

Multa iocis pateant, liceat quoque ludere fictis;   260
sed lingua mulcente gravem interlidere dentem,
ludere blanditiis urentibus et male dulces
fermentare iocos satirae mordacis aceto
saepe poetarum, numquam decet esse parentum.
namque fides pietasque petunt, ut, quod mala nectens
insinuat castis fama auribus, hoc bona voti   266
mens patris adfigi fixumque haerescere cordi
non sinat.   et vulgus scaevo rumore malignum
ante habitos mores, non semper flectere vitam
crimen habet: namque est laudi bene vertere.   cum me
inmutatum audis, studium officiumque require.   271
si pravo rectum, si relligiosa profanis,
luxurie parcum, turpi mutatur honestum,
segnis, iners, obscurus ago, miserere sodalis
in mala perversi: blandum licet ira parentem   275
excitet, ut lapsum rectis instauret amicum
moribus et monitu reparet meliora severo.

---

[1] Elsewhere (*e.g. Epist.* xxvi. 44) called Lucaniacus.

official robe grows shabby in some mouldering shrine; whereas in fact it hangs in the renowned city of Roman Quirinus along with the imperial palm-broidered robes, trophies of like distinction, there gleaming, long venerable, with unfrayed gold, keeping fresh the glorious bloom of thy deathless achievement? Or when thou art lodged under the roof of Lucanus,[1] thy country house, inhabiting a pile vying with the halls of Rome, shall we take the pretext afforded by the place which gives its name to the vicinity, saying thou dwellest in the hamlet of Condate[2]?

[260] Let much admit of jests, let sportive fiction also be allowed; but with a smooth tongue to strike against an aching tooth, to sport with stinging compliments, and to season jests ill-relished with the vinegar of tart satire, oft befits a poet, never a father. For loyalty and natural affection demand that what slander-spinning Rumour instils into guileless ears, that the good-hoping mind of a father should not suffer to take hold and gain firm lodgment in the heart. Even the common herd, malignant in its brutal sneers towards habits formerly observed, does not always hold it crime to alter one's life: for to alter wisely is accounted praise. When thou hearest I am changed, ask what is my pursuit and my business. If 'tis a change from right to wrong, from godliness to wickedness, from temperance to luxury, from honour to baseness, if I live slothf l, sluggish, ignoble, take pity on a comrade strayed into evil; a gentle father well may be stirred with anger to restore a fallen friend to right living and by stern reproof to bring him back to better things.

[2] Cognac, near Saintes.

At si forte itidem, quod legi et quod sequor, audis,
corda pio vovisse deo venerabile Christi
imperium docili pro credulitate sequentem,   280
persuasumque dei monitis aeterna parari
praemia mortali damnis praesentibus empta,
non reor id sancto sic displicuisse parenti,
mentis ut errorem credat sic vivere Christo,
ut Christus sanxit.   iuvat hoc nec paenitet huius 285
erroris.   stultus diversa sequentibus esse
nil moror, aeterno mea dum sententia regi
sit sapiens.   breve, quidquid homo est, homo corporis
          aegri,
temporis occidui et sine Christo pulvis et umbra:
quod probat aut damnat tanti est, quanti arbiter ipse.
ipse obit atque illi suus est comitabilis error   291
cumque suo moriens sententia iudice transit.
    Et nisi, dum tempus praesens datur, anxia nobis
cura sit ad domini praeceptum vivere Christi,
sera erit exutis homini querimonia membris,   295
dum levia humanae metuit convicia linguae,
non timuisse graves divini iudicis iras;
quem patris aeterni solio dextraque sedentem,
omnibus impositum regem et labentibus annis
venturum, ut cunctas aequato examine gentes   300
iudicet et variis referat sua praemia gestis,
credo equidem et metuens studio properante laboro,
si qua datur, ne morte prius quam crimine solvar.
    Huius in adventum trepidis mihi credula fibris

[278] But if perchance thou dost likewise hear—and 'tis what I have chosen and what I pursue—that I have vowed my heart to our holy God, following in accord with obedient belief the awful behest of Christ, and that I am convinced by God's word that deathless rewards are laid up for man, purchased by present loss, that, methinks, has not so displeased my revered father that he thinks it a perversion of the mind so to live for Christ as Christ appointed. This is my delight, and this "perversion" I regret not. That I am foolish in the eyes of those who follow other aims gives me no pause, if only in sight of the eternal King my opinion be wise. A short-lived thing is man at best, man with his frail body and passing season, dust and a shadow without Christ: his praise and blame are so much worth as the arbiter himself. Himself he perishes and his own mistake must bear him company, and with the judge who pronounced it a verdict dies and passes.

[293] And unless, while this present time is granted, we take careful heed to live according to the command of Christ our Lord, too late, when man has put off his mortal frame, will be his complaint that while he feared the light rebuke of human tongues, he feared not the severe wrath of the Heavenly Judge. And that He sitteth on the throne at the right hand of the eternal Father, that He is set over all as king, and that as years roll away He will come to try all races with even-balanced judgment, and bestow due rewards upon their several deeds, I for my part believe, and, fearing, toil with restless zeal that, if so it may be, I be not cut off by death ere I am cut off from sin.

[304] Against His coming my believing heart trembles

corda tremunt gestitque anima id iam cauta futuri, 305
praemetuens, ne vincta aegris pro corpore curis
ponderibusque gravis rerum, si forte recluso
increpitet tuba vasta polo, non possit in auras
regis ad occursum levibus se tollere pinnis,
inter honora volans sanctorum milia caelo,   310
qui per inane levis neque mundi conpede vinctos
ardua in astra pedes facili molimine tollent
et teneris vecti per sidera nubibus ibunt,
caelestem ut medio venerentur in aere regem
claraque adorato coniungant agmina Christo.   315

    Hic metus est, labor iste, dies ne me ultimus atris
sopitum tenebris sterili deprendat in actu,
tempora sub vacuis ducentem perdita curis.
nam quid agam, lentis si, dum coniveo votis,
Christus ab aetheria mihi proditus arce coruscet 320
et, subitis domini caelo venientis aperto
praestrictus radiis, obscurae tristia noctis
suffugia inlato confusus lumine quaeram?

    Quod mihi ne pareret vel diffidentia veri,
vel praesentis amor vitae rerumque voluptas   325
curarumque labor, placuit praevertere casus
proposito et curas finire superstite vita
communemque adeo ventura in saecula rebus
expectare trucem securo pectore mortem.

    Si placet hoc, gratare tui spe divite amici: 330
si contra est, Christo tantum me linque probari.

with fluttering strings and my soul, even now aware
of what shall be, quakes with foreboding lest,
shackled with paltry cares for the body and weighted
with a load of business, if perchance the awful trump
should peal from the opened heaven, it should fail
to raise itself on light pinions into the air to meet
the Lord,[1] flitting in Heaven amid glorified thousands
of the saints, who through the void up to the stars
on high shall with unlaborious effort uplift light feet,
unshackled with the world's fetters, and wafted on
soft clouds shall pass amid the stars to worship the
Heavenly King in mid air and join their glorious
companies with Christ whom they adore.

[316] This is my fear, this my task, that the Last Day
overtake me not asleep in the black darkness of
profitless pursuits, spending wasted time amid empty
cares.   For what shall I do if, while I drowse amid
sluggish hopes, Christ, disclosed to me from his
heavenly citadel, should flash forth, and I, dazzled by
the sudden beams of my Lord coming from opened
Heaven, should seek the doleful refuge of murky
night, confounded by the o'erwhelming light?

[324] Wherefore, that neither doubt of the truth, nor
love of this present life with delight in worldly
things and anxious toil should bring this on me, I
am resolved to forestall calamity by my plan of life,
to end anxieties while life remains, awaiting with
untroubled heart fierce Death, the general doom of
things for ages yet to come.

[330] If this thou dost approve, rejoice in thy friend's
rich hope : if otherwise, leave me to be approved by
Christ alone.

[1] cp. 1 *Thessalonians* iv. 16 f.

XXXII.—Oratio Paulini

Omnipotens genitor rerum, cui summa potestas,
exaudi, si iusta precor.   ne sit mihi tristis
ulla dies, placidam nox rumpat nulla quietem.
nec placeant aliena mihi, quin et mea prosint
supplicibus nullusque habeat mihi vota nocendi   5
aut habeat nocitura mihi.   male velle facultas
nulla sit ac bene posse adsit tranquilla potestas.
mens contenta suo nec turpi dedita lucro
vincat corporeas casto bene conscia lecto
inlecebras, turpesque iocos obscenaque dicta   10
oderit illa nocens et multum grata malignis
auribus effuso semper rea lingua veneno.
non obitu adfligar cuiusquam aut funere crescam,
invideam numquam cuiquam nec mentiar umquam.
adsit laeta domus epulisque adludat inemptis   15
verna satur fidusque comes nitidusque minister,
morigera et coniunx caraque ex coniuge nati.

   Moribus haec castis tribuit deus : hi sibi mores
perpetuam spondent ventura in saecula vitam.

XXXIII.—<Paulinus Gestidio>

Domino merito suspiciendo Gestidio Paulinus.

   Iniuria quidem est patri familias maritimis deliciis
abundanti terrenum aliquid et agreste praebere ;
sed ego, ut et causa mihi esset aput unanimitatem

THE EPISTLES

XXXII.—A Prayer of Paulinus

Almighty Father of all things, to whom supreme power belongs, hear, if I pray aright. Let no day be passed by me in sadness, no night disturb my calm repose. Let others' goods not attract me, but rather let my own avail such as implore my aid: may none have a wish to hurt me or the means to hurt me. Let me have no occasion to will ill and let the unruffled power to do well be with me. Let my mind, content with its own and not given to base gains, overcome bodily enticements keeping the conscience of chaste conduct. Let that offending member, the ever-guilty tongue, well-pleasing to malicious ears for the poison it sheds, hate lewd jesting and unseemly words. Let me not be overcome by any man's decease, nor prosper through the death of any; let me never envy any man nor ever tell a lie. Be mine a cheerful home, and at my unpurchased [1] repasts may a well-fed slave bred in my house, my trusty comrade and prosperous henchman, serve blithely; and mine an obedient wife with children born of my dear wife.

[18] Upon pure conduct God bestows such gifts: such conduct assures itself of life unending against the world to come.

XXXIII.—Paulinus to Gestidius

Paulinus to the justly respected lord Gestidius.

It is an insult to present a man of standing who has plenty of sea dainties with anything derived from the land and country-side. But, that I might have

[1] *i.e.* consisting of "home-grown" products, and so homely, not luxurious.

tuam aliquid conloquendi et aliquod sermoni huic
obsequium viderer adiungere, pauculas de paucis-
simis, quas pueruli vespere inferunt, ficedulas misi.
quarum cum erubescerem paucitatem, plura etiam
versiculis verba subtexui, quasi vero numerum
loquacitate facturus.   sed quia utraque culpabilia
sunt, tu utrisque benigne ac familiariter ignoscendo
facies, ut nec inhumana videatur paucitas nec
odiosa garrulitas.

Sume igitur pastas dumoso in rure volucres,
quas latitans filicis sub tegmine callidus auceps,
dum simili mentitur aves fallitque susurro,
agmina viscatis suspendit credula virgis.
tunc referens tenuem non parvo munere praedam   5
digerit aucupium tabulis : et primus opimis
ordo nitet, sensim tenuatus ad ima tabellae.
ut minus offendat macies, praelata saginae
gratia praeventos pingui iuvat alite visus.

XXXIV.—Ad Eundem

Pauperis ut placeat carum tibi munus amici,
munera ne reputes, quae mittis ditia nobis.
nam tibi quid dignum referam pro piscibus illis,
quos tibi vicinum locupleti gurgite litus
suppeditat miros specie formaque diremptos ?   5
at mihi vix alto vada per saxosa profundo

excuse for some converse with you, my bosom friend, and to make a show of accompanying these words of mine with some token of respect, I am sending a poor few of the very few fig-peckers which my lads bring home of an evening. And since I blush for their small number, I added on more words to my verses, as though indeed I could increase their number by my chatter. But since both alike are open to criticism, you will do a kind and friendly action by pardoning both, so as to make the fewness of the birds not appear mean, and my wordiness not tiresome.

Take, then, these fowl fed in the thickets of the country-side, which the cunning fowler, lurking beneath a screen of bracken, while he beguiles and decoys birds with a call like their own, has taken hanging on his limed twigs—a silly tribe. Then, bringing home his light prey of no slight price, he sets out the catch upon his stall : and the array makes goodly show of prime birds in front gradually thinning out towards the back of the counter. That the more skinny may not displease, the fat birds with their attractive plumpness hold the foremost place, forestalling and delighting the gaze.

XXXIV.—To the same

That thy poor friend's loving gift may find favour with thee, think not on the rich gifts which thou sendest me. For what fit return can I make thee for those fish which the neighbouring shore supplies thee from its teeming pools, so wondrous in appearance, so diverse in shape ? But for me in the deep pools amid

rarus in obscura generatur sphondylus alga.
hinc te participans bis quinque et bis tibi ternas
transmisi aequoreo redolentes nectare testas,
quas viscus praedulce replet bicolore medulla.　　10
　　Oro libens sumas, nec vilia dedigneris,
quae sunt parva modum magno metitus amore.

XXXV.—Fragmenta Epistularum

1　Redite sursum flumina!

2　investigatum ferre dolo leporem.

3　quae tantae tenuere morae rumore sub omni?

the rocky shallows only a few shell-fish are bred among the dark seaweed. Of these I give thee a share sending across to thee twice five and twice three shells smelling of the sea's fragrance, filled with delicious meat and substance of double hue.

" I pray thee accept them gracefully and despise them not as little worth : if they are few, use great love in measuring their quantity.

XXXV.—FRAGMENTS OF EPISTLES [1]

1 YE rivers, backwards return !

2 To carry off a hare tracked down by craft.

3 What things have kept thee lingering so long, while Rumour is rife ?

[1] These three citations from epistles no longer extant are preserved by an anonymous grammarian of the seventh century.

LIBER XIX

EPIGRAMMATA AUSONII DE DIVERSIS REBUS

I

I.—Προσωποποιία in Chartam

Si tineas cariemque pati te, charta, necesse est,
    incipe versiculis ante perire meis.
"malo, inquis, tineis." sapis, aerumnose libelle,
    perfungi mavis quod leviore malo.
ast ego damnosae nolo otia perdere Musae,   5
    iacturam somni quae parit atque olei.
"utilius dormire fuit, quam perdere somnum
    atque oleum." bene ais: causa sed ista mihi est:
irascor Proculo, cuius facundia tanta est,
    quantus honos. scripsit plurima, quae cohibet. 10
hunc studeo ulcisci; et prompta est ultio vati:
    qui sua non edit carmina, nostra legat.
huius in arbitrio est, seu te iuvenescere cedro,
    seu iubeat duris vermibus esse cibum.
huic ego, quod nobis superest ignobilis oti,   15
    deputo, sive legat, quae dabo, sive tegat.

---

[1] Possibly the son of Titianus, Count of the East in 382-3, executed 392 A.D.

BOOK XIX

EPIGRAMS OF AUSONIUS ON VARIOUS MATTERS

I

I.—A Personal Address to his Paper

If worms and decay must needs be thy lot, my sheet, begin to perish under my verses first. "Rather," thou sayest, "the worms." Wisely, my woeful little book, dost thou choose to endure the lesser evil. But I like not to lose the leisure given to the wasteful Muse, who causes loss of slumber and lamp-oil too. "It had been better to sleep than to lose both slumber and oil." Well said : but this is my reason for it. I am angry with Proculus [1] whose eloquence is equal to his rank. He has written reams, but keeps all close. On him I long to be avenged, and a poet has vengeance ready to hand : let him who publishes not his own verse read mine. For him is it to decide whether to bid thee keep thy youth with cedar oil,[2] or to be food for cruel worms. To him I commit all that I have to show for my inglorious leisure, either to scan what I shall give him or to ban it.

---

[2] Cedar-oil was used to preserve books from the attacks of worms.

II.—Exhortatio ad Modestiam

Fama est fictilibus cenasse Agathoclea regem
    atque abacum Samio saepe onerasse luto,
fercula gemmatis cum poneret horrida [1] vasis
    et misceret opes pauperiemque simul.
quaerenti causam respondit : " Rex ego qui sum   5
    Sicaniae, figulo sum genitore satus."
fortunam reverenter habe, quicumque repente
    dives ab exili progrediere loco.

III.—In Eumpinam [2] Adulteram

Toxica zelotypo dedit uxor moecha marito,
    nec satis ad mortem credidit esse datum.
miscuit argenti letalia pondera vivi,
    cogeret ut celerem vis geminata necem.
dividat haec si quis, faciunt discreta venenum ;   5
    antidotum sumet, qui sociata bibet.
ergo inter sese dum noxia pocula certant,
    cessit letalis noxa salutiferae.
protinus et vacuos alvi petiere recessus,
    lubrica deiectis qua via nota cibis.   10
quam pia cura deum ! prodest crudelior uxor :
    et, cum fata volunt, bina venena iuvant.

IV.—In Eunomum Medicum

Languentem Gaium moriturum dixerat olim
    Eunomus. evasit fati ope, non medici.

[1] So *V* : aurea, *Z*.
[2] So *VZ* : Euripulam ? (= Euripylam), *Peiper* : Euripinam ?,
Schenkl.

EPIGRAMS ON VARIOUS MATTERS

II.—An Exhortation to Moderation

'Tis said that Agathocles[1] when king dined off earthen plates and that his sideboard oft bare a load of Samian ware, whereas he used to lay his rustic trays with jewelled cups, thus mingling wealth and poverty together. To one who asked his reason he replied : " I, who am king of Sicily, was born a potter's son."

[7] Bear good fortune modestly, whoe'er thou art who from a lowly place shall rise suddenly to riches.

III.—To Eumpina a faithless Wife

A FAITHLESS wife gave poison to her jealous spouse, but believed that not enough was given to cause death. She added quicksilver of deadly weight, that the poison's redoubled strength might force on a speedy end. If one keep these apart, separate they act as poison ; whoso shall drink them together, will take an antidote. Therefore while these baleful draughts strove with each other, the deadly force yielded to the wholesome. Forthwith they sought the void recesses of the belly by the accustomed easy path for swallowed food.

[11] Mark well the loving kindness of the gods ! A wife too ruthless is a gain, and, when the Fates will, two poisons work for good.

IV.—To Eunomus a Physician

Eunomus had once pronounced that Gaius would die of his sickness. He slipped away, Fate—not the

---

[1] King or tyrant of Sicily, 317-289 B.C.

paulo post ipsum videt, aut vidisse putavit,
 pallentem et multa mortis in effigie.
"Quis tu?" "Gaius," ait. "Vivisne?" hic abnuit. 5
 "Et quid
nunc agis hic?" "Missu Ditis, ait, venio,
ut, quia notitiam rerumque hominumque tenerem,
 accirem medicos." Eunomus obriguit.
tum Gaius: "Metuas nihil, Eunome. dixi ego et
 omnes,
 nullum, qui saperet, dicere te medicum." 10

V.—In Hominem Vocis absonae

Latratus catulorum, hinnitus fingis equorum,
 caprigenumque pecus lanigerosque greges
balatu adsimulas; asinos quoque rudere dicas,
 cum vis Arcadicum fingere, Marce, pecus.
gallorum cantus et ovantes gutture corvos 5
 et quidquid vocum belua et ales habet,
omnia cum simules ita vere, ut ficta negentur,
 non potes humanae vocis habere sonum.

VI.—De Auxilio Grammatico

Emendata potest quaenam vox esse magistri,
 nomen qui proprium cum vitio loquitur?
auxilium te nempe vocas, inscite magister?
 da rectum casum: iam solicismus eris.

---

[1] i.e. asses.

doctor—aiding. A little afterwards the doctor saw, or thought he saw, the man, pale, and in death's very likeness. "Who art thou?" he asked. "Gaius," he answered. "Art thou alive?" He answered "No." "And what now dost thou here?" "I come," said he, "at the behest of Dis, because I still retained knowledge of the world and men, to summon to him doctors." Eunomus grew stiff with fright. Then Gaius: "Fear nothing, Eunomus: I said, as all men say, that no man who is wise calls you a doctor."

V.—To a Man with a discordant Voice

WHELPS' barking, horses' neighing thou dost copy, and imitate the bleating of herds of goats and woolly flocks, and a man would say asses were bray-ing, when thou, Marcus, wouldst mimic the Arcadian herd.[1] The cock's crow, the raven's throaty caw and whatever cry is uttered by beast or bird—though these thou canst imitate so naturally that no one believes them feigned, thou canst not command the sound of the human voice.

VI.—On Auxilius a Grammar-Master

How can a master speak a word correctly who cannot utter his own name without mistake? "*Aux-ilium*[2]" (a help) callest thou thyself forsooth, ignorant usher? Give the nominative: straightway thou wilt be a solecism!

[2] There is a play on the word as both a proper and a common noun.

AUSONIUS

VII.—De Philomuso Grammatico

Emptis quod libris tibi bibliotheca referta est,
  doctum et grammaticum te, Philomuse, putas?
hoc genere et chordas et plectra et barbita condes:
  omnia mercatus cras citharoedus eris.

VIII.—De Rufo Rhetore

" Reminisco " Rufus dixit in versu suo:
cor ergo versus, immo Rufus, non habet.

IX.—In Statuam eiusdem Rhetoris

Rhetoris haec Rufi statua est: nil verius; ipse est,
  ipse, adeo linguam non habet et cerebrum.
et riget et surda est et non videt: haec sibi constant;
  unum dissimile est: mollior ille fuit.

X.—Idem

" Ore pulcro, et ore muto, scire vis quae sim? "
    " Volo."
  " Imago Rufi rhetoris Pictavici."
" Diceret set ipse, vellem, rhetor hoc mi."   " Non
    potest."
  " Cur? "   " Ipse rhetor est imago imaginis."

XI.—Idem

" Rhetoris haec Rufi statua est? "   " Si saxea, Rufi."
  " Cur id ais? "   " Semper saxeus ipse fuit."

---

¹ For *reminiscor*: *cor* in l. 2 = wit, intelligence.

EPIGRAMS ON VARIOUS MATTERS

VII.—On Philomusus a Grammar-Master

Because with purchased books thy library is crammed, dost think thyself a learned man and scholarly, Philomusus? After this sort thou wilt lay up strings, keys, and lyres, and, having purchased all, to-morrow thou wilt be a musician.

VIII.—On Rufus a Rhetorician

Reminisco,[1] wrote Rufus in his verse: so then the verse—nay, Rufus—has no *cor* (wit).

IX.—For a Statue of the same Rhetorician [2]

This is a statue of Rufus the Rhetorician; nothing more life-like: 'tis the man himself, so much lacks it tongue and brain. 'Tis stiff and dumb and sees not: in these points it tallies. One single point of difference is there—he was a little softer.

X.—The same Subject

" With lips so fair and lips so dumb, wouldst know who I am?" " I would." " I am a figure of Rufus the Pictavian rhetorician." " Nay, I would have the rhetorician tell me this himself." " He cannot." "Why?" " The real rhetorician is an image of this image."

XI.—The same Subject [3]

" Is this a statue of Rufus the rhetorician?" " If 'tis of stone, 'tis Rufus's." " Why sayest thou so?" " Rufus himself was always made of stone."

[2] *cp. Anth. Pal.* xi. 145, 149, 151.
[3] *cp. id.* xvi. 317.

AUSONIUS

XII.—Idem

Elinguem quis te dicentis imagine pinxit?
  dic mihi, Rufe. taces? nil tibi tam simile est.

XIII.—Idem

"Haec Rufi tabula est." "Nil verius. ipse ubi
  Rufus?"
  "In cathedra." "Quid agit?" "Hoc, quod et in
  tabula."

XIV.—De eo qui Thesaurum repperit cum se Laqueo vellet suspendere
[ex Graeco]

Qui laqueum collo nectebat, repperit aurum
  thesaurique loco deposuit laqueum.
at qui condiderat, postquam non repperit aurum,
  aptavit collo quem reperit laqueum.

XV.—Ex Graeco
ἀρχὴ δέ τοι ἥμισυ παντός

Incipe: dimidium facti est coepisse. superfit
  dimidium: rursum hoc incipe et efficies.

XVI.—Ex Graeco
ἁ χάρις ἁ βραδύπους ἄχαρις χάρις

Gratia, quae tarda est, ingrata est. gratia namque
  cum fieri properat, gratia grata magis.

---

[1] = *Anth. Pal.* xvi. 318.   [2] = *id.* ix. 44.   [3] Lucian, *Somn.* 3.
162

XII.—The same Subject [1]

Who painted thee, Rufus, tongue-tied, in the likeness of a speaking man? Tell me, Rufus. Thou art silent? Nothing is more like you.

XIII.—The same Subject

"This is a picture of Rufus." "Nothing more lifelike. Where is Rufus himself?" "In his chair." "What is he doing?" "The same as in the picture."

XIV.—On the Man who found a Treasure when he meant to hang himself (from the Greek) [2]

He who was knotting a halter for his own neck, found gold and buried the halter in the treasure's place. But he who had hidden the gold, not finding it, fitted about his neck the halter which he found.

XV.—From the Greek

The beginning is half the whole. [3]

Begin: to have commenced is half the deed. Half yet remains: begin again on this and thou wilt finish all.

XVI.—From the Greek [4]

" Favours slow-footed are unfavoured favours."

Favours which tarry meet small favour. For a favour when it hastes to be performed, is a favour more favoured. [5]

[4] = *Anth. Pal.* x. 30.   [5] *i.e.* more acceptable.

AUSONIUS

XVII—Ex eodem

Si bene quid facias, facias cito. nam cito factum
gratum erit. ingratum gratia tarda facit.

XVIII.—De eo qui Capaneum saltans ruit

Deceptae felix casus se miscuit arti:
histrio, saltabat qui Capanea, ruit.

XIX.—In Dodralem

Dodra ex dodrante est. sic collige: ius, aqua, vinum,
sal, oleum, panis, mel, piper, herba: novem.

XX.—Idem

"Dodra vocor." "Quae causa?" "Novem species
gero." "Quae sunt?"
"Ius, aqua, mel, vinum, panis, piper, herba, oleum,
sal."

XXI.—Idem

Δόδρα ποτὸν καὶ ἀριθμός, ἔχω μέλι, οἶνον, ἔλαιον,
ἄρτον, ἅλας, βυτάνην, ζωμόν, ὕδωρ, πέπερι.

XXII.—Ad Marcum Amicum de Discordia quam habet cum Puellis

"Hanc amo quae me odit, contra illam quae me
amat, odi.
compone inter nos, si potes, alma Venus!"

---

[1] *i.e.* the acrobat made a slip and fell, but as he was in the
part of Capaneus, the accident was appropriate. *cp. Anth.*

EPIGRAMS ON VARIOUS MATTERS

XVII.—From the same

If thou doest aught good, do it quickly. For what is done quickly will be acceptable. Favours slow granted are unfavourably received.

XVIII.—On an Acrobat who fell while dancing as Capaneus

A happy chance combined with a fault in skill: a tumbler, dancing the part of Capaneus, fell to the ground.[1]

XIX.—On a Brew called "Dodra"

Dodra[2] ("nines") is from *dodrans* (nine-twelfths). Thus compound: broth, water, wine, salt, oil, bread, honey, pepper, herbs: there's nine!

XX.—The same Subject

"I am called *dodra*." "Why so?" "I am made of nine ingredients." "What are they?" "Broth, water, honey, wine, bread, pepper, herbs, oil, salt."

XXI.—The same Subject

I, *dodra*, brew and number both, contain honey, wine, oil, bread, salt, herbs, broth, water, pepper.

XXII.—To Marcus a Friend on his Lack of Concord with Girls

"I love one girl who hates me, and again another who loves me I hate. Settle the trouble between us,

Pal. xi. 254, 1–4. Capaneus, one of the Seven against Thebes, was smitten by a thunderbolt and fell from the walls.

[2] A drink compounded of nine ingredients.

" Perfacile id faciam : mores mutabo et amores ;
　oderit haec, amet haec." " Rursus idem patiar."
" Vis ambas ut ames ?" " Si diligat utraque, vellem." 5
　" Hoc tibi tu praesta, Marce : ut ameris, ama."

XXIII.—Dyseros

" Suasisti, Venus, ecce, duas dyseros ut amarem.
　odit utraque : aliud da modo consilium."
" Vince datis ambas." " Cupio : verum arta domi res."
　" Pellice promissis." " Nulla fides inopi."
" Antestare deos." " Nec fas mihi fallere divos." 5
　" Pervigila ante fores." " Nocte capi metuo."
" Scribe elegos." " Nequeo, Musarum et Apollinis
　　expers."
　" Frange fores." " Poenas iudicii metuo."
" Stulte, ab amore mori pateris : non vis ob amorem ?"
　" Malo miser dici, quam miser atque reus." 10
" Suasi, quod potui : tu alios modo consule." " Dic
　quos ?"
　" Quod sibi suaserunt, Phaedra et Elissa dabunt,
quod Canace Phyllisque et fastidita Phaoni." [1]
　" Hoc das consilium ? tale datur miseris."

XXIV.—De eo qui Testam Hominis inmisericor-
diter dissipare voluit

Abiecta in triviis inhumati glabra iacebat
　testa hominis, nudum iam cute calvitium.

---

[1] So V : Phaedra et Elissa tibi dent laqueum aut gladium,
praecipitem pelago vel Leucados elige rupem, Z.

sweet Venus, if thou canst." "Right easily will I:
I will change thy leanings and thy loves; the one
shall hate, the other love." "Again I shall suffer
the same fate." "Wouldst love them both?" "If
both should love me, I would." "Bestow this, Marcus,
on thyself: to be beloved, love."

XXIII. ·A POOR LOVER

"Lo, Venus, thou hast persuaded me to love two
girls, a luckless lover. Each hates me: give me
another counsel now." "Overcome both with gifts."
"Fain would I: but scant is my store at home."
"Tempt them with promises." "A poor man has no
credit." "Swear by the gods." "But 'twere a sin
to deceive the gods." "Keep watch before their
doors." "I fear to be caught at night." "Write
sonnets." "I cannot, having no skill of the
Muses and Apollo." "Break down their doors."
"I fear the legal penalties." "Fool, thou dost let
thyself be killed by love: wouldst thou not die for
love?" "I would rather be called poor fellow than
poor prisoner." "I have advised thee all I can:
now take others' counsel." "Tell me whose?"
"Phaedra and Elissa will give the advice they gave
themselves, Canace, too, and Phyllis, and she whom
Phaon scorned." "Do you give this counsel? Such
is given to the unhappy!"

XXIV.—ON THE MAN WHO PITILESSLY TRIED TO BREAK IN PIECES A HUMAN SKULL

THE bare skull of an unburied man lay cast away
where three roads met—a bald thing now stripped of

fleverunt alii : fletu non motus Achilas,
    insuper et silicis verbere dissicuit.
eminus ergo icto rediit lapis ultor ab osse   5
    auctorisque sui frontem oculosque petit.
sic utinam certos manus impia dirigat ictus,
    auctorem ut feriant tela retorta suum.

II

XXV.—Commendatio Codicis

Est quod mane legas, est et quod vespere ; laetis
    seria miscuimus, tempore uti placeant.
non unus vitae color est nec carminis unus
    lector ; habet tempus pagina quaeque suum ;
hoc mitrata Venus, probat hoc galeata Minerva ;   5
    Stoicus has partes, has Epicurus amat ;
salva mihi veterum maneat dum regula morum,
    plaudat permissis sobria musa iocis.

XXVI.—[De Augusto [1]]

Phoebe potens numeris, praeses Tritonia bellis,
tu quoque ab aerio praepes Victoria lapsu,
come serenatum duplici diademate frontem
serta ferens, quae dona togae, quae praemia pugnae.
bellandi fandique potens Augustus honorem   5
bis meret, ut geminet titulos, qui proelia Musis
temperat et Geticum moderatur Apolline Martem.

[1] Suppl. *Pulmann.*

---

[1] This collection as a whole is found only in the *Z* group of
MSS., *i.e.* in the first published collection of Ausonius's
work : see *Introduction.*

skin. Other men wept: by weeping all unmoved, Achilas even struck and cleft it with a stone. And so the avenging stone, glancing from the skull, flew back and caught the face and eyes of him who threw it. So may an impious hand ever aim its deadly blows, that the weapon may rebound and smite the wielder.

II [1]

XXV.—A Recommendation of his Book

Here is what thou mayest read at morn, here also what at eve; I have mingled grave with gay, each to give pleasure at its season. Life wears not one hue, nor has my verse one reader only; each page has its due season; mitred Venus approves this, helmed Minerva that; the Stoic loves this part, Epicurus that. So long as the code of ancient manners remains by me unbroken, let the grave Muse applaud at lawful jests.

XXVI.—On Augustus

Phoebus, thou lord of song and thou, Tritonia, queen of war, thou also, Victory, down-swooping in dizzy flight, deck with a two-fold diadem an unknitted brow [2]: bring garlands, those which are gifts in peace, those which are prizes in fight. Mighty in war and eloquence, Augustus [3] doubly wins renown, so that he claims a two-fold title, since by the Muses' aid he allays wars and by Apollo's restrains

[2] *i.e.* on the Emperor's brow, no longer sternly knitted in war.
[3] *i.e.* Gratian.

arma inter Chunosque truces furtoque nocentes
Sauromatas, quantum cessat de tempore belli,
indulget Clariis tantum inter castra Camenis.　　10
vix posuit volucres stridentia tela sagittas:
Musarum ad calamos fertur manus, otia nescit
et commutata meditatur arundine carmen:
sed carmen non molle modis; bella horrida Martis
Odrysii Thraessaeque viraginis arma retractat.　　15
exulta, Aeacide: celebraris vate superbo
rursum Romanusque tibi contingit Homerus.

XXVII.—[DE FERA A CAESARE INTERFECTA[1]]

CEDERE quae lato nescit fera saucia ferro
　　armatique urget tela cruenta viri,
quam grandes parvo patitur sub vulnere mortes
　　et solam leti vim probat esse manum!
mirantur casusque novos subitasque ruinas:　　5

　•　.　.　.　.　.　.　.　.　.　.　.　.

nec contenta ictos letaliter ire per artus,
　　coniungit mortes una sagitta duas.
plurima communi pereunt si fulminis ictu,
　　haec quoque de caelo vulnera missa putes.　　10

XXVIII.—AD FONTEM DANUVII IUSSU VALENTINIANI AUGUSTI

ILLYRICIS regnator aquis, tibi, Nile, secundus
　　Danuvius laetum profero fonte caput.

　　　　　　[1] Suppl. *Avantius.*

_____

　[1] The Muses are called Clarian from their connection with
Apollo, who was worshipped at Claros, near Colophon.

the Getic Mars. 'Midst arms and Huns ferocious and
Sauromatae dangerous in stealth, whatever rest he
has from hours of war, in camp he lavishes it all
upon the Clarian [1] Muses. Scarce has he laid aside
his swift arrows, those whirring darts : 'tis to the
Muses' shafts he turns his hand, repose he knows
not, and setting the reed to new employ essays a
song : yet 'tis a song not soft of strain ; the frightful
wars of Odrysian Mars and the prowess of the
Thracian warrior-maid he treats anew. Rejoice,
thou son of Aeacus! Thou art sung once more by
a lofty bard and thou art blessed with a Roman
Homer.[2]

XXVII.—On a Wild Beast slain by Caesar

The beast which knows not how to yield when
pierced with the broad steel, but hurls itself upon
the gory spear of a full-armed man, how marvellous
the death it suffers from a tiny wound, showing that
on the hand alone death's might depends. Men
wonder at swift disasters and sudden downfalls

. . . .

and not content to drive its deadly course through
the stricken limbs, a single arrow deals two deaths
at once. If full many deaths come from one light-
ning stroke, these wounds also thou mayest deem
sent from heaven.

XXVIII.—On the Source of the Danube. Written by Command of the Emperor Valentinian

Lord among streams of Illyricum, next to thee
in greatness, O Nile, I, Danube, from my source put

[2] Gratian appears to have been composing an epic on
Achilles.

salvere Augustos iubeo, natumque patremque,
    armiferis alvi quos ego Pannoniis.
nuntius Euxino iam nunc volo currere ponto,   5
    ut sciat hoc superum cura secunda Valens,
caede, fuga, flammis stratos periisse Suebos
    nec Rhenum Gallis limitis esse loco.
quod si lege maris refluus mihi curreret amnis,
    huc possem victos inde referre Gothos.   10

XXIX.—Valentiniano Iuniori in Signum marmoreum

Nunc te marmoreum pro sumptu fecimus: at cum
Augustus frater remeaverit, aureus esto.

XXX.—Picturae subditi ubi Leo una Sagitta a Gratiano occisus est

Quod leo tam tenui patitur sub harundine letum,
    non vires ferri, sed ferientis agunt.

XXXI.—Ad Fontem Danuvii Jussu Valentiniani Augusti

Danuvius penitis caput occultatus in oris
    totus sub vestra iam dicione fluo:
qua gelidum fontem mediis effundo Suebis,
    imperiis gravidas qua seco Pannonias,

---

[1] Valentinian I. and Gratian : Valentinian's father, another Gratian, was a Pannonian.

[2] For the events commemorated see *Introduction*.

forth my head in joy. I bid the Emperors hail, father and son,[1] whom I have nurtured amid the sword-wearing Pannonians. As herald to the Euxine Sea even now I long to speed, that Valens, who is Heaven's next care, may learn of this—that with slaughter, flight, and fire the Swabians[2] are hurled to destruction, and Rhine no longer is accounted the frontier of Gaul. But if at the sea's behest my stream should flow backwards may I hither bring from there news that the Goths are vanquished.

XXIX.—To Valentinian the Younger. For a marble Statue

Now we have made thee of marble, as our means afford : but when thine Emperor-brother is returned, be thou of gold.[3]

XXX.—Lines inscribed under a Picture showing a Lion slain by Gratian with a single Arrow

The death which the lion suffers through so frail a reed is due, not to the weapon's power, but to the wielder's.

XXXI.—To the Source of the Danube. By Command of the Emperor Valentinian

I, Danube, whose head was once concealed in lands remote, now flow at full length under your sway : where 'midst the Suebi I pour forth my chill source, where I divide the Pannonias pregnant with

[3] *cp.* Virgil, *Ecl.* vii. 35 f. : nunc te marmoreum pro tempore fecimus ; at tu, Si fetura gregem suppleverit, aureus esto.

. et qua dives aquis Scythico solvo ostia ponto,   5
    omnia sub vestrum flumina mitto iugum.
Augusto dabitur sed proxima palma Valenti :
    inveniet fontes hic quoque, Nile, tuos.

XXXII.—In Echo Pictam

Vane, quid adfectas faciem mihi ponere, pictor,
    ignotamque oculis sollicitare deam?
Aeris et Linguae sum filia, mater inanis
    indicii, vocem quae sine mente gero.
extremos pereunte modos a fine reducens,   5
    ludificata sequor verba aliena meis.
auribus in vestris habito penetrabilis Echo :
    et, si vis similem pingere, pinge sonum.

XXXIII.—In Simulacrum Occasionis et Paenitentiae

Cuius opus?   Phidiae : qui signum Pallados, eius
    quique Iovem fecit ; tertia palma ego sum.
sum dea quae rara et paucis occasio nota.
    quid rotulae insistis?   stare loco nequeo.
quid talaria habes?   volucris sum.   Mercurius quae 5
    fortunare solet, trado ego, cum volui.
crine tegis faciem.   cognosci nolo.   sed heus tu
    occipiti calvo es?   ne tenear fugiens.
quae tibi iuncta comes?   dicat tibi.   dic rogo, quae sis.
    sum dea, cui nomen nec Cicero ipse dedit.   10

---

[1] Because Valentinian was of Pannonian origin.

empire,[1] and where with wealth of waters I open my mouth to the Scythian sea, all my streams I cause to pass beneath your Roman yoke. To Augustus shall the chief palm be given, but the next to Valens: he too shall find out sources—even thine, O Nile.

XXXII.—To a Painting of Echo

Fond painter, why dost thou essay to limn my face, and vex a goddess whom eyes never saw? I am the daughter of Air and Speech, mother of empty utterance, in that I have a voice without a mind. From their dying close I bring back failing strains and in mimicry repeat the words of strangers with my own. I am Echo, dwelling in the recesses of your ears: and if thou wouldst paint my likeness paint sound.

XXXIII.—For a Figure of Opportunity and Regret

" Whose work art thou?" "Pheidias's: his who made Pallas' statue, who made Jove's: his third masterpiece am I. I am a goddess seldom found and known to few, Opportunity my name." "Why stand'st thou on a wheel?" "I cannot stand still." "Why wearest thou winged sandals?" "I am ever flying. The gifts which Mercury scatters at random I bestow when I will." "Thou coverest thy face with thy hair." "I would not be recognised." "But—what!—art thou bald at the back of thy head?" "That none may catch me as I flee." "Who is she who bears thee company?" "Let her tell thee." "Tell me, I beg, who thou art." "I am a goddess to whom not even Cicero himself gave

sum dea, quae factique et non facti exigo poenas,
    nempe ut paeniteat.   sic METANOEA vocor.
tu modo dic, quid agat tecum.   quandoque volavi,
    haec manet; hanc retinent, quos ego praeterii.
tu quoque dum rogitas, dum percontando moraris, 15
    elapsam dices me tibi de manibus.

XXXIV.—Ad Gallam Puellam iam senescentem

Dicebam tibi : "Galla, senescimus; effugit aetas,
    utere rene tuo : casta puella anus est."
sprevisti.   obrepsit non intellecta senectus
    nec revocare potes, qui periere, dies.
nunc piget et quereris, quod non aut ista voluntas 5
    tunc fuit, aut non est nunc ea forma tibi.
da tamen amplexus oblitaque gaudia iunge.
    da : fruar, et si non quod volo, quod volui.

XXXV.—De Lepore capto a Cane Marino

Trinacrii quondam currentem in litoris ora
    ante canes leporem caeruleus rapuit.
at lepus : "In me omnis terrae pelagique rapina est,
    forsitan et caeli; si canis astra tenet."

---

[1] = μετάνοια, primarily change of disposition and purpose,
then the emotion accompanying such change, and finally
"regret," "remorse" generally.

a name. I am a goddess who exacts penalties for what is done and what undone, to cause repentance. So I am called *Metanoea.*[1] " " Do thou [2] now tell me what does she along with thee ? " "When I have flown away she remains : she is retained by those I have passed by. Thou also whilst thou keepest asking, whilst thou tarriest with questioning wilt say that I have slipped away out of thy hands."

XXXIV.—To a Maid, Galla, now growing old [3]

I used to say to thee : "Galla, we grow old, Time flies away, enjoy thy life : a chaste girl is an old woman." Thou didst scorn my warning. Age has crept upon thee unperceived, nor canst thou call back the days that are gone. Now thou art sorry and dost lament, either because then thou wert disinclined, or because now thou hast not that former beauty. Yet give me thine embrace and share forgotten joys with me. Give : I will take, albeit not what I would, yet what I once would.

XXXV.—On a Hare caught by a Sea-Dog [4]

Once on the strand of Sicily a sea-dog snapped up a hare speeding before the hounds. Then said the hare : "Against me both sea and land direct their ravages, perchance heaven also ; since there is a Dog among the stars."

[2] The poet here turns again to Opportunity.
[3] After *Anth. Pal.* v. 21.
[4] *id.* ix. 18.

XXXVI.—De Pergamo Scriptore fugitivo qui captus fuerat

Tam segnis scriptor, quam lentus, Pergame, cursor,
    fugisti et primo captus es in stadio.
ergo notas scripto tolerasti, Pergame, vultu
    et quas neglexit dextera, frons patitur.

XXXVII.—<In eundem Pergamum [1]>

Pergame, non recte punitus fronte subisti
    supplicium, lentae quod meruere manus.
at tu, qui dominus, peccantia membra coherce:
    iniustum falsos excruciare reos.
aut inscribe istam, quae non vult scribere, dextram,
    aut profugos ferri pondere necte pedes.

XXXVIII.—De Myrone qui Laidis Noctem rogaverat

Canus rogabat Laidis noctem Myron:
    tulit repulsam protinus
causamque sensit et caput fuligine
    fucavit atra candidum.
idemque vultu, crine non idem Myron   5
    orabat oratum prius.
sed illa formam cum capillo comparans
    similemque, non ipsum, rata
(fortasse et ipsum, sed volens ludo frui)
    sic est adorta callidum: 10
"Inepte, quid me, quod recusavi, rogas?
    patri negavi iam tuo."

    [1] Combined in the MSS. with the foregoing epigram.

XXXVI.—On Pergamus, a Runaway Scribe, who had been caught

As lazy a scribe as a sluggish runner, thou, Pergamus, didst run away and wert caught at the first lap. Therefore thou hast felt letters[1] branded, Pergamus, upon thy face, and those which thy right hand neglected thy brow endures.

XXXVII.—On the same Pergamus

Pergamus, when thou wast punished 'twas not just thy brow should bear the penalty which thy slow hands earned. Nay, do thou, their master, control thy errant limbs: it is unfair to torment those not really guilty. Either mark that right-hand which will not make a mark, or shackle those errant feet with an iron weight.

XXXVIII.—On Myron who asked Laïs for an Assignation[2]

Hoar-headed Myron asked Laïs for an assignation, and was refused outright: he understood the cause, and dyed his white poll with black soot. In face—though not in hair—the selfsame Myron, he begged what he had begged before. But she, contrasting his features with his hair, and thinking him like, though not the same (perchance even thinking him the same, but wishing to enjoy the jest), thus addressed the artful gallant: "Fool, why askest thou what I have refused? I have already rejected thy father."

---

[1] *i.e.* FUG = *fugitivus.*
[2] *cp.* Spartianus, *Vita Hadriani*, xx. 8.

XXXIX.—De Opinione quam de illo habebat eius Uxor

Laidas et Glyceras, lascivae nomina famae,
  coniunx in nostro carmine cum legeret,
ludere me dixit falsoque in amore iocari.
  tanta illi nostra est de probitate fides.

XL.—Ad Uxorem

Uxor, vivamus quod viximus, et teneamus
  nomina, quae primo sumpsimus in thalamo:
nec ferat ulla dies, ut commutemur in aevo;
  quin tibi sim iuvenis tuque puella mihi.
Nestore sim quamvis provectior aemulaque annis   5
  vincas Cumanam tu quoque Deiphoben;
nos ignoremus, quid sit matura senectus.
  scire aevi meritum, non numerare decet.

XLI.—In Meroen Anum ebriosam

Qui primus, meroe, nomen tibi condidit, ille
  Thesidae nomen condidit Hippolyto.
nam divinare est, nomen componere, quod sit
  fortunae et morum vel necis indicium.
Protesilae, tibi nomen sic fata dederunt,   5
  victima quod Troiae prima futurus eras.
Idmona quod vatem, medicum quod Iapyga dicunt,
  discendas artes nomina praeveniunt.
et tu sic Meroe, non quod sis atra colore,
  ut quae Niliaca nascitur in Meroe;   10

---

[1] *i.e.* the Sibyl of Cumae, daughter of Glaucus (see Virgil, *Aen.* vi. 36).
[2] See *Epitaphia*, xii. 1-2 (note).

XXXIX.—How highly the Poet's Wife thought of him

OF Laïs and Glycera, ladies of naughty fame, whene'er my wife read in my verse, she said I did but play and feign strange loves in jest. Such is her confidence in my integrity.

XL.—To his Wife

DEAR wife, as we have lived, so let us live and keep the names we took when first we wedded : let no day ever make us change in lapse of time; but I will be thy " Lad " still and thou wilt be my " Lass." Though I should outlive Nestor, and thou too shouldst outstrip Deïphobe of Cumae[1] in rivalry of years, let us refuse to know the meaning of ripe age. Better to know Time's worth than count his years.

XLI.—To Meroë, a drunken Hag

WHO first compounded thee thy name, Meroë, he for Hippolytus, Theseus' son, compounded a name. For 'tis divining to make such a name as betokens lot, or character, or death. So, Protesilaüs, the Fates gave thee thy name, because thou wert to be Troy's first victim.[2] When men call a poet Idmon,[3] a physician Iapyx,[4] the names anticipate the arts they are to learn. Even so art thou Meroë, not because thou art dusky-hued as one born in Nile-washed

---

[3] Idmon (from the root ιδ-) was the bard and seer who accompanied the Argonauts.

[4] Iapyx was the physician who tended Aeneas (Virgil, *Aen.* xxii. 391 ff.).

infusum sed quod vinum non diluis undis,
  potare inmixtum sueta merumque merum.

XLII.—Ex Graeco traductum de Statua Nemesis

Me lapidem quondam Persae advexere, tropaeum
  ut fierem bello : nunc ego sum Nemesis.
ac sicut Graecis victoribus adsto tropaeum,
  punio sic Persas vaniloquos Nemesis.

XLIII.—De Thrasybulo Lacedaemonio qui fortissime dimicans occubuit

Excipis adverso quod pectore vulnera septem,
  arma super veheris quod, Thrasybule, tua,
non dolor hic patris est, Pitanae sed gloria maior.
  rarum, tam pulchro funere posse frui.
quem postquam maesto socii posuere feretro,   5
  talia magnanimus edidit orsa pater :
"Flete alios.   natus lacrimis non indiget ullis,
  et meus, et talis, et Lacedaemonius."

XLIV.—Ex Graeco traductum de Matre magnanima

Mater Lacaena clipeo obarmans filium,
  "Cum hoc," inquit, "aut in hoc redi."

---

[1] The play upon *Meroë . . . merum* cannot be reproduced.
[2] = *Anth.* xvi. 263.
[3] See *Epist.* xxvii. 53 ff. and note.

Meroë ; but because thou never slakest wine with water, being used to drink draughts unallayed of wine, pure wine.[1]

XLII.—Translated from the Greek.[2] On a Statue of Nemesis

As a stone the Persians once brought me here to be a trophy of war ; now am I Nemesis. And even as I stand here a trophy of Greek victory, so as Nemesis I requite the idly-boasting Persians.[3]

XLIII.—On Thrasybulus the Lacedaemonian who fell fighting most bravely [4]

That thou receivest seven gashes all in front, that thou art borne, Thrasybulus, upon thy shield, this grieves not thy sire, but adds greater glory to Pitana.[5] Rare is the opportunity of so fair a death. After thy comrades laid thee upon the mournful bier, these words did thy stout-hearted sire pronounce : " Weep ye for others : a son needs not any tears, being mine, so glorious, and a Spartan."

XLIV.—Translated from the Greek.[6] On a brave Mother

A Spartan mother slinging her son's shield, "Return with this," said she, " or upon it."

---

[4] = *Anth. Pal.* vii. 229.
[5] A Spartan town on the Eurotas.
[6] Plut. *Apophth. Lacaen. Incert.* 15 : τέκνον, ἔφη, ἢ τὰν ἢ ἐπὶ τᾶς.

XLV.—In Degenerem divitem Moecho genitum

Quidam superbus opibus et fastu tumens
 tantumque verbis nobilis
spernit vigentis clara saecli nomina,
 antiqua captans stemmata,
Martem Remumque et conditorem Romulum   5
 privos parentes nuncupans.
hos ille Serum veste contexi iubet:
 hos caelat argento gravi,
ceris inurens ianuarum limina
 et atriorum pegmata.   10
credo, quod illi nec pater certus fuit
 et mater est vere lupa.

XLVI.—Antisthenis Cynici Imagini subditi

Inventor primus Cynices ego. "Quae ratio istaec?
 Alcides multo dicitur esse prior."
Alcida quondam fueram doctore secundus:
 nunc ego sum Cynices primus, et ille deus.

XLVII.—[De Eodem]

Discipulus melior nulli meliorve magister
 εἰς ἀρετὴν συνέβη καὶ Κυνικὴν σοφίην.
dicere me novit verum, qui novit utrumque,
 καὶ θεὸν Ἀλκείδην, καὶ κύνα Διογένην.

---

[1] Antisthenes, pupil first of Gorgias, then of Socrates, founder of the Cynic school, used to quote Heracles as illus-

EPIGRAMS ON VARIOUS MATTERS

XLV.—To a rich Degenerate basely born

A FELLOW, purse-proud and swollen-headed, high born in words alone, scorns the illustrious names of the current age, hankering after an ancient pedigree and claiming Mars, Remus, and Romulus our founder as his own special forebears. Their figures he bids be woven in his silken robes, theirs he chases on his massy plate, or paints in encaustic on his threshold and on the ceiling of his halls. True for him! For his father was not known and his mother surely is a bitch.

XLVI.—Written under a Portrait of Antisthenes the Cynic

"I AM the first discoverer of the Cynic rule." "How can that be? Men say Alcides [1] long preceded thee." "Once I was second with Alcides for my master; now I am the first Cynic and he a god."

XLVII.—On the same

NONE had a better pupil or a better master in virtue and the Cynic lore. He knows that I speak truth who knows each of the two, Alcides the god and Diogenes the dog (Cynic).

trating his doctrine that labour is a good. Diogenes (412–323 B.C), disciple of Antisthenes, compared his mantle to the lion's skin of Heracles.

XLVIII.—Mixobarbaron Liberi Patris Signo mar-
moreo in Villa nostra omnium Deorum
Argumenta habenti

Ogygidae[1] me Bacchum vocant,
Osirin Aegypti putant,
Mysi Phanacen nominant,
Dionyson Indi existimant,
Romana sacra Liberum, 5
Arabica gens Adoneum,
Lucaniacus Pantheum.

XLIX.—Libero Patri

Αἰγυπτίων μὲν Ὄσιρις ἐγώ, Μυσῶν δὲ Φανάκης,
Βάκχος ἐνὶ ζωοῖσιν, ἐνὶ φθιμένοισιν Ἀδωνεύς,
πυρογενής, δίκερως, Τιτανολέτης, Διόνυσος.

L.—In Corydonem marmoreum

Αἲξ χίμαρος πήδη ποιμὴν ῥαβδοῦχος ἐλαίη
εἷς λίθος ἐκ πάντων λιτὸς ἐγὼ Κορυδών.

LI.—In Simulacrum Sapphus

Lesbia Pieriis Sappho soror addita Musis,
εἰμ᾽ ἐνάτη λυρικῶν, Ἀονίδων δεκάτη.

LII.—Deae Veneri

Orta salo, suscepta solo, patre edita Caelo,
Aeneadum genetrix, hic habito alma Venus.

[1] cp. Statius, Theb. ii. 586: Ogygiae, MSS.

---

[1] i.e. the Thebans: Ogyges was the mythieal founder of
the city.   [2] Ausonius' estate.

EPIGRAMS ON VARIOUS MATTERS

XLVIII.—An outlandish Medley to a marble Statue of Liber Pater in my Country House, having the Attributes of various Gods

THE sons of Ogyges[1] call me Bacchus, Egyptians think me Osiris, Mysians name me Phanaces, Indians regard me as Dionysus, Roman rites make me Liber, the Arab race thinks me Adoneus, Lucaniacus[2] the Universal God.

XLIX.—To Liber Pater

I AM Osiris of the Egyptians, Phanaces of the Mysians, Bacchus among the living, Adoneus among the dead, Fire-born, Twy-horned, Titan-slayer, Dionysus.

L.—To a marble Statue of Corydon

A GOAT, a ram, a wallet, a shepherd with his staff, an olive-tree, all in a monolith make up lithe[3] Corydon.

LI.—To a Figure of Sappho[4]

I, LESBIAN Sappho, adopted sister of the Muses, am ninth of the lyrists,[5] tenth of the Aonides.

LII.—To the Goddess Venus

RISEN from the firth, received by earth, Heaven's child by birth, mother of Aeneas' line, I, kindly Venus, here do dwell.

[3] The play on λίθος . . . λιτός cannot fully be reproduced.
[4] cp. Anth. Pal. ix. 506, 571 (ll. 7 f.).
[5] In reference to the Alexandrine Canons of standard authors (Nine Lyrists, Ten Orators, and so forth).

AUSONIUS

LIII.—Versus in Veste contexti

Laudet Achaemenias orientis gloria telas :
  molle aurum pallis, Graecia, texe tuis ;
non minus Ausoniam celebret dum fama Sabinam,
  parcentem magnis sumptibus, arte parem.

LIV.—Item

Sive probas Tyrio textam subtemine vestem
  seu placet inscripti commoditas tituli,
ipsius hoc dominae concinnat utrumque venustas,
  has geminas artes una Sabina colit.

LV.—De eadem Sabina

Licia qui texunt et carmina, carmina Musis,
  licia contribuunt, casta Minerva, tibi.
ast ego rem sociam non dissociabo Sabina,
  versibus inscripsi quae mea texta meis.

LVI.—De Puella quam amabat

Hanc volo, quae non vult ; illam, quae vult, ego nolo :
  vincere vult animos, non satiare Venus.
oblatas sperno illecebras, detrecto negatas :
  nec satiare animum nec cruciare volo.
nec bis cincta Diana placet nec nuda Cythere :   5
  illa voluptatis nil habet, haec nimium.
callida sed mediae Veneris mihi venditet artem
  femina, quae iungat, qucd volo nolo vocant.

---

[1] Again *Ausonia* bears a double meaning, " western " and
" wife of Ausonius."
[2] *cp. Anth. Pal.* xii. 200.

EPIGRAMS ON VARIOUS MATTERS

LIII.—Lines woven in a Robe

Let the proud Orient extol its Achaemenian looms: weave in thy robes, O Greece, soft threads of gold; but let fame equally renown Ausonian[1] Sabina who, shunning their costliness, matches their skill.

LIV.—A Second Set

Whether thou dost admire robes woven in Tyrian looms, or lovest a motto neatly traced, my mistress with her charming skill combines the twain: one hand—Sabina's—practises these twin arts.

LV.—On the same Sabina

Some weave yarn and some weave verse: these of their verse make tribute to the Muses, those of their yarn to thee, O chaste Minerva. But I, Sabina, will not divorce mated arts, who on my own webs have inscribed my verse.

LVI.—On the Maid whom he loved[2]

Her I would have who will not, and her, who will, I would not: Venus would vanquish, not satisfy, the heart. Charms offered me I scorn, depreciate those denied: I would neither sate my heart nor torture it. Neither twice-girt Dian pleases, nor nude Cythere: the one gives no delight, the other overmuch. Be mine a mistress skilfully to display the art of attempered love, who can unite what " I would," " I would not " mean.[3]

[3] *i.e.* " who can unite the two attitudes these words imply."

AUSONIUS

LVII.—De duobus Fratribus

Χρῆστος, Ἀκίνδυνος, αὐτοαδελφεοί, οἰκτρὰ δὲ τέκνα,
    moribus ambo malis nomina falsa gerunt :
οὐδ᾽ οὗτος χρηστός, οὐδ᾽ οὗτος ἀκίνδυνός ἐστιν.
    una potest ambos littera corrigere.
αἴ κεν Χρῆστος ἔχῃ παρ᾽ ἀδελφοῦ Ἀκινδύνου ἄλφα,   5
    κίνδυνος hic fiet, frater ἄχρηστος erit.

LVIII.—De Chresto et Acindyno quibus fuerat male Nomen impositum

Germani fratres sunt, Chrestos, Acindynos alter.
falsum nomen utrique : sed ut verum sit utrique,
alpha suum Chresto det Acindynos, ipse sine alpha
    permaneat ; verum nomen uterque geret.

LIX.—Quoddam quasi Aenigma de tribus Incestis

" Tres uno in lecto : stuprum duo perpetiuntur,
    et duo committunt." " Quattuor esse reor."
" Falleris : extremis da singula crimina et illum
    bis numera medium, qui facit et patitur."

LX.—De his qui dicunt Reminisco quod non est Latinum

Qui reminisco putat se dicere posse latine
hic ubi co scriptum est, faceret cor, si cor haberet.

EPIGRAMS ON VARIOUS MATTERS

LVII.—On two Brothers

CHRESTUS and Acindynus, own brothers but hapless children, bear names which belie their unhappy qualities: neither this one is "Gracious," nor this "Riskless." One letter can correct them both. If Chrestus should borrow *alpha* ("-less"), from his brother Acindynus, one will become "Risk" and his brother will be "Graceless."

LVIII.—On Chrestus and Acindynus who had been inappropriately named

THESE are two own brothers, Chrestus and Acindynus. Both have been wrongly named: but that both may be set right, let Acindynus give his *alpha* to Chrestus, himself remaining without *alpha*; each will be an appropriate name.

LIX.—A Kind of Riddle on three lewd Fellows [1]

" THREE lewd fellows in a single bed: two are practising depravity and two are suffering it." "Why, that makes four." "Not at all: give a role each to those on the outside and count the middle one twice: he is both active and passive."

LX.—On those who say "Reminisco," which is not Latin

HE who thinks he can say *reminisco* and speak Latin, would put *cor* where *co* is written, if he had any sense.

[1] = *Anth. Pal.* xi. 225.

AUSONIUS

LXI.—DE VERBIS RUFI

Rufus vocatus rhetor olim ad nuptias,
  celebri ut fit in convivio,
grammaticae ut artis se peritum ostenderet,
  haec vota dixit nuptiis :
"Et masculini et feminini gignite   5
  generisque neutri filios."

LXII.—DE GLAUCIA INMATURA MORTE PRAEVENTO

Laeta bis octono tibi iam sub consule pubes
  cingebat teneras, Glaucia adulte, genas.
et iam desieras puer anne puella videri :
  cum properata dies abstulit omne decus.
sed neque functorum socius miscebere vulgo   5
  nec metues Stygios flebilis umbra lacus,
verum aut Persephonae Cinyreius ibis Adonis,
  aut Iovis Elysii tu Catamitus eris.

LXIII.—IN SIGNUM MARMOREUM NIOBES

Vivebam : sum facta silex, quae deinde polita
  Praxiteli manibus vivo iterum Niobe.
reddidit artificis manus omnia, sed sine sensu :
  hunc ego, cum laesi numina, non habui.

LXIV.—DE PALLADE VOLENTE CERTARE ARMIS CUM VENERE

Armatam vidit Venerem Lacedaemone Pallas.
  "Nunc certemus," ait, "iudice vel Paride."
cui Venus : "Armatam tu me, temeraria, temnis,
  quae, quo te vici tempore, nuda fui ?"

---

[1] cp. generally *Anth. Pal.* ix 489.
[2] Meaning apparently that a rhetorician was often invited
and expected to make a speech.

EPIGRAMS ON VARIOUS MATTERS

LXI.—On an Utterance of Rufus [1]

Rufus the rhetorician, being once invited to a wedding—a thing oft done at crowded festivals [2]—to show his skill in grammar, expressed these wishes for the wedded pair : "May ye get sons of gender masculine, feminine and neuter."

LXII.—On Glaucias, cut off by an untimely Death

Glad youth verging upon thy sixteenth year already was encircling thy soft cheeks with down, young Glaucias. And already thou hadst ceased to seem boy or maid indifferently when the day came too hurriedly and bare off all thy comeliness. Yet neither shalt thou join company with the common throng of dead, nor shalt thou, a piteous shade, dread the Stygian pools, but thou shalt go thither as Persephone's Adonis, the son of Cinyras, or thou shalt be the Ganymede of Elysian Jove.

LXIII.—For a marble Statue of Niobe [3]

I used to live : I became stone, and then being polished by the hand of Praxiteles, I now live again as Niobe. The artist's hand has restored me all but sense : that, when I offended gods, I had not.

LXIV.—On Pallas offering to do Combat with Venus [4]

At Lacedaemon Pallas saw Venus armed. "Now," quoth she, "let us contend, even with Paris for judge." Venus replied : "When I am armed, rash maid, dost thou despise me, seeing that when I conquered thee I was bare ? "

[3] *cp. Anth.* xvi. 129.   [4] *= Anth.* xvi. 174.

AUSONIUS

LXV.—De Laide dicante Veneri Speculum suum

Lais anus Veneri speculum dico : dignum habeat se
    aeterna aeternum forma ministerium.
at mihi nullus in hoc usus, quia cernere talem,
    qualis sum, nolo, qualis eram, nequeo.

LXVI.—[De Castore, Polluce et Helena]

Istos tergemino nasci quos cernis ab ovo,
    patribus ambiguis et matribus adsere natos.
hos genuit Nemesis, sed Leda puerpura fovit ;
    Tyndareus pater his et Iuppiter : hic putat, hic scit.

LXVII.—De Imagine Veneris sculpta a Praxitele

Vera Venus Gnidiam cum vidit Cyprida, dixit :
    "Vidisti nudam me, puto, Praxitele."
"Non vidi, nec fas : sed ferro opus omne polimus.
    ferrum Gradivi Martis in arbitrio.
qualem igitur domino scierant placuisse Cytheren, 5
    talem fecerunt ferrea caela deam."

LXVIII.—In Buculam Aeream Myronis

Bucula sum, caelo genitoris facta Myronis
    aerea : nec factam me puto, sed genitam,
sic me taurus init, sic proxima bucula mugit,
    sic vitulus sitiens ubera nostra petit.

---

[1] *cp. Anth. Pal.* vi. 1.   [2] *cp.* Gorgias, *Helen*, § 3.

EPIGRAMS ON VARIOUS MATTERS

LXV.—On Laïs dedicating her Mirror to Venus [1]

I, Laïs, grown old, to Venus dedicate my mirror:
let eternal beauty have the eternal service which
befits it. But for me there is no profit in this, for to
behold myself such as I am I would not, such as I
was I cannot.

LXVI.—On Castor, Pollux, and Helen

Those whom thou seest springing from a triple
egg, declare their ancestry doubtful on either side.
These Nemesis conceived, but pregnant Leda bare
them in her womb; Tyndareus to them was father
and Juppiter: the one believes he is, the other
knows. [2]

LXVII.—On a Statue of Venus sculptured by Praxiteles [3]

The real Venus, when she saw the Cnidian Cypris,
said: "Methinks, Praxiteles, thou hast seen me un-
clad." "I have not seen thee, 'twould be sin: but
'tis with steel I finish every work. Steel is at the
disposal of Mars Gradivus. Therefore my steel chisel
has fashioned a goddess such as the Cythera whom
it knew to have pleased its lord."

LXVIII.—On the Bronze Heifer of Myron [4]

I am a heifer, wrought in bronze by the chisel
of Myron my creator: nay, I think I was not
wrought but born, so does the bull make for me, so
does the heifer by my side low, so the calf athirst

[3] *Anth.* xvi. 160 (*cp.* 162).
[4] *cp. Anth. Pal.* ix. 713, 726, 730.

miraris, quod fallo gregem? gregis ipse magister 5
inter pascentes me numerare solet.

LXIX.—De eadem Bucula Myronis

Ubera quid pulsas frigentia matris aenae,
    o vitule, et sucum lactis ab aere petis?
hunc quoque praestarem, si me pro parte parasset
    exteriore Myron, interiore deus.

LXX.—Ad Daedalum de eadem Bucula

Daedale, cur vana consumis in arte laborem?
    me potius clausa subice Pasiphae.
illecebras verae si vis dare, Daedale, vaccae,
    viva tibi species vacca Myronis erit.

LXXI.—De eadem Myronis Bucula iam habente Spiritum

Aerea mugitum poterat dare vacca Myronis;
    sed timet artificis deterere ingenium.
fingere nam similem vivae, quam vivere, plus est;
    nec sunt facta dei mira, sed artificis.

LXXII.—De eadem Bucula iam habente Spiritum

Aerea bos steteram; mactata est vacca Minervae;
    sed dea proflatam transtulit huc animam.
et modo sum duplex: pars aerea, pars animata.
    haec manus artificis dicitur, illa deae.

seeks my udders. Dost wonder that the herd mistakes me? The master of the herd himself oft reckons me with his grazing beasts.

LXIX.—On the same Heifer of Myron

Why thrustest thou at the cold udders of a brazen dam, O calf, and seekest milky liquid from bronze? That also would I supply had Heaven made me within as Myron without.

LXX.—To Daedalus on the same Heifer

Daedalus, why wastest thou pains in idle craft? Rather expose me with Pasiphaë enclosed within. If thou wouldst offer the allurement of a real cow, Myron's shall be for thee a living image.

LXXI.—On the same Heifer of Myron now endowed with Breath

Myron's brazen heifer could low aloud, but fears to spoil the artist's craftsmanship. For to make me seem alive is more than to make me live; and not the works of God are wondrous, but the artist's.[1]

LXXII.—On the same Heifer now endowed with Breath

I had stood here a brazen heifer; a cow was slaughtered to Minerva; but the goddess transferred to me the life breathed forth. And now I am twofold: part is brazen, part alive. This is ascribed to the artist's skill, that to the goddess.

[1] *i.e.* natural objects are taken for granted and excite no wonder: it is the artificial which meets with admiration.

LXXIII.—Ad Taurum de eadem Bucula

Quid me, taure, paras specie deceptus inire?
non sum ego Minoae machina Pasiphaae.

LXXIV.—De eadem Myronis Bucula

Necdum caduco sole, iam sub vespere,
ageret iuvencas cum domum pastor suas,
suam relinquens me monebat ut suam.

LXXV.—De eadem Myronis Bucula

Unam iuvencam pastor forte amiserat,
   numerumque iussus reddere
me defuisse conquerebatur, sequi
   quae noluissem ceteras.

LXXVI.—<Quae Sexum mutarint>

Vallebanae (nova res et vix credenda poetis,
   sed quae de vera promitur historia)
femineam in speciem convertit masculus ales
   pavaque de pavo constitit ante oculos.
cuncti admirantur monstrum : sed mollior agna   5
   [talia virginea voce puella refert:[1]]
" Quid stolidi ad speciem notae novitatis hebetis?
   an vos Nasonis carmina non legitis?
Caenida convertit proles Saturnia Consus
   ambiguoque fuit corpore Tiresias.   10
vidit semivirum fons Salmacis Hermaphroditum :
   vidit nubentem Plinius Androgynum.

[1] Suppl. *Translator*

EPIGRAMS ON VARIOUS MATTERS

LXXIII.—To a Bull on the same Heifer

Why seekest thou to make for me, lord of the herd, beguiled by appearance? I am no contrivance of Pasiphaë, Minos' wife.

LXXIV.—On the same Heifer of Myron

Ere the sinking sun was set, evening now drawing on, the neatherd, while he drove his heifers home, left one of his own and chid me as though one of his.

LXXV.—On the same Heifer of Myron

A neatherd chanced to have lost a single heifer, and, bidden to deliver up the tale, complained that I was missing because I would not follow the others home.

LXXVI.—They who have changed their Sex

At Vallebana [1] (a thing strange and scarce credible in a poet, but which is taken from a truthful tale) a male bird changed into female form, and an erstwhile peacock stood a peahen before men's eyes. All marvelled at the portent; but a girl softer than any lamb spake thus with maiden voice: "Fools, why so amazed to see a thing strange yet not unknown? Or do ye not read Naso's verse? Consus, old Saturn's son, changed Caenis to a boy and Tiresias was not always of one sex. The fount Salmacis saw Hermaphroditus the half-man [2]; Pliny [3] saw a man-woman

---

[1] Unknown.
[2] See Ovid, *Metam.* xii. 189 ff.; iii. 323 ff.; iv. 285 ff.
[3] See Pliny *N.H.* vii. 36.

nec satis antiquum, quod Campana in Benevento
    unus epheborum virgo repente fuit.
nolo tamen veteris documenta arcessere famae.   15
    ecce ego sum factus femina de puero."

LXXVII.—Ad Pythagoram de Marco qui
dicebatur Pullaria

" Pythagora Euphorbi, reparas qui semina rerum
    corporibusque novis das reduces animas,
dic, quid erit Marcus iam fata novissima functus,
    si redeat vitam rursus in aeriam?"
"Quis Marcus?"   "Feles nuper pullaria dictus,   5
    corrupit totum qui puerile secus,
perversae Veneris postico vulnere fossor,
    Lucili vatis subpilo pullipremo."
" Non taurus, non mulus erit, non hippocamelus,
    non caper aut aries, sed scarabaeus erit."   10

LXXVIII.—De Castore Fellatore qui suam
lingebat Uxorem

Lambere cum vellet mediorum membra virorum
    Castor nec posset vulgus habere domi,
repperit, ut nullum fellator perderet inguen :
    uxoris coepit lingere membra suae.

LXXIX.—Subscriptum Picturae Mulieris
impudicae

Praeter legitimi genialia foedera coetus
repperit obscenas veneres vitiosa libido :
Herculis heredi quam Lemnia suasit egestas,

in the act. Nor is the tale yet old that in Campanian Beneventum a certain lad suddenly became a maid. Yet I would not cite you instances of old report : lo, I was changed from boy to girl.''

LXXVII.—To Pythagoras on Marcus who was said to be a Kidnapper

" Pythagoras, Euphorbus' son, thou who dost renew the seeds of nature and to fresh bodies dost assign souls brought back to earth, say, what will Marcus be who has now felt fate's final stroke, if he return again to live in our air ? " " Who is Marcus ? " " One lately known as seducer and kidnapper, who has debauched the entire sex, an unnatural scoundrel, or, as the bard Lucilius says, a pilfering paederast." " No bull, no mule, no hippocamel shall he be, no goat or ram, but he shall be a scarabaeus." [1]

LXXVIII.—On Castor, A Fellator who used to lick his Wife

When Castor wanted to mouth the genitals of men and was unable to have clients at home, he found a way to practise his trade without polluting males : he took to licking his own wife's body.

LXXIX.—Written under the Portrait of a lewd Woman

Besides the enjoyable union of legitimate congress depraved passion has discovered unnatural forms of love : what the lack of Lemnian women suggested to Philoctetes, what Afranius's plays in Roman dress

[1] The Egyptian dung-beetle.

quam toga facundi scaenis agitavit Afrani
et quam Nolanis capitalis luxus inussit.   5
Crispa tamen cunctas exercet corpore in uno:
deglubit, fellat, molitur per utramque cavernam,
ne quid inexpertum frustra moritura relinquat.

LXXX.—De Alcone Medico qui Haruspicem vaniloquum fecit

Languenti Marco dixit Diodorus haruspex
ad vitam non plus sex superesse dies.
sed medicus divis fatisque potentior Alcon
falsum convicit illico haruspicium
tractavitque manum victuri, ni tetigisset;   5
illico nam Marco sex periere dies.

LXXXI.—De Signo Iovis tacto ab Alcone Medico

Alcon hesterno signum Iovis attigit.   ille
quamvis marmoreus vim patitur medici.
ecce hodie iussus transferri e sede vetusta
effertur, quamvis sit deus atque lapis.

LXXXII.—In Eunum Ligurritorem

Eune, quid adfectas vendentem Phyllida odores?
diceris hanc mediam lambere, non molere.
perspice, ne mercis fallant te nomina, vel ne
aere Seplasiae decipiare cave,
dum κύσθον κόστονque putas communis odoris   5
et nardum ac sardas esse sapore pari.

represented on the stage, and what branded the people of Nola as utterly immoral. However, in her single person Crispa supplies her customers with all three: lest she leave aught untried and die frustrated, she masturbates, she sucks, and she makes herself available at either orifice.

LXXX.—On Alcon a Doctor who made a Soothsayer a false Prophet

When Marcus was sick, Diodorus the soothsayer told him that no more than six days of life remained. But the doctor, Alcon, more potent than the gods and fates, straightway proved the divination false and touched his patient's hand who might have lived had he not touched; for straightway Marcus' six days came to an end.

LXXXI.—On a Statue of Jove touched by Alcon the Doctor

Yesterday Alcon touched Jove's statue. He, though of marble, felt the doctor's influence. To-day, lo, he is being carried off, bidden to be removed from his ancient place, for all he is a god and made of stone.

LXXXII.—To Eunus a lecherous Fellow

Eunus, why are you wooing Phyllis, the scent-seller? Rumour has it that you serve her with your tongue, and not in the ordinary way. See that you are not led into error over the names of her wares or the scent of Seplasia,[1] by thinking that quims and quinces have a like smell and nards and sardines the same savour.

[1] A street in Capua where scents were sold.

AUSONIUS

LXXXIII.—<In eundem Eunum>

Diversa infelix et lambit et olfacit Eunus :
dissimilem olfactum naris et oris habet.

LXXXIV.—Ad eundem Eunum quod non velit bene nec male olere

Salgama non hoc sunt, quod balsama : cedite odores.
nec male olere mihi, nec bene olere placet.

LXXXV.—<Ad eundem Eunum>

Lais Eros et Itys, Chiron et Eros, Itys alter
nomina si scribis, prima elementa adime,
ut facias verbum, quod tu facis, Eune magister.
dicere me Latium non decet opprobrium.

LXXXVI.—Ad Eunum qui Uxoris suae Inguina lambebat

Eune, quod uxoris gravidae putria inguina lambis,
festinas glossas non natis tradere natis.

LXXXVII.—Ad Eunum Ligurritorem Paedagogum

Eunus Syriscus, inguinum ligurritor,
opicus magister (sic eum docet Phyllis)
muliebre membrum quadriangulum cernit :
triquetro coactu .Δ. litteram ducit.
de valle femorum altrinsecus pares rugas   5
mediumque, fissi rima qua patet, callem
.Ψ. dicit esse : nam trifissilis forma est.
cui ipse linguam cum dedit suam, .Λ. est :

EPIGRAMS ON VARIOUS MATTERS

LXXXIII.—To the same Eunus

UNHAPPY Eunus tastes and smells things much unlike: his nose has one sense, his tongue another.

LXXXIV.—To the same Eunus, because he would smell neither sweet nor rank

PICKLES are one thing, balsam another: away with scents! Neither to smell rank nor to smell sweet pleases me.

LXXXV.—To the same Eunus

LAÏS, Eros, and Itys, Chiron and Eros, Itys again, these names write down and take their initials, that thou mayest form a word describing what thou dost, schoolmaster Eunus. To name the infamy in Latin becomes me not.

LXXXVI.—To Eunus, who used to put Tongue to his Wife's Private

IN putting tongue to the smelly private of your pregnant wife, Eunus, you hasten to gloss the buttocks of your unborn sons (*glossa* = schoolmaster's explanation *and* tongue).

LXXXVII.—To Eunus, a lecherous Schoolmaster

EUNUS the Syrian, who is a crude and sex-crazed schoolmaster—so says Phyllis (cf. LXXXII)—, sees the female private as a quadrangle: with triangular abbreviation he draws it as the letter *delta* (Δ). Concerning the valley of the thighs he says that the two creases at the sides and the defile in the middle, where opens the parting of the slit, are a *psi* (Ψ), for this letter has a three-pronged shape. When he

veramque in illis esse .Φ. notam sentit.
quid, imperite, .P. putas ibi scriptum,   10
ubi locari .I. convenit longum?
miselle doctor, .ȣ. tibi sit obsceno,
tuumque nomen .Θ. sectilis signet.

LXXXVIII.—Ad Crispam quae a quibusdam dicebatur deformis

Deformem quidam te dicunt, Crispa : ego istud
  nescio : mi pulchra es, iudice me satis est.
quin etiam cupio, iunctus quia zelus amori est,
  ut videare aliis foeda, decora mihi.

LXXXIX.—Qualem velit habere Amicam

Sit mihi talis amica velim,
iurgia quae temere incipiat,
nec studeat quasi casta loqui ;
pulcra procax petulante manu,
verbera quae ferat et regerat   5
caesaque ad oscula confugiat.
nam nisi moribus his fuerit,
casta modesta pudenter agens,
dicere abominor, uxor erit.

XC.—Ex Graeco traductum ad Cupidinem

Hoc, quod amare vocant, solve aut misceto, Cupido :
  aut neutrum flammis ure vel ure duo.

XCI.—Ad Dionen de Amore suo

Aut restingue ignem, quo torreor, alma Dione,
  aut transire iube : vel fac utrimque parem.

puts his tongue to it, that is *lambda* (Λ = λείχειν, to lick); but he realises that the proper symbol there is *phi* (Φ = φαλλός, penis). What makes you think *rho* (Ρ= penis and scrotum) is meant, you imbecile, where nothing but a tall *iota* (I= simply the letter) has been written? Wretched teacher, an *ou* (O = a noose) to you for your depravity, and may the cleft letter *theta* (Θ = θάνατος, death) be recorded against your name.

LXXXVIII.—To Crispa, said by some to be deformed

Some say that thou art deformed, Crispa: that I know not : for me thou art fair, 'tis enough since I am judge. Nay more, I long—for jealousy is yoked with love—that thou mayest seem to others ugly, comely to me alone.

LXXXIX.—What Sort of Mistress he would have

Fain would I have such a mistress as may lightly start a quarrel, nor be careful to speak as if an honest woman ; pretty, saucy, hasty of hand, one to take blows and return them, and, if beaten, to take refuge in kisses. For if she be not of this character, but live chaste, subdued, shamefastly—I shudder to say it—she will be a wife.

XC.—To Cupid. Translated from the Greek [1]

This thing which they call love bring to an end or spread evenly, Cupid : either burn neither with thy flame or burn both.

XCI.—To Dione on his Passion [2]

Either put out this fire wherein I burn, sweet Dione, or bid it pass over from me, or make it equal on both sides.

[1] cp. *Anth. Pal.* v. 68.   [2] cp. *id.* v. 88.

XCII.—De Iuris Consulto qui Uxorem habebat adulteram

Iuris consulto, cui vivit adultera coniunx,
  papia lex placuit, iulia displicuit.
quaeritis, unde haec sit distantia? semivir ipse
  scantiniam metuens non metuit titiam.

XCIII.—Ad quendam qui leuia sibi Inguina faciebat

Inguina quod calido levas tibi dropace, causa est :
  irritant volsas levia membra lupas.
sed quod et elixo plantaria podice vellis
  et teris incusas pumice Clazomenas,
causa latet : bimarem nisi quod patientia morbum   5
  adpetit et tergo femina, pube vir es.

XCIV.—Ad Zoilum qui Uxorem moecham duxerat

Semivir uxorem duxisti, Zoile, moecham :
  o quantus fiet quaestus utrimque domi,
cum dabit uxori molitor tuus et tibi adulter,
  quantum deprensi damna pudoris ement !
sed modo quae vobis lucrosa libido videtur,   5
  iacturam senio mox subeunte feret :
incipient operas conducti vendere moechi,
  quos modo munificos lena iuventa tenet.

XCV.—Pulchrum Dei Responsum

Doctus Hylas caestu, Phegeus catus arte palaestrae,
  clarus Olympiacis et Lycus in stadiis,

---

[1] The Lex Papia Poppaea (9 a.d.), intended to promote marriage (cp. Tac. Ann. ii. 32 ; iii 25, 28).
[2] Lex Iulia de Adulteriis, promulgated by Augustus (17 b.c.).

EPIGRAMS ON VARIOUS MATTERS

XCII.—To a Lawyer who had a faithless Wife

A lawyer who had a faithless wife approved of the Papian statute [1] but disapproved of the Julian.[2] Do ye ask why this difference? Effeminate himself, fearing the Scantinian,[3] he feared not the Titian Law.[4]

XCIII.—To a Man who used to remove the Hair from his Groin

For you to smooth your groin with a depilatory is understandable: smooth lovers stimulate satin-skinned prostitutes. But why you pluck hairs from your backside after a bath and polish your anus with pumice remains obscure, unless it be that pathicism leads to a double depravity, you being a woman in the rear as well as a man in front.

XCIV.—To Zoïlus who had married a lewd Woman

Effeminate thyself, Zoïlus, thou hast wedded an unchaste wife: how great a profit will ye twain earn at home, when thy debaucher pays thy wife, and her lover thee, the fees of shame! But lust, which now seems to you profitable, will soon, as age creeps on, cause loss: lovers will begin to sell you their services for pay, whom prostituted youth now makes your customers.

XCV.—A neat Answer of the Oracle [5]

Hylas, the boxer, with Phegeus, skilled in wrestling, and Lycus, famous on the Olympian track,

---

[3] *sc.* de nefanda Venere : the date is uncertain.
[4] ? 31 B.C.: it directed provincial governors to appoint guardians to safeguard orphans.   [5] *Anth. Pal.* xi. 163.

an possent omnes venturo vincere agone,
    Hammonem Libyae consuluere deum.
sed deus, ut sapiens : " Dabitur victoria vobis   5
    indubitata equidem, si caveatis " ait,
" ne quis Hylam caestu, ne quis certamine luctae
    Phegea, ne cursu te, Lyce, praetereat."

XCVI.—<De Hermiones Zona>

Punica turgentes redimibat zona papillas
    Hermiones : zonae textum elegeon erat :
" Qui legis hunc titulum, Paphie tibi mandat, ames me
    exemploque tuo neminem amare vetes."

XCVII.—De Hyla quem Naiades rapuerunt

Adspice, quam blandae necis ambitione fruatur
    letifera experiens gaudia pulcher Hylas.
oscula et infestos inter moriturus amores
    ancipites patitur Naidas Eumenidas.

XCVIII.—Nymphis quae Hylam merserunt

Furitis procaces Naides
amore saevo et irrito :
ephebus iste flos erit.

XCIX.—Ad Narcissum qui sui ipsius Amore captus erat

Si cuperes alium, posses, Narcisse, potiri.
    nunc tibi amoris adest copia, fructus abest.

asked Ammon at his Libyan shrine [1] whether they all would win at the approaching games. But the god (so wise was he) replied : " Victory shall be assured you, if only ye take heed that none excel Hylas with the gloves, Phegeus in clinching, and thee, Lycus, in speed of foot."

XCVI.—On Hermione's Girdle [2]

A crimson girdle bound Hermione's swelling breasts : and on the girdle this couplet was embroidered : " Thou who dost read this inscription, know that the Paphian commands thee to love me, and by thy conduct to forbid none to love."

XCVII.—On Hylas seized by the Nymphs

Behold with how sweet and proud a death is fair Hylas blessed, tasting of joys that bring destruction ! Doomed to perish amid kisses and fatal love, 'twere hard to say whether Naiads or Eumenides so afflict him.

XCVIII.—To the Nymphs who drowned Hylas

Ye rave, ye wanton Nymphs, with love as cruel as 'tis fruitless. That lad shall be a flower.

XCIX.—To Narcissus seized with Love for himself

Wert thou to desire another, Narcissus, then mightest thou win him. Of love thou hast abundance ; 'tis the enjoyment fails.

[1] In the Oasis of Siwah in the Libyan desert.
[2] *Anth. Pal.* v. 158.

C.—De Eodem

Quid non ex huius forma pateretur amator,
 ipse suam qui sic deperit effigiem?

CI.—De Echo dolente propter Mortem Narcissi

Commoritur, Narcisse, tibi resonabilis Echo,
 vocis ad extremos exanimata modos:
et pereuntis adhuc gemitum resecuta querellis,
 ultima nunc etiam verba loquentis amat.

CII.—De Hermaphrodito et eius Natura

Mercurio genitore satus, genetrice Cythere,
nominis ut mixti, sic corporis Hermaphroditus,
concretus sexu, sed non perfectus, utroque:
ambiguae Veneris, neutro potiendus amori.

CIII.—De Coniunctione Salmacis cum Hermaphrodito

Salmacis optato concreta est nympha marito.
 felix virgo, sibi si scit inesse virum:
et tu formosae, iuvenis, permixte puellae
 bis felix, unum si licet esse duos.

CIV.—Ad Apollinem de Daphne fugiente

Pone arcum, Paean, celeresque reconde sagittas:
 non te virgo fugit, sed tua tela timet.

EPIGRAMS ON VARIOUS MATTERS

C.—On the same Subject

What would a lover not suffer through the beauty of this youth who thus pines away for his own reflection?

CI.—On Echo grieving for Narcissus' Death

Along with thee, Narcissus, dies resounding Echo, her spirit passing with the last tones of thy voice: both while thou wert pining away, thy sighs she has hitherto answered with her plaints, and now also when she loves the latest words of thy voice.

CII.—On Hermaphroditus and his Nature [1]

By Mercury begotten, conceived by Cythera, Hermaphroditus, compound alike in name and frame, combining either sex, complete in neither, neutral in love, unable to enjoy either passion.

CIII.—On the Union of Salmacis and Hermaphroditus

The nymph Salmacis grew one with the mate she desired. Ah, happy maid, if she is conscious of a man's embrace. And twice happy thou, O youth, united with a lovely bride, if one being may still be two.

CIV.—To Apollo : on Daphne fleeing him

Put by thy bow, Paean, and hide thy swift arrows : not thee the maid flees, but fears thy shafts.

[1] *cp. Anth. Pal.* ix. 783.

CV.—De Daphne tecta Cortice

Invide, cur properas, cortex, operire puellam?
laurea debetur Phoebo, si virgo negatur.

CVI.—In scabiosum Polygitonem

Thermarum in solio si quis Polygitona vidit
ulcera membrorum scabie putrefacta foventem,
praeposuit cunctis spectacula talia ludis.
principio tremulis gannitibus aera pulsat
verbaque lascivos meretricum imitantia coetus   5
vibrat et obscenae numeros pruriginis implet.
brachia deinde rotat velut enthea daemone Maenas;
pectus, crura, latus, ventrem, femora, inguina, suras,
tergum, colla, umeros, luteae Symplegadis antrum,
tam diversa locis vaga carnificina pererrat,   10
donec marcentem calidi fervore lavacri
blandus letali solvat dulcedine morbus.
desectos sic fama viros, ubi cassa libido
femineos coetus et non sua bella lacessit,
irrita vexato consumere gaudia lecto,   15
titillata brevi cum iam sub fine voluptas
fervet et ingesto peragit ludibria morsu:
torpida non aliter Polygiton membra resolvit.
et, quia debentur suprema piacula vitae,
ad Phlegethonteas sese iam praeparet undas.   20

CVII.—De quodam Silvio Bono qui erat Brito

Silvius ille Bonus, qui carmina nostra lacessit,
nostra magis meruit disticha, Brito bonus.

---

[1] Apparently "a good man" and "a Briton" were re-
garded as a contradiction in terms, and a Briton surnamed

EPIGRAMS ON VARIOUS MATTERS

CV.—On Daphne covered with Bark

Too envious bark, why hastest thou to overlap the maid? Laurel is Phoebus' due, if the damsel is denied.

CVI.—On mangy Polygiton

Whoe'er has seen Polygiton in a tub at the baths chafing the caked and rotting ulcers on his limbs, ranks such a sight above every comic show. First, he makes the air ring with his quavering howls, yells words suggestive of a brothel and sounds the full gamut of impurity. Next, he whirls his arms like a Maenad possessed by some spirit, while the itch strays at random, now in this part now in that, over his breast, legs, flanks, belly, thighs, loins and calves, his back, neck, shoulders, and his hinder parts. At length he droops with the heat of his scalding bath, and kind exhaustion makes him relax in a death-like swoon. Just as they say that men emasculate, when vain desire attacks them, exhaust themselves without fruition, mocked by pleasure unachieved; even so Polygiton relaxes his nerveless limbs. And, since at the last he must expiate his life, let him now make ready for the waters of Phlegethon.

CVII.—On one Silvius "Good" who was a Briton

That Silvius "Good" who attacks my verse, has the more fully earned my lampoon, being a good Briton.[1]

Bonus as something extremely humorous. The expression "good Indian" (= a dead Indian) is somewhat similar.

AUSONIUS

CVIII.—Idem

Silvius hic Bonus est. "Quis Silvius?" Iste Britannus.
"Aut Brito hic non est Silvius, aut malus est."

CIX.—Idem

Silvius esse Bonus fertur ferturque Britannus:
quis credat civem degenerasse bonum?

CX.—Idem

Nemo bonus Brito est.   si simplex Silvius esse
incipiat, simplex desinat esse bonus.

CXI.—Idem

Silvius hic Bonus est, sed Brito est Silvius idem:
simplicior res est, credite, Brito malus.

CXII.—Idem

Silvi, Brito Bonus: quamvis homo non bonus esse
ferris nec <se quit> iungere Brito Bono.

CVIII.—The Same

"This is Silvius 'Good.'" "Who is Silvius?" "He is a Briton." "Either this Silvius is no Briton, or he is Silvius 'Bad.'"

CIX.—The Same

Silvius is called Good and called a Briton: who would believe a good citizen had sunk so low?

CX.—The Same

No good man is a Briton. If he should begin to be plain Silvius, let the plain man cease to be good.

CXI.—The Same

This is Silvius Good, but the same Silvius is a Briton: a plainer thing—believe me—is a bad Briton.

CXII.—The Same

Thou Silvius art Good, a Briton : yet 'tis said thou art no good man, nor can a Briton link himself with Good.

LIBER XX

AUSONII BURDIGALENSIS VASATIS[1] GRATIARUM ACTIO AD GRATIANUM IMPERATOREM PRO CONSULATU

I. Ago tibi gratias, imperator Auguste; si possem, etiam referrem. sed neque tua fortuna desiderat remunerandi vicem neque nostra suggerit restituendi facultatem. privatorum ista copia est inter se esse munificos: tua beneficia ut maiestate praecellunt, ita mutuum non reposcunt. quod solum igitur nostrae opis est, gratias ago: verum ita, ut apud deum fieri amat, sentiendo copiosius quam loquendo. atque non in sacrario [loco] imperialis oraculi, qui locus horrore tranquillo et pavore venerabili raro eundem animum praestat et vultum tui; sed usquequaque gratias ago, tum tacens, tum loquens, tum in coetu hominum, tum ipse mecum, et cum voce patui, et cum meditatione secessi, omni loco actu habitu et tempore. nec mirum, si ego terminum non statuo tam grata profitendi, cum tu finem facere nescias

---

[1] *i.e.* belonging (by origin) to Bazas, the birthplace of the orator's father.

BOOK XX

THE THANKSGIVING OF AUSONIUS OF BORDEAUX, THE VASATE,[1] FOR HIS CONSULSHIP, ADDRESSED TO THE EMPEROR GRATIAN

I. I EXPRESS my thanks to you, most gracious Emperor ; could I do so, I would also make repayment. But neither does your estate need any interchange of bounty, nor does mine supply the ability to return it. Men of private station alone have the opportunity for being liberal to one another : your favours at once surpass all others in their princely scale and demand no requital. And so I express my thanks—all that is in my power to do : yet in such a way as one is wont to do in the presence of God, with greater fulness of feeling than of speech. And it is not in the shrine of the imperial oracle, a place where feelings of subdued fear and reverent awe rarely permit your subject to exhibit outwardly all that he feels within ; but it is at all times and in all places that I express my thanks, now silently in my own heart, now with my tongue, now in company with others, now by myself, whether I speak openly or reflect inwardly and apart, in every place, deed, habit, and season. Nor is it surprising that I set no limit to the expression of my gratitude, seeing that you do not know how to

honorandi. quis enim locus est aut dies, qui non me
huius aut similis gratulationis admoneat? admoneat
autem? o inertiam significationis ignavae! quis,
inquam, locus est, qui non beneficiis tuis agitet, in-
flammet? nullus, inquam, imperator Auguste, quin
admirandam speciem tuae venerationis incutiat: non
palatium, quod tu, cum terribile acceperis, amabile
praestitisti; non forum et basilicae, olim negotiis
plena, nunc votis pro tua salute susceptis: nam de
sua cui non te imperante securitas? non curia
honorificis modo laeta decretis, olim sollicitis maesta
querimoniis; non publicum, in quo occursus gauden-
tium plurimorum neminem patitur solum gratulari;
non domus commune secretum. lectus ipse, ad
quietem datus, beneficiorum tuorum reputatione
tranquillior. somnus, abolitor omnium, imagines
tuas offert. ista autem sedes honoris, sella curulis,
gloriosa pompis imperialis officii, in cuius me fastigio
ex qua mediocritate posuisti, quotiens a me cogitatur,
vincor magnitudine et redigor ad silentium, non
oneratus beneficiis, sed oppressus. ades enim locis
omnibus, nec iam miramur licentiam poetarum, qui

set any bound to your gracious favours. For what
place, what time is there which does not remind me
of this or some similar cause for thankfulness? Do
I say " remind "? What a weak and feeble conno-
tation has that word! Is there any place, I say,
which does not thrill and fire me with a sense of
your bounty? There is no place, I say, Most
Gracious Emperor, but stamps my consciousness with
the wondrous image of your most worshipful majesty;
not the Court, which was so formidable when you
succeeded, and which you have made so agreeable;
not the forum and basilicas, which once reechoed
with legal business, but now with the taking of vows
for your well-being—for under your rule who is there
whose property is not secure?—; not the Senate-
house, now happy in the business of passing reso-
lutions in your honour as formerly gloomy and
troubled with complaints; not the public highways
where the sight of so many joyous faces suffers no
one to be alone in showing delight; not the univer-
sal privacy of the home. The very bed, destined
for our repose, is made more restful as we reflect
upon your benefits: slumber, which blots out every-
thing, nevertheless presents your picture to our gaze.
As for that throne of honour, the curule chair
surrounded with all the splendid circumstance
which belongs to a rank which confers the
imperium, to the proud elevation of which you
have exalted me from so ordinary a station, as
often as I think of it, its grandeur overpowers me
and I am reduced to silence, being not merely loaded
by your bounty, but overwhelmed. Your presence,
indeed, is felt in all places and we are no longer
surprised at the supposed extravagance of the poets

omnia deo plena dixerunt. spem superas, cupienda
praevenis, vota praecurris: quaeque animi nostri
celeritas divinum instar adfectat, beneficiis praeeun-
tibus anteceditur. praestare tibi est, quam nobis
optare, velocius.

II. Ago igitur gratias, optime imperator. ac si
quis hunc sermonem meum isdem verbis tam saepe
repetitum inopiae loquentis adsignat, experiatur hoc
idem persequi, et nihil poterit proferre facundius.
aguntur enim gratiae non propter maiestatis ambitum
nec sine argumentis imperatori fortissimo: testis est
uno pacatus in anno et Danuvii limes et Rheni;
liberalissimo: ostentat hoc dives exercitus; indul-
gentissimo: docet securitas erroris humani; consul-
tissimo: probat hoc tali principe oriens ordinatus;
piissimo: huius vero laudis locupletissimum testi-
monium est pater divinis honoribus consecratus,
instar filii ad imperium frater adscitus, a contumelia
belli patruus vindicatus, ad praefecturae collegium
filius cum patre coniunctus, ad consulatum praeceptor
electus. possum ire per omnes appellationes tuas,

---

[1] *cp.* Virgil, *Ecl.* iii. 60.
[2] After the defeat of the Alamanni at Argentaria in
378 A.D.
[3] Valentinian II., raised to the purple as emperor of the
East in 375 A.D.
[4] Valens was killed in battle with the Goths at Adrianople
in 378 A.D. and his body burned. The Goths were actually
driven out by Theodosius.

who have declared that "all things are full of God."[1]
You surpass our hopes, you anticipate all we can
desire, you outstrip our fondest wishes; and the
swiftness of our thought, which claims to be some-
thing divine, is outdistanced by your benefits which
outrun it. For you to fulfil a wish is more in-
stantaneous than for us to conceive it.

II. Therefore I express my thanks, most gracious
Emperor. And if anyone attributes so frequent a
repetition in the same words of this phrase of mine
to the speaker's poverty of speech, let him try to
work out this same theme, and he will not be able to
produce anything more eloquent. For I am now
expressing thanks, not with intent to flatter any royal
vanity and not without proofs of my assertions, to a
most valiant emperor—as witness the pacification in
a single year of the Danubian and Rhenish frontiers:[2]
to one most generous; the wealth of the Army shows
as much: to one most merciful; the safety which
man's waywardness enjoys declares this: to one
most statesmanlike; the organization of the east by
so great a prince is proof enough: to one most
dutiful; there is the amplest evidence to confirm
this tribute—the canonization of his father with
divine honours, the association of his brother,[3] just as
though he were a son, with himself in the imperial
authority, the avenging of the outrage suffered by his
uncle in war,[4] the pairing of a son and father together
in joint control of a praefecture,[5] and the election
of his tutor to the consulate. I could enumerate all
those titles which your valour has won for you in the

[5] In 378 A.D. Ausonius and his son Thalassius were col
leagues in the administration of the double prefecture of the
Gauls and Italy.

223

quas olim virtus dedit, quas proxime fortuna concessit,
quas adhuc indulgentia divina meditatur : vocarem [1]
Germanicum deditione gentilium, Alamannicum tra-
ductione captorum, vincendo et ignoscendo Sarma-
ticum ; conecterem omnia merita virtutis et cogno-
mina felicitatis : sed alia est ista materia et suo
parata secreto, cum placuerit signanter et breviter
omnia, quae novimus, indicare nec persequi, ut qui
terrarum orbem unius tabulae ambitu circumscribunt
aliquanto detrimento magnitudinis, nullo dispendio
veritatis.

Nunc autem, quod diei huius proprium, de con-
sulatu gratias agam.   Sed procurrunt et aliae dig-
nitates atque in vocem gratulationis erumpunt ac se
prius debere profitentur.   tot gradus nomine comitis
propter tua incrementa congesti : ex tuo merito te ac
patre principibus quaestura communis et tui tantum
praefectura beneficii, quae et ipsa non vult vice sim-
plici gratulari, liberalius divisa quam iuncta : cum
teneamus duo integrum, neuter desiderat separatum.

III. Sed illa, ut paulo ante promisi, habebunt sui
muneris peculiare secretum.   consulatus hic meus

---

[1] *Acidalius* : voca, *Z, Peiper.*

[1] The Sarmatae were actually conquered by Theodosius in
378-379 A.D.

past, those which Fortune has granted you so recently, and those which Heaven's favour is still designing for you : I might call you Germanicus in virtue of the surrender of that race to you ; Alamannicus, because of the prisoners whom you transplanted; Sarmaticus,[1] because you conquered and forgave that people : I might string together all the distinctions won by your valour, and all the titles earned by your good fortune ; but that is another theme and one which will be treated in its own separate place, when I decide that the time has come to sketch distinctly and briefly all my facts without following them out in detail—like those who confine a map of the world to the compass of a single sheet, thereby causing it to lose something in impressiveness, but without any sacrifice of truth.

But now for the special business of this day, which is to express thanks for my consulate. And yet there are other distinctions besides, which push to the front and burst out into cries of acknowledgment, claiming that they have the right to do this first. All those honours heaped upon me at once under the title of "companion" in acknowledgment of your upbringing ; the quaestorship for which I have to thank you, though it was held under the joint sovereignty of your father and yourself, and the praefecture which I owe to your kindness alone. This latter in its very self is not content with a single acknowledgment for the larger bounty which divided rather than kept it one : since two of us now possess it complete, neither desires it apart.

III. But these honours, as I promised just now, shall have their special place apart for paying their tribute. At the present moment my consulship

orat atque obsecrat, ut obnoxiam tibi uni sinas fieri eius dignitatem, quem omnibus praetulisti. quot quidem et ipse sibi invenit gradus [1] cum clarissimo viro collega meo honore coniunctus, nuncupatione praelatus, consul ego, imperator Auguste, munere tuo non passus saepta neque campum, non suffragia, non puncta, non loculos : qui non prensaverim manus nec salutantium confusus occursu aut sua amicis nomina non reddiderim, aut aliena imposuerim : qui tribus non circumivi, centurias non adulavi, vocatis classibus non intremui, nihil cum sequestre deposui, cum distributore nil pepigi. Romanus populus, Martius campus, equester ordo, rostra, ovilia, senatus, curia, unus mihi omnia Gratianus. iure meo, Auguste maxime, adfirmare possum incolumi omnium gratia, qui ad hunc honorem diversa umquam virtute venerunt venturique sunt (suus enim cuique animus, suum meritum sibique mens conscia est), iure, inquam meo adfirmare possum me mihi videri a ceteris esse secretum. sunt quos votorum cruciat inanitas : non optavi ; quos exercet ambitus : non petivi ; qui adsiduitate exprimunt : non coegi ; qui offeruntur occasione : non adfui ; quos iuvat opulentia : obstat

---

[1] This was Q. Clodius Hermogenianus Olybrius.
[2] *i.e.* they happen to be before the Emperor when he is designating the consuls.

begs and prays you to allow one whom you have set above all to submit his high degree to yourself alone. And how many further degrees were added to this honour! Not only was I associated in this high office with a distinguished colleague,[1] and designated as the senior, but by your favour, most gracious Emperor, I became consul without undergoing the ordeal of the hustings, the Campus Martius, the canvassing, the registration, the gratuities; I have not had to shake hands, nor have I been so confused by crowds of people pressing to greet me as to have been unable to call my friends by their proper names, or to have given them names which were not theirs: I have not had to visit the tribes, to flatter the centuries, I have not trembled as the classes were called upon to vote. I have made no deposit with a trustee, nor given any pledge to a financial agent. The Roman people, the Field of Mars, the Equestrian Class, the Rostra, the hustings, the Senate and the Senate House—Gratian alone was all of these for me. I have the right to declare, most mighty Emperor, and that without offending any of those who have ever attained or shall attain hereafter to this distinction in right of various qualities (for everyone has his own spirit, his own deserts, his own conscience): I can, I repeat, rightfully declare that my consulship seems to stand apart from the consulships of other men. Some are cruelly grieved by the disappointment of their hopes: I longed for nothing; some busy themselves in canvassing for this honour: I never sought it; some extort it by their importunity: I brought no pressure to bear; some owe their designation to the accident of their presence:[2] I was not at the court; some use

temporum disciplina : non emi, nec possum con-
tinentiam iactare : non habui. unum praestare
temptavi, et hoc ipsum quasi meum vindicare non
possum : in tua enim positum est opinione, si merui.

IV. Fecisti autem et facies alios quoque consules,
piissime Gratiane, sed non et causa pari. viros
gloriae militaris : habent enim tecum, ut semper
laboris, ita dignitatis plerumque consortium, virtutis
quam honoris antiquiore collegio ; viros nobilitatis
antiquae : dantur enim multa nominibus et est fama
pro merito ; viros fide inclitos et officiis probatos :
quorum me etiamsi non secerno numero, tamen, quod
ad honoris viam pertinet, ratione dispertio.

Quartum hunc gradum novi beneficii[1] tu, Auguste,
constituis : differre tibi ipsi, quo alter ornetur, bona
animi tui ad alienam referre praestantiam eruditio-
nemque naturae, quam deo et patri et tibi debes, ad
alterius efficaciam gratius retorquere quam verius.
tua haec verba sunt a te mihi scripta : *solvere te, quod
debeas et adhuc debere, quod solveris.* o mentis aureae
dictum bratteatum ! o de pectore candidissimo

---

[1] *i.e.* in addition to the three detailed immediately above.

their wealth to help them: the morality of our age forbids such a practice ; I did not buy this honour, yet cannot boast any self-restraint : I had no money. One thing only I have tried to make sure of, and even that I cannot claim as my own ; for it depends upon your valuation whether I have been deserving.

IV. You have appointed, and will appoint others also as consuls, most kindly Gratian, but never on similar grounds. Men of military renown: and as these are always associated with you in the toils of empire, so they, in common with you, hold the greater share in its distinctions, having been your colleagues in soldierly virtue before they became so in civil dignities; men of ancient and famous lineage : for an illustrious name secures much, and distinction may serve as a substitute for achievements ; men distinguished for their trustworthiness and tested by official duties : and though I do not place myself outside this category, yet, so far as the path to honours is concerned, I differ in my qualifications.

And to this new favour of yours, your Majesty, you add a fourth degree,[1] in that you disparage yourself to do another honour, give the credit of the excellences of your mind to the efficacy of exterior influence, and with greater generosity than truth, misrepresent those natural accomplishments which you owe to God, to your father, and to yourself as the product of a stranger's efforts. Your own words written to me in your own hand declare: *that you are discharging a debt which you owe, and still owe what you have discharged.* Oh, how that sentence is overlaid with the gold of your nature ! How

lactei sermonis alimoniam! quisquamne tam parcus
est in ostentatione beneficii? quisquam pondus
gratiae suae vim meriti profitetur alieni? quisquam
denique quod indulget, quasi ab obnoxio deferatur,
pretium mavult vocare quam donum? certent huic
sententiae veteres illi et Homerici oratores, subtilis
deducta oratione Menelaus et instar profundae gran-
dinis ductor Ithacensius et melleo delibutus eloquio
iam tertiae Nestor aetatis: sed neque ille concinnius
eloquetur, qui se Laconica brevitate collegit, nec ille
contortius, qui cum sensibus verba glomeravit, nec
iste dulcius, cuius lenis oratio mulcendo potius quam
extorquendo persuasit. solvere te dicis, quod debeas
et debiturum esse, cum solveris. Auguste iuvenis,
caeli tibi et humani generis rector hoc tribuat, ut
praelatus antiquis, quos etiam elegantia sententiae
istius antecessisti, vincas propria singulorum: in
Menelao regiam dignationem, in Ulixe prudentiam,
in Nestore senectutem.

V. Subiciet aliquis: ista quidem adeptus es, sed
effare, quo merito? quid me oneras, sciscitator?
rationem felicitatis nemo reddit. deus et qui deo
proximus tacito munera dispertit arbitrio et benefi-
ciorum suorum indignatus per homines stare iudicium,

sustaining is the milk of these words, springing from the sincerest of breasts! Is there anyone who shrinks so modestly from arrogant display of his generosity? Anyone who thus alleges that his favours have no other weight but the receiver's work? Anyone who, in a word, prefers to call his gifts payment as though rendered by a debtor? Let those famous spokesmen of old, those orators of Homer—Menelaus, with his subdued but subtle mode of speech, the chieftain of Ithaca, so like a heavy storm of hail, Nestor, the survivor of three generations, whose lips were steeped in honey—let those seek to rival such a sentence! Yet for all his compression and Spartan conciseness, the first will utter nothing neater; the second, though he heap up words and ideas, nothing more forcible; the last, nothing sweeter, although his gentle speech persuaded rather by charming than overbearing. You say that you are paying a debt you owe and will still be in debt when you have paid. My young sovereign, may He who is the Ruler of heaven and of mankind grant that you may excel those ancients, even above whom the choiceness of that one sentence has placed you, and outstrip each one of them in his peculiar quality—Menelaus in kingly majesty, Ulysses in discretion, and Nestor in length of days.

V. Someone will interpose: "It is true you have received all these benefits, but, tell me, how have you deserved them?" Why do you cast this burden upon me, Master Inquisitor? No man gives a reason for his prosperity. God, and he who stands next to God, distributes blessings at will, and disdaining to await man's verdict on his favours, chooses rather in the persons of the uplifted to perform a

mavult de subditis dedisse miraculum.   quo, inquis,
merito?   ego nullum scio, nisi quod tu, piissime
imperator, debere te dicis : et hoc debere latissime
pertinet, sive hoc eruditionis tuae faenus existimas,
sive sine faenore gloriam liberalitatis adfectas, sive
te pondere conceptae sponsionis exoneras, seu fidei
commissum patris exsolvis, seu magnanimitate caelesti,
ostentatione suppressa, dei munus imitaris.   debere
te dicis.   cui?   quando?   quo nomine?   lege syngra-
pham, nomina creditorem ; accepti et expensi tabulae
conferantur : videbis alio summae istius transire ra-
tionem.   tibi coepit deus debere pro nobis.   quid
autem mihi debes, gratissime imperator?   patitur
enim humanitas tua, ut praeter regias virtutes privata
appellatione lauderis.   quid tu mihi debes?   et contra
quid non ego tibi debeo?   anne quod docui?   hoc ego
possum verius retorquere, dignum me habitum, qui
docerem ; tot facundia doctrinaque praestantes in-
clinata in me dignatione praeteritos, ut esset quem
tu matura iam aetate succinctum per omnes honorum
gradus festinata bonitate proveheres ; timere ut vide-
reris, ne in me vita deficeret, dum tibi adhuc aliquid,
quod deberes praestare, superesset.

   VI. Negat Cicero consularis ultra se habere, quod

----

¹ There is of course a play on *gratissime* and the Emperor's
own name.

miracle. "How have I deserved them," you ask?
I know of no grounds, except that you, most kindly
Emperor, say that you owe a debt: and this word
"owe" admits of very wide interpretation. Either
you consider this debt to be the interest on the
principal of your education; or, apart from this
interest, you seek after the renown which bounty
earns; or you are discharging yourself of the burden
of a pledge which you have incurred; or else with a
heavenly loftiness of soul and without a trace of
vanity you are imitating God's function. You say
you owe a debt. To whom then? Or when did you
contract it? On what account? Read the bill over:
name the creditor: let the accounts for receipts and
expenditure be laid before the court. When this is
done you will see that the debit balance is not
against you but against another. It is God who now
begins to owe you a debt on my behalf. But what
do you owe me, most gracious Emperor—for your
kindly nature permits me to set aside your kingly
qualities and use this familiar form of complimentary
address?[1] What do you owe me? And on the other
side, what do I not owe you? Is it because I was
your tutor? I can turn this about and say more
exactly that I was deemed worthy to teach you;
that so many men superior to me in eloquence and
learning were passed over; that the honourable
choice fell upon me, in order that you might have a
man equipped with ripe years whom your impetuous
generosity might advance through all the stages of
a distinguished career; and that you seemed to fear
that my life might fail while there still remained
unbestowed something which you ought to bestow.

VI. Cicero, after his consulate, declared that he

cupiat. ego autem iam consul et senex adhuc avidi-
tatem meam fatebor. te videre saepius in hoc magi-
stratu, Gratiane, desidero, ut et sex Val. Corvini et
septem C. Marii et cognominis tui Augusti tredecim
consulatus unus aequiperes. plures tibi potest aetas
et fortuna tua praestare ; verum ego in numero par-
cior, quia tu in munere liberalior : ipsum enim te
saepius hoc honore defraudas, ut et aliis largiaris.
scis enim, imperator doctissime (rursum enim utar
laude privata), scis, inquam, septem ac decem Domi-
tiani consulatus, quos ille invidia alios provehendi
continuando conseruit, ita in eius aviditate derisos, ut
haec eum pagina fastorum suorum, immo fastidiorum,
fecerit insolentem nec potuerit praestare felicem.
quod si principi honoris istius temperata et quae
vocatur aurea debet esse mediocritas, quid privati
status hominibus, quid aequanimis, quid iam senibus
erga se oportet esse moderaminis ? ego quidem,
quod ad honores meos pertinet, et vota saturavi : tu
tamen, imperator optime, tu piissime, tu quem non
fatigat liberalitas, nisi quando cessavit : tu, inquam,
indulgentissime Gratiane, ut ad benefaciendum
subito es necopinus ingenio, adhuc aliquid, quod hoc
nomine mihi praestetur, invenies. invenies ? sic,
intellexere omnes, sic nobis ordinem ipse fecisti,

---

[1] *pro Planco*, 25.   [2] *cp.* Suet. *Augustus*, 26.
[3] See Suet. *Dom.* 13.

had nothing more to long for.[1] I for my part, though I am a consul and an old man to boot, will confess to a ravenous appetite. I long to see you, Gratian, holding this office so many more times that your total may equal the sum of the six consulships of Valerius Corvinus,[2] the seven of Caius Marius, and the thirteen of Augustus, whose name you bear. Your youth and your exalted station can secure for you a still greater number; but I am sparing in my estimate, because you are so generous in bestowing this honour. For too often you cheat yourself of it to lavish it upon others. You know, most learned Emperor (for once again I will use a personal mode of complimentary address), you know, I say, that the seventeen consulates of Domitian[3] which, in his jealousy of the advancement of others, he held in an unbroken series, brought down such ridicule upon his selfishness that this page of his annals, nay, rather, of his arrogance, made him overbearingly proud but could not make him happy. But if the Sovereign ought to observe a well-calculated and, as the saying goes, a golden mean in holding this dignity, what moderation ought men of private station, of calm judgment, and lastly, of advanced age to observe? For myself, I have sated even my desires, so far as my own distinctions are concerned; but you, my most excellent, my most gracious Sovereign, you who never weary in your generosity except when you have no scope for it, you, I repeat, most bountiful Gratian, have such a quick and surprising inventiveness in conferring favours, that even now some addition to be conferred upon me under this head will be found. "Will be found"? Such a conviction have all men felt, in such wise have you yourself created this

sic amicus deo es, ut a te iam impetratum sit, quod optatur, a quo et quod nondum optamus, adipiscimur.

VII. Et rursum aliquis adiciet aut sermone libere aut cogitatione liberius : nonne olim et apud veteres multi eiusdem modi doctores fuerunt? an tu solus praeceptor Augusti? immo ego cum multis con- iunctus officio, sed cum paucissimis secretus exemplo. nolo Constantini temporum taxare collegas : Caesares docebantur. superiora contingam. dives Seneca, nec tamen consul, arguetur rectius quam praedica- bitur non erudiisse indolem Neronis, sed armasse saevitiam. Quintilianus consularia per Clementem ornamenta sortitus honestamenta nominis potius videtur quam insignia potestatis habuisse. quo modo Titianus magister, sed gloriosus ille, munici- palem scholam apud Visontionem Lugdunumque variando non aetate equidem, sed vilitate consenuit. unica mihi et amplectenda est Frontonis imitatio : quem tamen Augusti magistrum sic consulatus orna- vit, ut praefectura non cingeret. sed consulatus ille cuius modi? ordinario suffectus, bimenstri spatio interpositus, in sexta anni parte consumptus, quae-

---

[1] Possibly T. Flavius Clemens, uncle of Domitian. Quin- tilian appears to have been a "consul suffectus," appointed to fill a vacancy due to death or some other cause.

[2] The tutor of the younger Maximin : *cp. Epist.* xii.

[3] M. Cornelius Fronto, of Cirta in Numidia, the tutor of Marcus Aurelius and Lucius Verus : *c.* 90–168 A.D.

rank for me, such is your intimacy with the deity, that what we hope for is straightway granted by you, and what we have not yet hoped for is bestowed upon us.

VII. But again someone will comment freely in speech, yet more freely in thought: "Were there not in the past and even in ancient times many such tutors? Or are you the only man who has had an Emperor for his pupil?" No, indeed! But while I am only one of many so far as my employment goes, I stand apart with very few in virtue of this distinction. I do not wish to cast reflections upon my fellows in this calling in the age of Constantine: there were princes and they were instructed. I will go back to earlier times. Fact proves more surely than words that Seneca, who for all his wealth was not a consul, did not discipline the nature of Nero, but merely gave arms to his cruelty. And though Quintilian obtained the consular distinction by grace of Clemens,[1] he seems to have held an honorary title rather than the actual emblems of power. So too with the tutor Titianus;[2] but for all his boastful assumption, while alternating between the provincial school of Visontio (Besançon) and Lugdunum (Lyons), not through years but through light esteem he fell into a decline. The one and only precedent and one which I must frankly accept is the case of Fronto;[3] and yet this tutor to an Emperor, though he had the distinction of a consulate, was never invested with the authority of a prefect. But what sort of a consulship was it which he held? Acting as the substitute to an ordinary[4] consul, made to fill up a gap of two months, and dismissed in the sixth part of a year, this

[4] The "consul ordinarius" is junior of the two, the senior (*i.e.* the first to be designated) giving his name to the year.

rendum ut reliquerit tantus orator, quibus consulibus
gesserit consulatum.

Ecce aliud, quod aliquis opponat : in tanti te ergo
oratoris fastigium gloriosus attollis ?   cui talia requi-
renti respondebo breviter : non ego me contendo
Frontoni, sed Antonino praefero Gratianum.   cele-
brant equidem sollemnes istos dies omnes ubique
urbes, quae sub legibus agunt, et Roma de more et
Constantinopolis de imitatione et Antiochia pro luxu
et Carthago discincta et donum fluminis Alexandria :
sed Treveri principis beneficio et mox cum ipso
auctore beneficii.   loca inter se distant, vota con-
sentiunt.   unus in ore omnium Gratianus, potestate
imperator, virtute victor, Augustus sanctitate, pon-
tifex religione, indulgentia pater, aetate filius, pietate
utrumque.

VIII. " Non possum fidei causa ostendere imagines
maiorum meorum," ut ait apud Sallustium Marius,
nec deductum ab heroibus genus vel deorum stemma
replicare, nec ignotas opes et patrimonia sparsa sub
regnis : sed ea, quae nota sunt, dicere potius, quam
praedicare : patriam non obscuram, familiam non

---

[1] The connection of thought with the foregoing seems to
be : Gratian's unique position is proved by the affectionate
popularity with which he is universally regarded.

[2] In imitation of Herodotus' dictum that " Egypt is the
gift of the Nile."   But Alexandria is not on a river.

great orator has left us to find out for ourselves in which year he held the consulate.

But here is another objection which may be raised: "Are you then so conceited as to exalt yourself to the height attained by that great orator?" To such a question I will answer briefly: No, I do not set myself up as Fronto's rival, but I rank Gratian before Antoninus. It is true[1] that all the world over, every city which lives under our governance observes these annual days of festival, Rome as a matter of custom, Constantinople out of imitation, Antioch out of love for indulgence, as also do degenerate Carthage and Alexandria, the gift of its river[2]; but Trèves is enabled to do this by the kindness of our prince, and will soon do so in company with the author of that kindness. All these places are far apart, but the prayers they offer up are all to one effect: one name is on the lips of all—the name of Gratian, Gratian who in virtue of his authority is styled Imperator; of his courage, the Victorious;[3] of his sacred person, Augustus; of his devotion, Pontifex; of his tenderness, Father; of his age, a Son; and of natural affection, both one and the other.

VIII. "I am not able to display portraits of my ancestors in proof of good faith," as Marius says in Sallust:[4] I cannot unroll a pedigree to show my descent from heroes, or that I am of the lineage of the gods: I cannot boast of uncounted wealth and ancestral estates dotted all over the kingdoms of the world: but I can mention without vaunting advantages which are less fabulous. I can mention my birthplace, a city not unrenowned; my family, of

---

[3] For most of these titles *cp. C.I.L.* vi. i. 1175.
[4] *Jugurtha*, lxxxv. 29.

paenitendam, domum innocentem, innocentiam non
coactam, angustas opes, verumtamen libris et litteris
dilatatas, frugalitatem sine sordibus, ingenium libe-
rale, animum non inliberalem, victum, vestitum,
supellectilem munda, non splendida: veteribus ut
illis consulibus (excepta, quae tum erant, bellicarum
conlatione virtutum) si quis me conferre dignetur,
seponat opulentiam non derogaturus industriam.

Verum quoniam gratiis agendis iamdudum suc-
cumbo materiae: tu orationi meae, Gratiane, succede.
tu, Gratiane, qui hoc nomen sic per fortunam adep-
tus es, ut nemo verius ambitione quaesierit: neque
enim iustius Metellus cognomento Pius patre revo-
cato, qui esset impius exulante; aut verius Sulla
Felix, qui felicior ante, quam vocaretur; quam tu,
Gratianus: cui et hoc nomen est, et illa Metelli
Sullaeque cognomina. tu, inquam, Gratiane, qui
hoc non singulis factis, sed perpetua grate agendi
benignitate meruisti; cui, nisi ab avo deductum
esset, ab omnibus adderetur: tu ipse tibi, inquam,
pro me gratiam refer, tu tuaeque virtutes: bonitas,
qua in omnes prolixus es, perpetuus in me; pietas,
qua orbem tuum temperas, quam in ulciscendo patruo

which I have no need to be ashamed; my unblemished home; my life passed of my own free will without a spot; my scanty means (though enriched with books and learning); my simple yet not stingy tastes; my liberal intellect; my not illiberal spirit; the unostentatious refinement of my diet, my dress and the appointments of my house; so that, if anyone should think me worthy of comparison with those famous consuls of past days (excluding from the comparison those war-like qualities which then flourished), let him deny me their wealth without belittling my diligence.

But in this expression of gratitude, my subject has long overpowered me: you, Gratian, must come to the help of my words. You, Gratian, who have received this name by chance, yet by so happy a chance that no one out of flattery has ever tried to find one more appropriate—for Metellus was less rightly surnamed the Dutiful when he recalled his father (since he would have been undutiful had he kept him in exile), and Sulla was less exactly called the Lucky (since he was luckier before he was so named), than you are named Gratian; you, who besides this name also bear those titles of Metellus and Sulla, you, Gratian, I repeat, who have earned your name not by isolated deeds but by the continual kindliness of your gracious life, you who would have received this as a surname by general consent had you not inherited it from your grandfather, you, I repeat, must yourself render thanks to yourself on my behalf. It is a task for you and for your high powers: for that kindness, so frequently shown to all, and so continually to me; for that natural affection with which you guide your subject world, and which

probas, tuendo in fratre cumulas, ornando in prae-
ceptore multiplicas. agat gratias clementia, quam
humano generi impertis ; liberalitas, qua ditas omnes ;
fortitudo, qua vincis, et mens ista aurea, quam de
communi deo plus quam unus hausisti. agant et pro
me gratias voces omnium Galliarum, quarum praefecto
hanc honorificentiam detulisti. ultra progredior, et
hoc quia debere te dicis : agat, quae optime agere
potest, vox ista, quam docui.

IX. Iamdudum autem quam grati animi, tam ser-
monis exigui, ut supra dictum est, succumbo materiae,
neque adhuc illa perstrinxi, quae ne infantissimus
quidem, nisi idem impiissimus, eminentia per famam
et omnium gaudiis testata supprimeret ; quae supra
vires dicendi meas posita cunctor attingere, aut ingrati
crimine arguendus aut temerarii professione culpan-
dus : tamen, alterum cum subeundum sit, audaciam
quam malevolentiam malo reprehendi. tu, Auguste
venerabilis, districtus maximo bello, adsultantibus tot
milibus barbarorum, quot Danuvii ora praetexitur,
comitia consulatus mei armatus exerces. tributa ista
quod in urbe Sirmio geruntur, an, ut quod in pro-

you proved by avenging your uncle's death, doubled
by maintaining your brother, and redoubled by
raising your tutor to distinction. Let that indulgence
which you vouchsafe to mankind render you thanks;
that generosity with which you enrich all; that
courage which enables you to conquer; and that
golden spirit which you have drawn more freely than
any single man from the God of us all. So also let
the voice of every province in the three Gauls render
thanks on my behalf, since it is upon their prefect
that you have bestowed this distinction. I go even
farther—and this I add because you say you are in
my debt: let that render you thanks which can best
render it, I mean that voice which I have trained.

IX. But grateful as my heart is, my words are all
too feeble, and, as I have already said, I have long
sunk under the theme. Moreover, I have not yet
touched upon those matters which not even the
sorriest speaker, unless he were likewise the most
sacrilegious, would pass over, exalted as they are by
fame and attested by universal delight—matters so
far beyond my powers of speech that I hesitate
to touch upon them, and I must either be proved guilty
on a charge of ingratitude, or be blamed for my rash
pretensions. And yet since I must suffer one of these
two things, I prefer to be censured for over boldness
than for ill-will. You, most worshipful Emperor,
amid all the distractions of a most serious war,
amid the onslaughts of all those thousands of
savages who dwell along the shores of the Danube,
held the elections for my consulate in full panoply.
Shall I speak of them as elections by the people in
tribes because they were held in the city of
Sirmium? Or in centuries, because they were held

cinctu, centuriata dicentur? an ut quondam ponti-
ficalia vocabuntur, sine arbitrio multitudinis sacer-
dotum tractata collegio? sic potius, sic vocentur
quae tu pontifex maximus deo participatus habuisti.

Non est ingenii mei, piissime imperator, talia com-
minisci. verba sunt litterarum tuarum : quibus apud
me auctoritatem summi numinis et tuae voluntatis
amplificas. sic enim loqueris : *cum de consulibus in
annum creandis solus mecum volutarem, ut me nosti atque
ut facere debui et velle te scivi, consilium meum ad deum
retuli. eius auctoritati obsecutus te consulem designavi et
declaravi et priorem nuncupavi.* cuius orationis ordo
lucidior? quae doctrina tam diligens propriis comi-
tiorum verbis loqui nec vocabulis moris antiqui
nomina peregrina miscere? valete modo, classes
populi et urbanarum tribuum praerogativae et cen-
turiae iure vocatae. quae comitia pleniora um-
quam fuerunt quam quibus praestitit deus consilium,
imperator obsequium?

X. Et nunc ego, piissime imperator, ne fastigium
auditorii sacri, dictorum tuorum timidus interpres,
offendam, divinitatis tuae pro! levi cum piaculo
verba transcurro. *cum de consulibus,* inquis, *in annum
creandis :* erudita vox et cura sollemnis! *mecum*

---

[1] The pontifices filled up vacancies in their college by co-
option until 102 B.C., when Cn. Domitius Ahenobarbus trans-
ferred the right of election to the people.

in the war-zone? Or shall we call them pontifical
elections, as in old days,[1] since they were held, as
elections to the priestly college were held, without
reference to the people's will? That is best, that
is their right description, seeing that you, who
presided over them, are the Pontifex Maximus and
a participator in the designs of God.

It is not a part of my character, most devout Em-
peror, to invent such words as these. They are the
words of your letter, in which you enlarge upon the
authority of the Supreme Disposer and of your own
will. This is what you say : *When I was privately con-
sidering the appointment of consuls for the year, I re-
ferred my purpose to God, as you know I do, and as I
was bound to do, and as I knew you wished me to do.
In obedience to his prompting I have designated you as
consul, proclaimed you as such, and given your name
the precedence.* What speech could be more clearly
arranged? What learned man more careful to use
only the terms customary at elections, without
mixing untechnical words with the time-honoured
phrases? No more of you henceforth, you classes
of the people, you privileged city-tribes and
centuries called up in due order! What elections have
ever been more adequately attended than these,
where God furnished the design, and the Emperor
gave it effect ?

X. And now, most devout Emperor, that I may not
insult the majesty of this sacred Audience-Chamber
by shrinking from interpreting your utterances, with
the forgiveness of your godhead, though not without
some slight sacrilege, I run over your words. *When,*
you say, *I was considering the appointment of consuls
for the year.* What a learned phrase ! What a

volutarem : o profundi altitudo secreti ! habes ergo
consiliatorem et non metuis proditorem. *ut me nosti :*
quid familiarius, *ut facere debui :* quid constantius, *ut
velle te scivi :* quid dici blandius potest? *consilium
meum ad deum retuli.* et quemadmodum *solus,* cui
praesto est tam grande consilium ? an plenius cum
senatu, cum equestri ordine, cum plebe Romana,
cum exercitu tuo et provinciis omnibus deliberasses ?
consilium meum ad deum retuli. non ut, credo, novum
sumeres, sed ut sanctius fieret, quod volebas. *eius
auctoritati obsecutus :* scilicet ut in consecrando patre,
in ulciscendo patruo, in cooptando fratre fecisti. *te
consulem designavi et declaravi et priorem nuncupavi.*
quis haec verba te docuit ? ego tam propria et tam
Latina nescivi. *designavi et declaravi et nuncupavi.*
non fit hoc temere. habet moras suas dispertitis
gradibus tam matura cunctatio. has ego litteras tuas
si in omnibus pilis atque porticibus, unde de plano
legi possint, instar edicti pendere mandavero, nonne
tot statuis honorabor, quot fuerint paginae libellorum ?

XI. Sed ad blandiora festino. ab hac enim litte-
rarum ad me datarum parte digressus, eo quoque
descendisti, ut quaereres, qualis ad me trabea mitte-
retur. omne largitionum tuarum ministerium solli-
citudine fatigasti. non ergo supra consulatum mihi

solemn task! *I was pondering inwardly.* What depths to the secrets of your heart! You have, then, a counsellor without fearing betrayal. *As you know I do:* what could be more intimate? *As I was bound to do:* what more uncompromising? *As I knew you wished:* what more courteous phrase could be used? *I referred my purpose to God:* how, then, can you say *privately* when such vast wisdom is ready to aid you? Could you have weighed the matter more thoroughly if the Senate, the Equestrian Order, and the People together with your army and all the provinces had been aiding you? *I referred my purpose to God.* Not, I am sure, in order to gain some new plan, but to consecrate your own inclination. *In obedience to his will:* that is to say, as you have acted in canonizing your father, in avenging your uncle, in associating your brother with you. *I have designated you as consul, proclaimed you as such, and given your name the preference.* Who taught you these words? I knew none so fitting, so thoroughly Roman. *I have designated, proclaimed, and named you.* This is no random writing. The ripe deliberation of these words with its pauses allows them to progress by well-marked degrees. If I have this letter of yours posted up like an edict on every pillar and in every portico where it could easily be read, shall I not have as many statues in my honour as there were placarded sheets?

XI. But I hasten on to what is still more agreeable. For in your letter which was delivered to me, you diverged from this subject, and so far condescended as to ask me what sort of robe should be sent me. With your anxiety you have worn out the whole staff of officials in charge of your bounties. Have I not then received over and above the con-

est adhibita per te cura tam diligens, pro me cura tam felix ? in Illyrico arma quatiuntur : tu mea causa per Gallias civilium decorum indumenta dispensas, loricatus de toga mea tractas, in procinctu et cum maxime dimicaturus palmatae vestis meae ornamenta disponis : feliciter et bono omine. namque iste habitus, ut in pace consulis est, sic in victoria triumphantis. parum est, si, qualis ad me trabea mittatur, interroges : te coram promi iubes. nec satis habes, ut largitionum ministri ex more fungantur : eligis ipse de multis et, cum elegeris, munera tua verborum honore prosequeris. *palmatam*, inquis, *tibi misi, in qua divus Constantius parens noster intextus est.* me beatum, cuius insignibus talis cura praestatur! haec plane, haec est picta, ut dicitur, vestis, non magis auro suo quam tuis verbis. sed multo plura sunt in eius ornatu, quae per te instructus intellego. geminum quippe in uno habitu radiat nomen Augusti. Constantius in argumento vestis intexitur, Gratianus in muneris honore sentitur.

XII. Accessit tam inpenso beneficio tuo pondus quorundam sciscitatione cumulatum. interrogatus, quem priorem decerneres consulem, *nec dubitandum*

---

[1] *sc.* the son of Constantine the Great, father of Faustina and grandfather of Constantia, Gratian's wife.

sulate an additional gift in these pains, which cost you so much trouble and caused me so much happiness? Swords are being drawn in Illyricum: for my sake, you distribute robes of civil dignities in Gaul: you, wearing your equipment, deal with the question of my gown; while prepared for battle and on the verge of a supreme struggle, you make arrangements for the decoration of my palm-broidered garb. Yet the omen was happy and auspicious. For just as in peace time this apparel marks the consul, so in victory it distinguishes the conqueror in his triumph. But it is not enough for you to ask what kind of robe shall be sent me: you must have it produced before your eyes. You are not content that the officials of your largess should perform their ordinary duties: you choose one robe out of many with your own hands, and having chosen it, follow up your gift with words of compliment. You say: *I have sent you a palm-broidered robe in which is worked a figure of the sainted Constantius* [1] *my ancestor.* Happy am I that such pains should be bestowed upon my vestments! It is, it most surely is, a broidered robe, as you say; but embroidered more richly with your words than with its own threads of gold. But, since it is you who have invested me, I perceive that its enrichment means far more. For the light which flashes from this single garment bespeaks two imperial personages: Constantius is embroidered in the actual fabric of the robe; but in the complimentary nature of the gift, I feel the presence of Gratian.

XII. To your favour, already so weighty, was added the weight which a question put by certain persons piled upon it. When they inquired whom you appointed senior of the two consuls, you replied

esse dixisti tu, et qui tecum boni sunt, dubitare
non poterant. sed tamen ad hoc dictum erexerant
animos, qui libenter clarissimum virum collegam
meum, quem praesentem habebat occasio, praelatum
credidissent. fatigantes tamen, quod intellexerant,
requirebant. hic tu, sicut mihi renuntiatum est,
noto illo pudore tuo paulisper haesisti non rationis
ambiguus, sed eorum dubitationem vultu et rubore
condemnans, qui studium suum interpretationis
errore palpabant. deinde illico subdidisti: *quid de
duobus consulibus designatis quaeritis, quis ordo sit nun-
cupationis? anne alius quam quem praefectura consti-
tuit?* o felicem verecundiam tuam, cui ista popularis
ratio tam prudenter occurrit! scisti aliud, Gratiane,
quod diceres: sed propter quorundam verecundiam
dicere noluisti. scopulosus hic mihi locus est et
propter eam, quam numquam adpetivi, gloriam, re-
cusandus. cum prior renuntiatus sim, satis est
tuum tenere iudicium: interpretes valete meritorum.
neque autem ego, sacratissime imperator, in tenui
beneficio gradum nuncupationis amplector. non est
haec gloria ignota Ciceroni: praetorem me, inquit,
populus Romanus primum fecit, consulem priorem.
ex ipsa eius sententia intellegitur commendabilius
uni videri quam pluribus esse praepositum. nulla

---

[1] *In Pisonem* i. 2, 3.

that *there could be no uncertainty as to that*; and the honourable men who surround you could not feel uncertainty. Nevertheless, this pronouncement aroused the expectations of those who would have been glad to think that the most distinguished man, who is my colleague, and who happened to be present at the time, had been awarded the precedence. At any rate, they made themselves wearisome by seeking for that meaning which they had read into your answer. Whereupon, as I am informed, your well-known modesty caused you for a while to hesitate, not through indecision as to your course, but to reprove with your flushed glance those who were flattering their own hopes by their affected inability to understand. Then you replied outright: *Why do you ask in what order of precedence the two consuls designate are to stand? Can they stand in any other order than that which the prefecture has already determined?* What happy modesty, so sagely to suggest that popular reason! You could have made another reply, Gratian, but refrained in order to spare the feelings of certain persons. But I find myself on dangerous ground and for the sake of that distinction which I never coveted, I must avoid it. Since I have been declared the senior, it is enough for me to keep to your decision: so farewell, you who would examine merits! I do not, however, regard this honour of precedence as a trifling favour, my most gracious Sovereign. It confers a glory of which Cicero was fully conscious: " The Roman People," he says, "made me chief praetor and senior consul."[1] His very form of expression makes us clearly understand that it is more honourable to receive precedence over one person, than over many; for while there is

enim est equidem contumelia secundi, sed in duobus
gloria magna praelati.

Alexandri Macedonis hoc fertur, cum legisset
illos versus Homericos, quibus Hectore provocante
de novem ducibus, qui omnes pugnare cupiebant,
unum deligi placeret sortis eventu, trepida ubi con-
tentione votorum Iovem optimum maximum totus
precatur exercitus, ut Aiacem vel Tydei filium aut
ipsum regem ditium Mycenarum sortiri patiatur
Agamemnonem : occiderem, inquit, illum, qui me
tertium nominasset. o magnanimitatem fortissimi
viri ! nominari inter novem tertius recusabat ; ubi
certe pluribus antecelleret quam subesset. quanta
hic verecundia gravaretur posterior de duobus ? est
enim in hoc numero arduae plena dignationis electio.
cum universis mortalibus duo, qui fiant consules,
praeferuntur, qui alteri praeponitur, non uni, sed
omnibus antefertur.

XIII. Expectare nunc aures praesentium scio et
eminere in omnium vultu intellego, quod desiderio
concipiatur animorum. existimant enim, cum ea,
quae ad grates agendas pertinebant, summatim et
tenuiore filo, sicut dicitur, deducta libaverim, aliqua
me etiam de maiestatis tuae laudibus debere per-
stringere. quamquam me istam dixerim seposuisse
materiam et in tempus aliud reservare ; nihilominus
tamen, ut nunc aliqua contingam, nutu et prope mur-
mure cohortantur. itaque faciam, quando cogunt

---

[1] H 161–180.   [2] Horace, *Epp.* ii. i. 225.

indeed no disgrace in taking the second place, the one of two who is preferred is signally distinguished.

It is said of Alexander of Macedon that, after reading that passage in Homer[1] relating the decision to select by lot one of the nine chiefs who were all eager to fight in answer to Hector's challenge, and how the whole host besought Jupiter the Best and Greatest with anxiously conflicting prayers to suffer Ajax, or the son of Tydeus, or even Agamemnon, the king of rich Mycenae, to be chosen; he exclaimed : " I would have killed the man who named me third ! " See the high spirit of the dauntless hero ! He scorned to be placed third in a list of nine persons, even though, of course, he would have more below him than above him. How deeply ashamed he would feel if he were the second of two persons only ! For where there are two candidates, the choice of one is rich in high distinction. If the two who are made consuls are exalted over all mankind, then the one who has precedence over his colleague is set not above one only, but over all.

XIII. I know that the ears of my audience are now eagerly waiting, I can read on every face the thought which springs from the longing of each heart. They think that now that I have touched on every topic which has reference to my Thanksgiving—however summarily, or, as our poet says,[2] " spun out with meagre thread " —I am bound to touch upon the praises of your Majesty. Although I have said that I have put that subject on one side and am keeping it for another occasion, nevertheless they all urge with nods, nay, almost with protests, to make some reference to it now. I will do as they bid (for I welcome this compulsion), but I must lay aside the

volentem, sed maioribus separatis tenuiora memorabo,
nulla spe ad plenum exequendi, sed universi ut
intellegant eorum, quae inter [familiaria] praedi-
canda sunt, a me poscendam esse notitiam, ab aliis
dignitatem. nec excellentia, sed cotidiana tractabo.

XIV. Nullum tu umquam diem ab adulescentia
tua nisi adorato dei numine et reus voti et illico
absolutus egisti, lautis manibus, mente pura, inmacu-
labili conscientia et, quod in paucis est, cogitatione
sincera. cuius autem umquam egressus auspicatior
fuit aut incessus modestior aut habitudo cohibitior
aut familiaris habitus condecentior aut militaris
accinctior? in exercendo corpore quis cursum tam
perniciter incitavit? quis palaestram tam lubricus
expedivit? quis saltum in tam sublime collegit?
nemo adductius iacula contorsit, nemo spicula crebrius
iecit aut certius destinata percussit. mirabamur
poetam, qui infrenos dixerat Numidas, et alterum,
qui ita collegerat, ut diceret in equitando verbera et
praecepta esse fugae et praecepta sistendi. obscurum
hoc nobis legentibus erat: intelleximus te videntes,
cum idem arcum intenderes et habenas remitteres
aut equum segnius euntem verbere concitares vel
eodem verbere intemperantiam coherceres. qui te
visi sunt hoc docuisse, non faciunt: immo qui visi

---

[1] Virgil, *Aen.* iv. 41.
[2] Nemesian, *Cyneg.* 268: verbera sunt praecepta fugae,
sunt verbera freni.

larger aspects of the subject and speak only of the slighter ; and this not with any hope of according them adequate treatment, but to let all men know that from me they are to expect a relation only of those personal qualities which deserve praise, and to look to others for an estimate of your higher virtues. I shall deal therefore not with your loftiest qualities, but those of your every-day life.

XIV. From your boyhood you have never let a single day pass without worshipping God, without discharging your vows the moment that they became due, with clean hands and a pure heart, a stainless conscience, and—a rare quality—with undivided thoughts. Was there ever a prince whose going forth was attended with better auguries, whose progress was less ostentatious, whose state was less extravagant, whose attire in private life was more seemly or in the field more severe ? In athletic pursuits who ever matched your fleetness of foot, who so supple in disengaging at wrestling, who cleared so great a height in leaping ? No one ever launched a javelin with a more forceful swing, no one hurled darts with greater speed or struck the mark more surely. We used to wonder at the poet[1] when he spoke of Numidians who use no reins, and at that other who summed up by saying that in riding it is with the lash alone that they urge their horses to full speed or make them stand.[2] While we read we could not understand this, but we realized it when we saw you drop the reins and at the same time draw your bow, or urge on your horse with the whip when he slackened speed and check his exuberance likewise with the whip. Those who were supposed to instruct you in this do not do these things : nay, rather,

255

sunt docuisse, nunc discunt. in cibis autem cuius
sacerdotis abstinentior caerimonia? in vino cuius
senis mensa frugalior? operto conclavis tui non
sanctior ara Vestalis, non pontificis cubile castius nec
pulvinar flaminis tam pudicum. in officiis amicorum
non dico paria reddis: antevenis et, quotiens in
obsequendo praecedimus, erubescis pudore tam ob-
noxio, quam in nobis esse deberet ab imperatore
praeventis. in illa vero sede, ut ex more loquimur,
consistorii, ut ego sentio, sacrarii tui, nullus umquam
superiorum aut dicenda pensius cogitavit aut con-
sultius cogitata disposuit aut disposita maturius
expedivit.

XV. Et aliqua de oratoriis virtutibus tuis dicerem,
nisi vererer mihi gratificari. non enim Sulpicius
acrior in contionibus nec maioris Gracchi commenda-
bilior modestia fuit nec patris tui gravior auctoritas.
qui tenor vocis, cum incitata pronuntias; quae inflexio,
cum remissa; quae temperatio, cum utraque dis-
pensas! quis oratorum laeta iucundius, facunda
cultius, pugnantia densius, densata glomerosius aut
dixit aut, quod est liberum, cogitavit? vellem, si
rerum natura pateretur, Xenophon Attice, in aevum

those who are supposed to instruct you are now learning from you. Again, in the matter of food, was ever a priest more self-denying on religious grounds? Or in the matter of wine, was there ever an old man more sparing at table? The altar of Vesta is not more hallowed than the privacy of your bed-chamber, the couch of a priest is not more pure, the bed of a prophet not more chaste. In your relations with your friends I do not say that you return like for like: you anticipate our services, or whenever we have the advantage in paying our duty to you, you flush up shyly with an embarrassment which we rather ought to feel when we have been anticipated by our Sovereign. In that place which we ordinarily speak of as your Consistory, but which I regard as your sanctuary, none of your predecessors ever thought out more deeply what he had to say, or arranged his thoughts more skilfully, or delivered them, when so arranged, in a more masterly style.

XV. I would also make some remarks on your excellence as a speaker, were I not afraid of flattering myself. Sulpicius was not more vehement in harangue, nor the elder Gracchus more deserving of praise for self-control, nor your own father more weighty, more impressive. How your voice rings out when you declaim some stirring theme! How gentle in unimpassioned passages! How skilfully regulated when you deal with both! Which of the orators either in speech or in the free domain of thought dealt with cheerful themes more charmingly, on eloquent themes more choicely, on the strenuous more intensely, on the intense more forcibly? Ah, Attic Xenophon, I would that it were possible in the nature of things for you to come to life again in

nostrum venires, tu, qui ad Cyri virtutes exequendas
votum potius, quam historiam commodasti: cum
diceres, non qualis esset, sed qualis esse deberet.
si nunc in tempora ista procederes, in nostro Gratiano
cerneres, quod in Cyro tuo non videras, sed optabas.
atque ista omnia, quae punctis quibusdam acuminata
signavi, si facundia pro voluntate suppeteret, quam-
quam non copiosius, exequerer, ubertatem stilo rerum
magnitudine suggerente. sed nec huius diei nec
huius ista materiae. qui dicturi estis laudes principis
nostri, habetis velut seminarium, unde orationum
vestrarum iugera compleatis. ego ista perstrinxi
atque, ut sciunt omnes, possum videri familiaris
notitiae secretus interpres domestica istaec non tam
praedicare quam prodere.

Atque ut ista dixi de cognitis mihi atque intra
aulam familiaribus, possem et foris celebrata memo-
rare, nisi omnia omnes et separatim sibi quisque
novisset. possem pari brevitate dicere, qua supe-
riora: *emendatissimi viri est pigenda non facere:* at
tu numquam paenitenda fecisti et semper veniam
paenitentibus obtulisti. *pulchrum est indulgere timen-*
tibus: sed tu perpetuae bonitatis edictis occurristi

this age—you who celebrated the virtues of Cyrus
by following the line of your own desires rather than
his actual history, since you described him not as he
was, but as he ought to have been. If you could
take a stride forward into these present times, you
would behold in our beloved Gratian not what you
actually saw in your favourite Cyrus, but what you
wished to see. All these qualities, the salient points
of which I have sketched in a few dashes, I would
describe in detail were my powers of speaking pro-
portionate to my will; for however much I may lack
fluency, the greatness of the subject would inspire
my pen. But all that is appropriate neither to this
occasion, nor to this subject. You, who hereafter
shall pronounce the praises of our Sovereign have
here, if I may call it so, a nursery-garden on which
you can draw to fill out the acres of your own dis-
courses. I have merely touched upon the subject,
and being—as all are aware—the exponent of secrets
known to me through my close intimacy, I may be
thought merely to divulge rather than to belaud
these personal virtues.

And as I have spoken of matters known to me
and to all who share the inner life of the
Court, I might also tell of those which are con-
stantly spoken of beyond its precincts, were it not
that they are all known to all men and individually
to each. I could say in as few words as I have
done above: *a most perfect hero does nothing of
which he need be ashamed;* but you have never
done anything which calls for repentance, while
you have always extended pardon to those who
repent. *It is noble to be merciful to those who fear;*
but so continual is your kindness that your edicts

omnibus, ne timerent. *magnificum largiri honores:*
tu honoratos et liberalitate ditasti. *laudabile est im-*
peratorem faciles interpellantibus praebere aditus nec de
occupatione causari : tu confirmas adire cunctantes;
et iam querimoniis explicatis, ne quid adhuc sileatur,
interrogas.

XVI. Celebre fuit Titi Caesaris dictum, *perdidisse*
se diem, quo nihil boni fecerat ; sed celebre fuit, quia
Vespasiani successor dixerat, cuius nimia parsimonia
et austeritas vix ferenda miram fecerat filii lenitatem.
tu Valentiniano genitus, cuius alta bonitas, praesens
comitas, temperata severitas fuit, parto et condito
optimo reipublicae statu, intellegis posse te esse
lenissimum sine dispendio disciplinae. neque vero
unum aliquod bonum uno die praestas : sed indul-
gentias singulares per singula horarum momenta
multiplicas. vel illud unum cuius modi est de con-
donatis residuis tributorum ? quod tu quam cumu-
lata bonitate fecisti ! quis umquam imperatorum
hoc provinciis suis aut uberiore indulgentia dedit,
aut certiore securitate prospexit, aut prudentia con-
sultiore munivit ? fecerat et Traianus olim, sed par-
tibus retentis non habebat tantam oblectationem
concessi debiti portio, quanta suberat amaritudo

---

[1] Suet. *Titus,* viii.
[2] Coins of Trajan bear references to this remission.

remove all cause for fear. *It is splendid to lavish dis-
tinctions :* you not only bestow distinctions, but also
generously enrich the recipients. *It is praiseworthy
in an Emperor to grant petitioners easy access and not to
refuse them on the pretext of engagements :* you encourage
those who hesitate to approach you, and when they
have declared their complaints, you ask them whether
they have left anything still unmentioned.

XVI. The saying of Titus Caesar [1] that *he had lost
that day in which he had not performed a good action,*
has become famous ; but it has become famous because
it was uttered by the successor of Vespasian, a man
whose excessive economy and almost intolerable
strictness made his son's easier rule seem remarkable.
You, the son of Valentinian, whose kindness was so
profound, whose affability was never lacking, whose
sternness was so well controlled—you realize that, now
that the State has gained and established a thoroughly
sound condition, you can show all the gentleness of
your nature without prejudice to good order. And,
indeed, it is not just one good deed a day that you
perform : every moment of every hour you increase
the sum of your momentous favours. How shall we
speak of that single measure by which the arrears of
tribute were remitted ? What a wealth of generosity
there was in this act ! What Emperor has ever granted
such a boon to his subject provinces with a more
generous consideration, or calculated its results with
a surer confidence, or safeguarded it with more
experience and wisdom ? Trajan [2] also did the same
thing in past times ; but since he retained a claim to
a certain amount of the arrears, the pleasure caused
by that portion of the debt which he forgave was less
than the underlying discontent left unremoved by

servati. et Antoninus indulserat, sed imperii, non
beneficii successor invidit, qui ex documentis tabu-
lisque populi condonata repetivit. tu argumenta
omnia flagitandi publicitus ardere iussisti. videre in
suis quaeque foris omnes civitates conflagrationem
salubris incendii. ardebant stirpes fraudium vete-
rum: ardebant semina futurarum. iam se cum
pulvere favilla miscuerat, iam nubibus fumus se
involverat: et adhuc obnoxii in paginis concrematis
ductus apicum et sestertiorum notas cum substan-
tiolae ratione cernebant, quod meminerant lectum,
legi posse metuentes. quid te, imperator Auguste,
indulgentius, quid potest esse consultius? quae bona
praestas, efficis, ne caduca sint: quae mala adimis,
prospicis ne possint esse recidiva. haec provin-
cialibus indulgentiae bona. quid illa nostro ordini?
quid illa militibus? Antoninorum cognita fuit et
iam ante Germanicorum in cohorte amicorum et
legionibus familiaris humanitas. sed ego nolo
benevolentiam tuam aliorum collatione praecellere.
abundant in te ea bonitatis et virtutis exempla, quae
sequi cupiat ventura posteritas et, si rerum natura
pateretur, adscribi sibi voluisset antiquitas.

XVII. Necesse est tamen aliquid comparari, ut
possit intellegi, bona nostra quo praestent. Aegro-

the amount which he retained. Antoninus, too,
granted the same favour; but he who inherited his
throne but not his kindliness, grudged this remission
of arrears and reclaimed from his people the full
amount as entered in the schedules and registers.
You gave orders for all these evidences of claim to be
burned publicly. Every township beheld in its own
market-place the blaze of the relieving fire. Burning
were the roots of by-gone wrongs: burning were the
seeds of those to come. Already the ashes had mingled
with the dust, already the smoke had been absorbed
in the clouds; but still the debtors beheld in the
charred pages the lines of lettering and the figures
in the cash-column together with the valuation of
their little properties: still they feared that what
they remembered to have heard read could even now
be read. What then can there be which is more
merciful, more sagacious than you, most gracious
Emperor? You give good gifts and make sure that
they shall not be transitory: you remove ills, and take
precautions against their revival. Such are the favours
you have lavished upon the provinces; but what of
those conferred upon our own order? Or upon the
Army? The personal interest taken by the Antonines,
and even earlier by the Germanici, in their suite of
friends and in their legions, was a recognized fact.
But I do not care to extol your benevolences by com-
paring others. You furnish a host of such instances
of goodness and virtue as generations to come will
long to imitate, and as ages past would have wished,
did the nature of things allow, to have attributed
to themselves.

XVII. Nevertheless, some comparison must be
made in order to make clear the superiority of our

tantes amicos Traianus visere solebat: hactenus in
eo comitas praedicanda est. tu et visere solitus et
mederi praebes ministros, instruis cibos, fomenta
dispensas, sumptum adicis medellarum, consolaris
adfectos, revalescentibus gratularis. in quot vias de
una eius humanitate progrederis! legionibus univer-
sis, ut in communi Marte evenit, si quid adversi
acciderat, vidi te circumire tentoria, "satin salvae?"
quaerere, tractare vulnera sauciorum et, ut salutiferae
adponerentur medellae atque ut non cessaretur, in-
stare. vidi quosdam fastidientes cibum te commen-
dante sumpsisse. audivi confirmantia ad salutem
verba praefari, occurrere desideriis singulorum: huius
sarcinas mulis aulicis vehere, his specialia iumenta
praebere, illis ministeria perditorum instaurare lixa-
rum, aliorum egestatem tolerare sumptu, horum
nuditatem velare vestitu, omnia agere indefesse et
benigne, pietate maxima, ostentatione nulla, omnia
praebere aegris, nihil exprobrare sanatis. inde
cunctis salute nostra carior factus meruisti, ut haberes
amicos obnoxios, promptos, devotos, fideles, in aevum
omne mansuros, quales caritas potius quam fortuna
conciliat.

blessings. Trajan was in the habit of visiting his friends when they were sick : so far we may grant that he had a considerate nature. Your practice is both to visit and to heal them : you provide them with attendants, you order their diet, you prescribe medicines, you furnish the cost of remedies, you comfort them in their pain, and you congratulate them on their recovery. See in how many ways you show advance beyond Trajan's single form of consideration! With the legions one and all, whenever any regrettable incident had occurred, as is the fortune of war, I have seen you go round the men's lines, asking " How goes it ? ", attending to the wounds of casualties, giving strict orders that healing remedies should be applied and that there should be no delay about it. I have seen men who turned from their food with loathing take it on your recommendation : I have heard you speak words which gave them heart to recover. You anticipated what each man sorely needed, causing this man's pack to be carried by the mules of the royal train, providing special beasts for some to ride, furnishing others with servants in place of those whom they had lost : sometimes you would relieve the poorer soldiers out of your own purse, sometimes cover the nakedness of the thinly clad. You would do all unwearyingly and cheerfully, with the deepest charity and without a trace of display, bestowing everything upon the sick and claiming nothing from the cured. Thus it is that you have become dearer to us than our lives, and have deservedly gained friends who are obedient, ready, devoted, faithful—men who will stand by you for ever, since it is affection rather than accident which makes them yours.

XVIII. Concludam deinceps orationem meam,
piissime Auguste, sermonis magis fine, quam gratiae.
namque illa perpetua est et spatio non transmeabili
terminum calcis ignorat. flexu tamen parvo, nec a
te procul, convertar ad deum. aeterne omnium
genitor, ipse non genite, opifex et causa mundi,
principio antiquior, fine diuturnior, qui templa tibi
et aras penetrabilibus initiatorum mentibus condi-
disti, tu Gratiano humanarum rerum domino eius-
modi semina nostri amoris inolesti, ut nihil in digressu
segnior factus meminisset et relicti, illustraret absen-
tem, praesentibus anteferret; deinde quia interesse
primordiis dignitatis per locorum intervalla non po-
terat, ad sollemnitatem condendi honoris occurreret,
beneficiis ne deesset officium. quae enim maiorum
umquam memoria transcursum tantae celeritatis
vel in audacibus Graecorum fabulis commenta est?
Pegasus volucer actus a Lycia non ultra Ciliciam
permeavit. Cyllarus atque Arion inter Argos Ne-
meamque senuerunt. ipsi Castorum equi, quod
longissimum iter est, non nisi mutato vectore trans-
currunt. tu, Gratiane, tot Romani imperii limites,
tot flumina et lacus, tot veterum intersaepta reg-
norum ab usque Thracia per totum, quam longum

---

[1] Possibly = the baptized.
[2] For Cyllarus (the steed of Pollux), see Virgil, *Georg.* iii.
90; Arion is the famous horse of Adrastus.

XVIII. After this I must bring my speech to a
close, most Sacred Majesty; though it is my words
rather than my gratitude which will end. For the
latter is unending: its course can never be run, for
it knows no stopping point. Yet I must make a
slight digression and turn not very far from you to
God. Eternal Begetter of all things, thyself un-
begotten, Creator and Cause of the universe, more
ancient than its beginning, outlasting its end, Thou
who hast built thine own temples and altars in the
inmost hearts of the initiated[1] worshippers: Thou
hast implanted in Gratian, the lord of this world
below, such seeds of love towards me that separation
has not weakened his remembrance of me though
parted from him. He has honoured me though I
was no longer in his presence, he has preferred
me above those who stand before him; and further:
because distance would not allow him to be present
at the opening ceremony of my elevation, he has
hastened to attend the solemnities of my laying down
office, that his bounties might be completed by his
courtesy. For what record is there, even in the
daring fables of the Greeks, of a journey so swiftly
accomplished? Winged Pegasus starting from Lycia
travelled no further than Cilicia: Cyllarus and Arion[2]
grew old between Argos and Nemea. Even the
steeds of a Castor do not accomplish that endless
journey of theirs without changing their riders.[3]
You, Gratian, speed across all those frontiers of the
Roman Empire, all those rivers and lakes, all those
barriers of old-established kingdoms, from distant
Thrace and along the whole coast, through all its

[3] Probably referring to the journey of Castor and Pollux
to and from the world below: *cp*. Virgil, *Aen.* **vi.** 121 f.

est, latus Illyrici, Venetiam Liguriamque et Galliam
veterem, insuperabilia Rhaetiae, Rheni vadosa, Se-
quanorum invia, porrecta Germaniae, celeriore trans-
cursu, quam est properatio nostri sermonis, evolvis,
nulla requie otii, ne somni quidem aut cibi munere
liberali, ut Gallias tuas inopinatus illustres, ut con-
sulem tuum, quamvis desideratus, anticipes, ut illam
ipsam, quae auras praecedere solet, famam facias
tardiorem.   hoc senectuti meae, hoc honori a te
datum.   supremus ille imperii et consiliorum tuorum
deus conscius et arbiter et auctor indulsit, ut sellam
curulem, cuius sedem frequenter ornabis, ut prae-
textam meam purpurae tuae luce fucatam, ut trabeam
non magis auro suo quam munere tuo splendidam,
quae ab Illyrico sermonis dignitas honestavit, apud
Gallias illustriora praestares, quaestorem ut tuum,
praefectum ut tuo praetorio, consulem tuum et, quod
adhuc cunctis meis nominibus anteponis, praecep-
torem tuum, quem pia voce declaraveras, iusta ratione
praetuleras, liberali largitate ditaveras, Augustae
dignationis officiis consecrares.

Finit gratiarum actio.

length, of Illyricum, through Venetia, Liguria, and old Gaul, over the forbidding peaks of Rhaetia, across the fords of the Rhine, through the thick country of the Sequani and across the plains of Germany; you speed across them, I repeat, swifter in your passage than my rapid speech, without stopping for rest, without indulging fully in sleep or in food; and all to shed the unexpected light of your presence upon your favourite Gaul, to surprise (how welcome the surprise!) your own consul while still in office, to make even Rumour, who is usually swifter than the winds, a slower traveller than yourself. This was your tribute to my age, this to my dignity! God, that supreme confidant, controller and author both of your throne and of your counsels, has graciously permitted that the curule chair (which you will often fill with so much grace), that my magisterial robe dyed with your glowing purple, that my consular apparel which is enriched less by its own gold than by your munificence—that all these favours, which your noble letter from Illyricum made yet more honourable, should gain yet further in lustre by your presence in Gaul; that your quaestor, your praetorian prefect, your consul, and—a name which you still rate above all my titles—your tutor, he whom you designated with your sacred lips, whom you named as senior consul on substantial grounds, whom you enriched with your generous bounty, should be hallowed by the condescension of your royal attentions.

End of the Thanksgiving.

APPENDIX TO AUSONIUS

THIS Appendix, corresponding to book XXII. of the Teubner edition, contains various poems of relatively ancient date which, though ordinarily edited with the works of Ausonius, are in fact anonymous. Two only of these works call for notice.

The elegiac poem *De Rosis Nascentibus* (II.) is interesting—apart from some trace of naturalistic feeling in ll. 7 ff.—both as the humble source of Herrick's *Gather ye Rosebuds* (ll. 49 f.), and as having once been attributed to Virgil himself. [1] It cannot, however, be regarded as earlier than the fourth century A.D., and was associated with the works of Ausonius by Aleander in the Paris edition of 1511.

Sulpicia's *Complaint on the State of the Commonwealth* (V.) seems to belong to the same age and is not unreasonably considered a school-piece or literary exercise. The real Sulpicia flourished in the later part of the first century A.D. and was famous for a series of amatory poems composed in a variety of metres (*see* ll. 4 ff.) and addressed to her husband Calenus. According to Martial (*Epigr.* x. 35. 1 ff.) her work was distinguished by its morality, though not perhaps by its delicacy (*id.* x. 38. 1 ff.), and Ausonius in his exculpatory address to Paulus at the close of the *Cento Nuptialis* [2] alleges that *prurire opusculum Sulpiciae, frontem caperare*. The piece was first published in an edition of Ausonius by Ugoletus in 1496 A.D.

[1] See Ribbeck's Virgil, iv. p. 181 (*Appendix Vergiliana*).
[2] See vol. i. p. 390.

APPENDIX AUSONIANA[1]

I.—Septem Sapientum Sententiae

(1) *Bias Prieneus*

Quaenam summa boni est? mens semper conscia recti.
pernicies homini quae maxima? solus homo alter.
quis dives? qui nil cupiet. quis pauper? avarus.
quae dos matronis pulcherrima? vita pudica.
quae casta est? de qua mentiri fama veretur.   5
quod prudentis opus? cum possis, nolle nocere:
quid stulti proprium? non posse et velle nocere.

(II) *Pittacus Mitylenaeus*

Loqui ignorabit, qui tacere nesciat.
bono probari malo quam multis malis.
demens superbis invidet felicibus;   10
demens dolorem ridet infelicium.
pareto legi, quisque legem sanxeris.
plures amicos re secunda compares:
paucos amicos rebus adversis probas.

[1] = *Peiper*, Book XXII.

APPENDIX TO AUSONIUS[1]

I.—SAYINGS OF THE SEVEN SAGES

(I) *Bias of Priene*

WHAT is the sum of all good? A heart ever conscious of right. What is man's greatest bane? His brother man alone. Who is the rich man? He who will long for nothing. Who is the poor man? The miser. What is the fairest dowry wedded wives can bring? A modest life. Who is the chaste woman? She about whom scandal fears to lie. What deed marks a wise man? To refuse to hurt another when he might. What is the fool's badge? To wish to hurt another though he cannot.

(II) *Pittacus of Mitylene*

He who cannot hold his tongue will not know how to speak. I would rather please one good man than many bad. A fool envies the proud man in prosperity, a fool laughs at the grief of the unhappy. Obey the law whoever you be who made the law. If Fortune smile, you gather many friends: if Fortune frowns, you find few true friends.

[1] The following poems, formerly included in the works of Ausonius, are by unknown authors.

AUSONIUS

(iii) *Cleobulus Lindius*

Quanto plus liceat, tam libeat minus.   15
fortunae invidia est immeritus miser.
felix criminibus non erit hoc diu.
ignoscas aliis multa, nihil tibi.
parcit quisque malis, perdere vult bonos.
maiorum meritis gloria non datur: 20
turpis saepe datur fama minoribus.

(iv) *Periander Corinthius*

Numquam discrepat utile ab decoro.
plus est sollicitus magis beatus.
mortem optare malum, timere peius.
faxis, ut libeat, quod est necesse.   25
multis terribilis caveto multos.
si fortuna iuvat, nihil laboris:
si non adiuvat, hoc minus laboris.

(v) *Solon Atheniensis*

Tunc beatam dico vitam, cum peracta fata sunt.
par pari iugator coniunx; quidquid inpar, dissidet. 30
non erunt honores umquam fortuiti muneris.
clam coarguas propinquum, quem palam laudaveris.
pulchrius multo parari quam creari nobilem.
certa si decreta sors est, quid cavere proderit?
sive sunt incerta cuncta, quid timere convenit?   35

(vi) *Chilon Lacedaemonius*

Nolo minor me timeat despiciatque maior.
vive memor mortis, item vive memor salutis,
tristia cuncta exsuperans aut animo, aut amico.
tu bene si quid facias, nec meminisse fas est;

APPENDIX TO AUSONIUS

(III) *Cleobulus of Lindos*

The greater your liberty, the less be your lusts. A just man suffering wrongfully is Fortune's indictment. A man may thrive on wrong, but not for long. Overlook much in others, nothing in yourself. He who spares the bad, seeks to corrupt the good. The good deeds of the fathers bring no glory to their posterity; but ill-repute is often inherited.

(IV) *Periander of Corinth*

The expedient and the honourable never disagree. The greater your fortune, the greater your cares. 'Tis bad to wish for death, but worse to fear it. See that you do willingly that which you needs must do. If many dread you, then beware of many. If Fortune aids, no need for toil: if she aids not, so much the less toil.[1]

(v) *Solon of Athens*

I only call a life happy after its fated course is run. Let like mate with like; the ill-matched never agree. True fame will never be in Chance's gift. Rebuke a kinsman privately, but praise him openly. 'Tis fairer far to win nobility than to be born to it. If our lot is certainly decreed, what profit is it to guard against it? Or if all is uncertain, what is the use of fear.

(VI) *Chilon of Lacedaemon*

I hate when one below me fears me, and one above me despises me. Live and forget not death, but also live and forget not safety: let courage or the support of friends conquer all your griefs. If you

---

[1] *i.e.* because you can do nothing to withstand her.

quae bene facta accipias, perpetuo memento.   40
grata senectus homini, quae parilis iuventae :
illa iuventa est gravior, quae similis senectae.

(VII) *Anacharsis Scythes*

Turpe quid ausurus te sine teste time.
vita perit, mortis gloria non moritur.
quod facturus eris, dicere distuleris.   45
crux est, si metuas, vincere quod nequeas.
cum vere obiurges, sic inimice iuvas :
cum falso laudes, tunc et amice noces.
nil nimium.   satis hoc, ne sit et hoc nimium.

II.—De Rosis Nascentibus

Ver erat et blando mordenti a frigore sensu
    spirabat croceo mane revecta dies.
strictior eoos praecesserat aura iugales
    aestiferum suadens anticipare diem.
errabam riguis per quadrua compita in hortis   5
    maturo cupiens me vegetare die.
vidi concretas per gramina flexa pruinas
    pendere aut holerum stare cacuminibus,
caulibus et teretes patulis conludere guttas

    10

vidi Paestano gaudere rosaria cultu
    exoriente novo roscida lucifero.
rara pruinosis canebat gemma frutectis
    ad primi radios interitura die.

---

[1] The poem *On the Seven Sages* (Peiper, I. viii.). a translation
of *Anth. Pal.* ix. 366, is omitted as spurious, being found

confer a benefit, never remember it; if you receive
one, never forget it. Old age may be sweet, if it be
made like youth; but youth is burdensome if it be
like old age.

(VII) *Anacharsis of Scythia*

When you would perpetrate some deed of shame,
fear yourself even without a witness. Life passes,
but a glorious death can never die. Avoid speaking
of what you plan to do. True torment is to fear
what you cannot overcome. A just reproof is an
unfriendly help, feigned praise a friendly injury. Do
nothing to excess. That is enough; or precept too
will run to excess.[1]

II.—On Budding Roses [2]

'Twas spring-time, and day brought back by saffron
morn was breathing with a pleasing influence after
the biting cold. A shrewder air had run before
Dawn's coursers, moving me to forestall heat-bringing
Day. I was straying along the paths dividing the
well-watered garden-plots, seeking to drink in the
freshness of day's prime. I saw the hoar-frost
hanging caked upon the bending grass or resting on
the tops of garden herbs, and round drops rolling
together upon the cabbage-leaves . . . . I saw
such rose-beds as Paestum cultivates smiling all dewy
at the new-risen harbinger of light. Upon the
frosted bushes a white pearl glimmered here and
there, to perish at the earliest rays of day. 'Twere

in no MS. and appearing first in the edition of Ugoletus, to
whom it is probably due.
    [2] This poem is sometimes attributed in MSS. to Virgil.

ambigeres, raperetne rosis Aurora ruborem   15
    an daret et flores tingueret orta dies.
ros unus, color unus et unum mane duorum ;
    sideris et floris nam domina una Venus.
forsan et unus odor : sed celsior ille per auras
    diffluit : expirat proximus iste magis.   20
communis Paphie dea sideris et dea floris
    praecipit unius muricis esse habitum.
Momentum intererat, quo se nascentia florum
    germina conparibus dividerent spatiis.
haec viret angusto foliorum tecta galero,   25
    hanc tenui folio purpura rubra notat.
haec aperit primi fastigia celsa obelisci
    mucronem absolvens purpurei capitis.
vertice collectos illa exsinuabat amictus,
    iam meditans foliis se numerare suis :   30
nec mora : ridentis calathi patefecit honorem
    prodens inclusi semina densa croci.
haec modo, quae toto rutilaverat igne comarum
    pallida conlapsis deseritur foliis.
mirabar celerem fugitiva aetate rapinam   35
    et, dum nascuntur, consenuisse rosas.
ecce et defluxit rutili coma punica floris,
    dum loquor, et tellus tecta rubore micat.
tot species tantosque ortus variosque novatus
    una dies aperit, conficit ipsa dies.   40
Conquerimur, Natura, brevis quod gratia talis :
    ostentata oculis illico dona rapis.
quam longa una dies, aetas tam longa rosarum :
    cum pubescenti iuncta senecta brevis.

hard to say whether Aurora were stealing blushes from the rose, or lending them and risen day were dyeing the flowers. One is the dew, one the tint, one the morn of both; for Venus is the one queen both of the morning-star and of the flower. Perchance, too, one is their fragrance; but that is diffused on the breezes far above us, this, near at hand, breathes forth a sweetness more perceptible. The queen of Paphos, goddess of the star and flower alike, bids both be habited in one ruddy hue.

23 The time was just at hand for the teeming buds to split in equal segments. One is close capped with a covering of green leaves; another flecks her narrow sheath with ruddy purple; a third is opening the tip of her tapering spire and freeing the point of her crimson head. Another was disengaging at her peak her furled array, already planning to take count of herself with her petals. Then on a sudden she has laid open the glories of her smiling calyx displaying the close-packed saffron seeds which lie within. Another, which but late had glowed with all the fires of her bloom, now fades, abandoned by her falling petals. I marvelled at the swift ruin wrought by the fleeting season, to see the roses all withered even while they bloom. See, even while I speak, a glowing flower has shed the ruddy honours of its head, and earth gleams carpeted with crimson. These many forms, these various births and changes, one day brings forth and the same day ends.

41 Nature, we grieve that such beauty is short-lived: once displayed to our eyes forthwith you snatch away your gifts. As long as is one day, so long is the life of the rose; her brief youth and age go hand in hand. The flower which the bright

quam modo nascentem rutilus conspexit Eous,   45
   hanc rediens sero vespere vidit anum.
sed bene, quod paucis licet interitura diebus
   succedens aevum prorogat ipsa suum.
collige, virgo, rosas, dum flos novus et nova pubes,
   et memor esto aevum sic properare tuum.   50

III.—Nomina Musarum

Clio gesta canens transactis tempora reddit.
dulciloquis calamos Euterpe flatibus urguet.
comica lascivo gaudet sermone Thalia.
Melpomene tragico proclamat maesta boatu.
Terpsichore affectus citharis movet, imperat, auget. 5
plectra gerens Erato saltat pede carmine vultu.
Urania motusque poli scrutatur et astra.
carmina Calliope libris heroica mandat.
signat cuncta manu loquiturque Polymnia gestu.
mentis Apollineae vis has movet undique Musas: 10
in medio residens complectitur omnia Phoebus.

IV.—De Signis Caelestibus

Ad Boreae partes Arctoe vertuntur et Anguis.
post has Arctophylax pariterque Corona, genuque
prolapsus, Lyra, Avis, Cepheus et Cassiopeia,
Auriga et Perseus, Deltoton et Andromedae astrum
Pegasus et Delphin Telumque, Aquila Anguitenensque.

Morning Star beheld just being born, that, returning
with late evening, he sees a withered thing. But 'tis
well; for though in a few days the rose must die,
she springs anew prolonging her own life. Then,
maidens, gather roses, while blooms are fresh and
youth is fresh, and be mindful that so your life-time
hastes away.[1]

III.—The Names of the Muses

Clio, singing of famous deeds, restores times past
to life. Euterpe's breath fills the sweet-voiced
flutes. Thalia rejoices in the loose speech of comedy.
Melpomene cries aloud with the echoing voice of
gloomy tragedy. Terpsichore with her lyre stirs,
swells, and governs the emotions. Erato bearing
the plectrum harmonises foot, song and voice in the
dance. Urania examines the motions of the heaven
and stars. Calliope commits heroic songs to writing.
Polymnia expresses all things with her hands and
speaks by gesture. The power of Apollo's will enlivens
the whole circle of these Muses: Phoebus sits in their
midst and in himself possesses all their gifts.

IV.—On the Heavenly Signs

Towards the realm of Boreas the two Bears and
the Snake turn in the sky. Next come the Bear-
warden and the Crown together, the Kneeling Man,
the Lyre, the Bird, Cepheus and Cassiopeia, the
Charioteer and Perseus, the Triangle and Andromeda's
constellation, Pegasus and the Dolphin and the

---

[1] Lines 45-50 inspired Herrick's stanza :—

> "Gather ye rosebuds while ye may ;
>   Old Time is still a-flying,
> And this same flower, that smiles to-day,
>   To-morrow will be dying."

AUSONIUS

Signifer inde subest, bis sex et sidera complent
hunc: Aries, Taurus, Gemini, Cancer, Leo, Virgo,
Libra, Scorpius, Arquitenens, Capricornus et urnam
qui tenet, et Pisces.   post sunt in partibus Austri
Orion, Procyon, Lepus, ardens Sirius, Argo,   10
Hydrus, Chiron, Turibulum quoque Piscis et ingens
hinc sequitur Pistrix simul Eridanique fluenta.

V.—Sulpicia queritur de Statu Reip. et Temporibus Domitiani

Musa, quibus numeris heroas et arma frequentas,
fabellam permitte mihi detexere paucis;
nam tibi secessi tecum penetrale retractans
consilium. quare nec carmine curro Phalaeco,
nec trimetro iambo, nec qui pede fractus eodem   5
fortiter irasci didicit duce Clazomenio.
cetera quin etiam, quot deinceps milia lusi
primaque Romanos docui contendere Grais
et salibus variare novis, constanter omitto
teque, quibus princeps et facundissima calles,   10
adgredior: precibus descende clientis et audi.
    Dic mihi, Calliope, quid iam pater ille deorum
cogitat? an terras et patria saecula mutat
quasque dedit quondam marcentibus eripit artes?

---

[1] A hendecasyllabic metre.
[2] Hipponax of Ephesus (*flor*. 546-520 B.C.) invented the variety of iambic metre known as "scazon" (limping), in which

282

Arrow, the Eagle and the Snake-holder. Below these comes the Zodiac which twelve constellations occupy: the Ram, the Bull, the Twins, the Crab, the Lion and the Virgin, the Scales, the Scorpion, the Archer, Capricornus, and He who holds the Water-Jar, and the Fishes. Next, in the Southern Hemisphere are found : Orion, Antecanis, the Hare with fiery Sirius, Argo and the Water-snake, Chiron, the Censer (Ara) also and the Great Fish. After these together follow the Whale and the streams of Eridanus.

V.—SULPICIA COMPLAINS OF THE CONDITION OF THE STATE AND OF THE TIMES OF DOMITIAN

MUSE, suffer me to weave in few words my tale, using those numbers wherewith thou celebratest heroes and deeds of war ; for 'tis for thee I have retired, with thee pondering my inward purpose. Wherefore my song trips not to the measure of Phalaecus,[1] nor to the iambic trimeter, nor to that which, limping on the last foot, learned under the guidance of him of Clazomenae boldly to be angry ![2] Nay, and all those other innumerable measures with which I have trifled, and wherein I first taught Romans to vie with Greeks and season their verse with an array of new flavours, I firmly pass by : thee I approach in that metre in which thou hast the chief and richest skill. Descend at thy suppliant's prayers and hearken.

[12] Tell me, Calliope, what ponders now that Father of the Gods ? Is he changing the whole earth and ages past, and is he snatching from our drooping hands the arts which he once gave us ? Is it his

the last foot is a spondee (– –) or trochee (– ◡) instead of an iambus (◡ –). This metre he used with effect in writing lampoons.

nosque iubet tacitos et iam rationis egentes,   15
non aliter, primo quam cum surreximus arvo,
glandibus et purae rursus procumbere lymphae?
an reliquas terras conservat amicus et urbes,
sed genus Ausonium Rutulique extirpat alumnos?
quid? reputemus enim : duo sunt, quibus extulit ingens
Roma caput, virtus belli et sapientia pacis.   21
sed virtus, agitata domi et socialibus armis,
in freta Sicaniae et Carthaginis exulat arces
ceteraque imperia et totum simul abstulit orbem.
deinde, velut stadio victor qui solus Achaeo   25
languet et immota sensim virtute fatiscit,
sic itidem Romana manus, contendere postquam
destitit et pacem longis frenavit habenis.
ipsa domi leges et Graia inventa retractans,
omnia bellorum terra quaesita marique   30
praemia consilio et molli ratione regebat :
stabat in his (neque enim poterat constare sine istis) :
haut frustra auctori mendaxque Diespiter olim,
" Imperium sine fine dedi" [1] dixisse probatur.

Nunc igitur qui rex Romanos imperat inter,   35
non trabe, sed tergo prolapsus et ingluvie albus,
et studia et sapiens hominum nomenque genusque
omnia abire foras atque urbe excedere iussit?
quid fugimus Graios hominumque reliquimus urbes,
ut Romana foret magis his instructa magistris,   40
iam (Capitolino veluti turbante Camillo

[1] Virgil, *Aen*. i. 279.

will that speechless and bereft of reason, even as
when first we rose up out of the soil, we feed on
acorns and again lap up unmixed water? Or does
he kindly keep all other lands and cities in their
former state, but roots out the Roman race and the
sons of Latium? What? Let us but reflect. Two
things there are whereby mighty Rome raised up her
head, valour in war and wisdom in peace. But valour,
exercised at home and in our Social Wars, travelled
abroad against the fleets of Sicily and the towers
of Carthage, pulled down those other empires and
seized upon the whole world at once. Then, as an
unmatched athlete on the Olympic course grows
feeble and with unstirred mettle declines gradually,
even so the might of Rome after it ceased to strive,
and gave loose rein to peace. She also, pondering at
home her laws and the discoveries of Greece, used to
govern the prizes won by her wars on land and sea
with wisdom and the gentle rule of reason : on these
she used to stand (for indeed without them she could
not have stood whole). Surely it was no vain or lying
word when to the father of our race Jupiter said of
old : " I have given you an Empire without bounds."

[85] Has he, then, who now reigns as king amongst
the Romans, bestial and dead-white through gluttony,
ordered learning and the whole name and race of
our philosophers to get gone and leave the city?[1]
Why do we flee the Greeks and have left the cities
of mankind that Rome might the better be sup-
plied[2] with such teachers, if now (as the Gauls fled
leaving the sword and scales when Camillus, the old

[1] Domitian expelled all the philosophers from Rome and
Italy. *cp.* Suet. *Dom.* x.
[2] *i.e.* by our absence, which gives the Greeks a free field.

ensibus [1] et trutina Galli fugere relicta)
si nostri palare senes adiguntur et ipsi
ut ferale suos onus exportare libellos?
ergo Numantinus Libycusque erravit in isto   45
Scipio, qui Rhodio crevit formante magistro,
ceteraque illa manus bello facunda secundo?
quos inter prisci sententia dia Catonis [2]
scire adeo magni fecisset, utrumne secundis
an magis adversis staret Romana propago.   50
scilicet adversis! nam, cum defendier armis
suadet amor patriae et caritura penatibus uxor,
convenit, ut vespis, quarum domus arce Monetae,
turba rigens strictis per lutea corpora telis;
ast ubi res secura redit, oblita furorum   55
plebs rectorque una somno moriuntur obeso:
Romulidarum igitur longa et gravis exitium pax.—

    Hic fabella modo pausam facit. optima, posthac,
Musa, velim moneas, sine qua mihi nulla voluptas
vivere: uti quondam, dum Smyrna Byblisque peribat,
nunc itidem migrare vacat. vel denique quidvis 61
ut dea quaere aliud: tantum Romana Caleno
moenia iucundos pariterque averte Sabinos.

    Haec ego. tum paucis dea me dignarier infit:

---

[1] So *MSS.*: censibus, *Peiper.* "Ensibus" is a jocular allusion
to the sword which Brennus cast into the scale.

[2] *cp.* Horace, *Sat.* I. ii. 32

---

[1] An allusion to the well-known deliverance of the Capitol
when besieged by Gauls under Brennus in 390 B.C.

hero of the Capitol, routed them [1]) our old sages are
forced to go a-wandering and to carry out their own
books like the deadly burden borne by criminals.[2]
Was Scipio, then, misguided in this, the hero of
Numantia and Libya [3] who prospered under the
guidance of a Rhodian director [4]; and the others
of that company who joined eloquence with success
in war?   And among these, how important would
old Cato with his heaven-sent prudence have held it
only to know whether the Roman race stood firmer in
prosperity or in adversity.   Surely in adversity!   For
when love of country and fear that their wives may
lose their homes moves them to defend themselves,
they muster; even as the wasps whose home is in
Moneta's stronghold, a swarm formidable with un-
sheathed weapons upon their yellow bodies; but
when security returns, the commons and their ruler
alike forgetful of their rage perish in full-fed sleep.
Therefore a long, heavy peace is the ruin of the sons
of Romulus.

[58] Here now my tale must rest.   Hereafter, sweetest
Muse, without whom I find no pleasure in life, I fain
would hear thy grave warnings : even as of old, while
Smyrna and Byblis were perishing, so now there is yet
time to go into other lands.   Or, as a goddess may,
find any other plan : only keep Calenus [5] from the
walls of Rome and from the pleasant Sabine land.

[64] Such was my prayer.   Then first the goddess

---

[2] *i.e.* the cross. Or, possibly, "as though their books
were some noxious load " (which needed to be got rid of).
[3] *sc.* Scipio Africanus Minor, who took Carthage in 146 B.C.
and Numantia in 133 B.C.
[4] Panaetius, the Stoic of Rhodes, the intimate friend of
Scipio and Laelius.
[5] Calenus was the husband of Sulpicia.

" Pone metus aegros, cultrix mea : summa tyranno 65
haec instant odia et nostro periturus honore est.
nam laureta Numae fontisque habitamus eosdem,
et comite Egeria ridemus inania coepta.
vive, vale ! manet hunc pulchrum sua fama dolorem :
Musarum spondet chorus et Romanus Apollo." 70

VI.—In Puerum Formosum

Dum dubitat natura, marem faceretne puellam :
  factus es, o pulcher, paene puella, puer.

VII.—De Matre Augusti

Ante omnes alias felix tamen hoc ego dicar,
  sive hominem peperi femina sive virum.

VIII.—Didoni

Infelix Dido, nulli bene nupta marito :
  hoc pereunte fugis, hoc fugiente peris.

IX.—Ad Amicam

Ecce rubes nec causa subest.   me teste pudicus
  iste tuus culpam nescit habere rubor.

vouchsafed me these few words: "Cast off your anxious fears, my devotee : hatred for these crowning offences threatens to overwhelm the tyrant, and he shall perish to expiate the slight he put upon me. For I dwell in the laurel groves that Numa haunted and by the same springs ; and, with Egeria for my companion, I laugh to scorn such vain attempts. Long life and farewell! So noble a grief shall find the fame that is its due ; an this the choir of Muses and Roman Apollo promise thee."

VI.—To a graceful Boy

WHILE Nature was in doubt whether to make a boy or girl, thou didst become almost a girl, my handsome boy.

VII.—On the Mother of an Emperor

YET for this cause [1] I shall be called happy above all others, whether I, a woman, have borne a man or hero.

VIII.—To Dido

AH! luckless Dido, unhappy in both husbands : this, dying, caused thy flight ; that, fleeing, caused thy death.

IX.—To a Mistress

SEE, thou dost blush ; and yet there is no secret cause. I can bear witness that this modest blush of

---

[1] *sc.* because I am mother of an Emperor, whatever his qualities may be. This couplet appears to be a fragment from the end of an epigram.

et vice populeae frondis tremis, et vice lunae
    puniceam maculant lutea signa cutem.
amplexus etiam nostros pudibunda recusas   5
    et, si testis adest, oscula sueta fugis.

X

CONSUETUDO oculis nil sinit esse novum.

thine is innocent of guilt. Now like a poplar-leaf thou tremblest, now like the moon pale marks dapple thy rosy cheeks. Shamefast, thou dost shun even my embrace, and if a witness is at hand, thou fleest my wonted kisses.

X

Custom suffers naught to be strange to the eye.

PAULINUS PELLÆUS

THE *EUCHARISTICUS*

INTRODUCTION

THE AUTHOR

THE author of the *Eucharisticus* is in some sense an
elusive personage; for while the one surviving MS.
states that the work is by an unknown writer
(*incerti auctoris*), the *editio princeps* attributes it to
St. Paulinus of Nola. This ascription was almost
certainly found in the MS. (now lost) used by the
first editor; and though quite impossible[1] as it stands,
it has so far been taken seriously by modern scholars
that the poem is ascribed, not to the Saint, but to
some other person of the same name.

Paulinus, as we may therefore call him, makes
certain allusions to his relatives which show at any
rate to what family he belonged. In ll. 26 ff. he
refers to his father as *vicarius* of Macedonia, and
again (l. 35) as proconsul of Africa: further on
(l. 48 f) he mentions a visit to Bordeaux in the same
year in which his grandfather was consul, and finally
(l. 332) alludes to Bazas as the native place of his
forefathers. The chronology of the author's life
leaves no room for doubt that the grandfather was
Decimus Magnus Ausonius, the poet-rhetorician,
who was consul in 379 A.D. But here our certainty
ends. Was Paulinus the son of Hesperius (as Brandes

---

[1] The history of the author is entirely different from the
known history of Paulinus of Nola.

argues), or of a daughter of Ausonius by Thalassius,[1] as Seeck and Peiper maintain? The complete arguments on either side are too minute and too complicated to be summarised here; nor, after all, is the question important. All that need be said is that the author's references to Gaulish estates inherited from his grandfather (*res avitae*, ll. 422, 570) and to others in Macedonia left by his mother (*materni census*, l. 414) strongly favour Brandes' view that Paulinus was a son of Hesperius by a Macedonian wife.

We may now turn to the life history of the author. He was born at Pella in Macedonia in 376 A.D. and carried to Carthage nine months later on his father's promotion to the Proconsulship of Africa (ll. 24–33). After eighteen months in this province he was taken first to Rome and then to Bordeaux, which he reached in 379 A.D. (ll. 34–49). Here his education began. After passing through the elementary stage, he was advanced to read Plato, Homer and Virgil; though, being used to converse in Greek and almost ignorant of Latin, he found the last-named a trying author (ll. 65–80). It is worthy of notice that at this early period he had a boyish ambition to be set apart—apparently for the monastic life (ll. 92 ff.). Just as he was beginning to take an interest in study and to show some promise, he was struck down by an ague. Doctors recommended exercise and amusement, with the result that horses, hounds and hunting took the place of books (ll. 113 ff.).

The youth, now rapidly growing up, next developed a love of finery and general magnificence, succeeded

[1] If so, "Paulinus" is really the grandson Ausonius of *Epist.* xxi.–xxii. (Above, pp. 68 ff.)

by indulgence in other amusements which he followed with a stronger sense of caution than of morality (ll. 140–175). Hereupon parents intervened with the remedy of a marriage of convenience. Paulinus gained a wife, for whom he shows scant affection, but found an outlet for his energies in restoring to order the neglected estate which was her portion (ll. 176 ff.). The independent means thus acquired were laid out in forming a comfortable and luxurious establishment, and Paulinus bade fair to settle down to an indolent, if blameless, life (ll. 202 ff.).

But this period of ease came to an abrupt end. In 406 A.D. his father died almost at the same time that the barbarians burst into the Roman Empire (ll. 226 ff.). The attempts of his brother to upset his father's will was the first and least of his troubles (ll. 248 ff.): Bordeaux was occupied by the Visigoths, who sacked the city ere they evacuated it in 414 A.D. Paulinus, absent at the time, had failed to take the precaution which might have saved his property; and consequently his house was given up to plunder (ll. 271 ff., 308 ff.). To make matters worse, the puppet-Emperor Priscus Attalus inflicted on him the empty but apparently burdensome title of Count of the Private Largesses. Driven from his home which was burned, Paulinus fled with his family to Bazas, only to be besieged in the town, where he narrowly escaped assassination (ll. 328 ff.). His attempts to extricate himself had the unexpected result of ending the siege by detaching the Alans from their Gothic allies (ll. 343 ff.).

His position, however, was now difficult. Hostile Goths and dishonest Romans had made away with

all, or nearly all, of his inherited property. Naturally he thought of removing to Macedonia, where his mother's estates remained intact, but was thwarted in this by his wife's obstinate refusal to make the voyage (ll. 404 ff., 480 ff., 494).

Probably it was in desperation at his difficulties that Paulinus sought to abandon the world (and his family) by becoming a monk (ll. 455 ff.); but from this purpose he was deterred by the advice of certain "holy men." A course of penance was imposed upon him, and at Easter, 421 A.D., he felt fitted to receive the Communion (ll. 464–478).

As years passed by, his position grew worse and worse; his mother-in-law, mother, and wife (of whom he speaks with some bitterness) died one after another; his sons left him to make their way at Bordeaux, where they too died (ll. 492–515). His means, too, were now so small that he retired to Marseilles and there endeavoured to make a livelihood by working a very small property which he owned there. But this effort also failed and he returned to Bordeaux to live, apparently, in dependence (ll. 520 ff.).

But at length his continuous ill-fortune was relieved. His estate at Marseilles, though somehow embarrassed, was purchased by an unknown Goth who paid, if not the fair price, yet a sum sufficient to make him independent once more (ll. 575 ff.). It is evident that Paulinus expects that the proceeds will suffice to support his remaining years; and we may therefore take it that the transaction was carried out not long before the *Eucharisticus* was written, and that it was the last incident of importance in this strange life.

INTRODUCTION

The poem was composed when the author was in his eighty-third year (ll. 12-14), *i.e.* in 459 A.D.: in the nature of things his death must have followed not long after that date.

THE *EUCHARISTICUS* AS LITERATURE

Paulinus openly avows that his purpose in writing the *Eucharisticus* is to show how his whole life had been ordered and directed by Providence, and thereby in some measure to return thanks for such guidance. He is careful to disclaim both literary merit and literary ambition. And indeed in any strictly literary sense the value of the poem must be regarded as slight.

It is probable that the nature of his subject—reflexions upon times long gone by—induced him to adopt a slow and deliberate style. Yet even if this is so, it cannot excuse the long and laboured periods in which he unfolds his experiences. In the tangle of absolute, temporal, and relative clauses, complicated by parentheses and conditions, the reader is often hard put to it to follow the trend of the author's thought; sometimes (as in ll. 149–153) a main verb is altogether lacking. A certain almost wilful ponderousness of expression (as in ll. 458 f.: "qui sibi servari consuetam indicere curam | posse viderentur"), and a habit of introducing sentence after sentence with a relative (ll. 81, 85, 92) only increase the monotonous effect. It is not that Paulinus scorns any form of literary refinement and embellishment. He imitates such authors as were known to him—Virgil among the ancients, and Ausonius, Paulinus of Nola, Juvencus,

Sedulius among the moderns. Moreover, as became
a grandson of Ausonius, he was by no means in-
different to rhetorical and verbal effects, indulging
largely in such antitheses as: " effectum . . . pro-
fectum " (l. 6), or " officeret . . . succedente . . . ce-
dente . . . sufficeret " (ll. 137–140). The note struck
by one word is frequently repeated with some
variation further on (as in ll. 4 f.: " placidus . . .
placita," or in 432–4 " complacuit . . . placatum ").
Alliteration also was frequently though not regularly
brought into play ; thus in ll. 182 ff. we have
" possessa placeret | ad praesens posset " followed
by " dudum desidia domini " ; in l. 209 " pretio
quam pondere praestans " ; in l. 149 " vegetus veloci
currere vectus | equo." Sometimes, but more rarely,
he indulges in such plays as " ponere finem | nescis
et ignaris solis succurrere nosti " (l. 445).

Of the metrical and rhythmic aspects of the
Eucharisticus no adequate account can here be
given.[1] Licences such as *statŭs* (l. 194, genitive)
and *compertă* (l. 197, ablative) may be due to the
changes which Latin had undergone and was under-
going ; but it is evident that Paulinus used the
hexameter as a purely conventional mould into
which his words were to be forced. As a result, his
verses move as regardless of rhythm as a slow train
over an ill-laid line.

But though we must deny to Paulinus literary
precision, technical ease and grace,[2] his work pre-
sents certain aspects which must not be ignored.

---

[1] On this see the *Prolegomena* to Brandes' edition, § iii.
[2] As Brandes observes, many of the blemishes in this
work may be due to the interruption of the author's training
ere he had attained an adequate knowledge of Latin.

INTRODUCTION

Consciously or unconsciously he chose a subject which has something of the unity and regular development of a Greek tragedy. The varying phases of the first half of the author's life unfold themselves in an atmosphere of almost insolent prosperity seeming to invite the catastrophe or "reversal of fortune" which forms the central point. Misfortune after misfortune follows until it seems likely that the "hero" will be overwhelmed; only towards the close is the picture brightened (as in the *Samson Agonistes*) by some measure of consolation. Here, moreover, as in Milton's drama, the pervading idea of continuous divine direction is an additional bond of unity. And lastly, if we seek for individual passages, most will admit that the conclusion at least (ll. 590 ff.) has a solemn and majestic dignity of its own. Paulinus lacks literary craftsmanship, but he has, what many literary craftsmen lack, sincerity and real experience of what he describes; his poem, though essentially religious, is quite pure of the mendacious assumption of emotions never experienced which poisons so many "religious poems."

HISTORICAL VALUE OF THE POEM

When all allowance has been made, we must still admit that it is as an historical document that the *Eucharisticus* deserves to be read. Even here it is not the few concrete facts recorded (the sack of Bordeaux, the siege of Bazas and the like) which are chiefly important. The phrases "barbarian invasion," "collapse of the Roman power," and such like mean little unless their implication is understood; and the *Eucharisticus* does indeed reveal in a single instance what these events implied for

thousands of happy and prosperous homes. First the free, gay and luxurious life of the well-to-do is depicted; then the storm breaks, and

> apparent rari nantes in gurgite vasto.

The surviving unfortunates struggle on for a time, catching at expedient after expedient, but always sinking deeper. If in the end certain of them found some ark of safety, they might well see in their preservation a token of divine mercy.

Nor is the poem unimportant for social and moral history. The author's account of his youth and early manhood well illustrates the life led by a young provincial squire—set upon having the best that money could buy in the way of horses, hounds, and the like; fond of hunting and a gallop across country, and withal, careful to be in the latest fashion. One passage at least (ll. 160 ff.) is a remarkable commentary on ancient slavery and the curious moral distinctions based upon it.

MSS. and Editions of the Poem

Only two MSS. of the *Eucharisticus* are known to have survived into modern times: (1) An MS. (*P*) used by the first editor. Of the earlier and later history of this, nothing is known. (2) A ninth-century MS. (*B*), now at Berne (No. 317), and showing corrections by three subsequent hands (distinguished as B²–B⁴). Both MSS. were derived from a single archetype.

The following have published editions of the *Eucharisticus*:—

(1) Marguarinus de la Bigne, in *Bibliotheca Sanctorum Patrum*, Appendix (Vol. III.), Paris, 1579 (*Editio Princeps*).

INTRODUCTION

(2) Caspar Barth, *Animadversiones*, Frankfurt, 1624 (republished with considerable augmentations and an emended text (pp. 150 ff.) in Christian Daum's *Paulinus Petricorius*, Leipzig, 1681).

(3) *Collectio Pisaurensis*, Vol. VI. (Pisauri, 1766).

(4) Ludovicus Leipziger, *Paulini Carmen Eucharisticum*, Wratislau, 1858.

(5) Wilhelm Brandes, in *Poetae Christiani Minores*, Pars I., Vienna, 1888. (*Corpus Scriptorum Ecclesiasticorum Latinorum*, Vol. XXVI.)

The text of the present edition is that of Brandes with a few negligible changes in punctuation.

There appears to be no English translation of the poem, and none in a foreign language is known to me. In the present version, intended as it is to stand side by side with the original, I have judged it better for the most part not to attempt to break up the author's long sentences. However desirable that process may be, it is calculated to perplex the reader who desires help in following the original rather than an independent version.

SANCTI PAULINI[1] ΕΥΧΑΡΙΣΤΙΚΟΝ

Praefatio

(1) Scio quosdam inlustrium virorum pro suarum
splendore virtutum ad perpetuandam suae gloriae
dignitatem ephemeridem gestorum suorum proprio
sermone conscriptam memoriae tradidisse. a quo-
rum me praestantissimis meritis tam longe profecto
quam ipsa temporis antiquitate discretum non utique
ratio aequa consilii ad contexendum eiusdem prope
materiae opusculum provocavit, cum mihi neque ulla
sint gesta tam splendida, de quibus aliquam possim
captare gloriolam, nec eloquii tanta fiducia ut facile
audeam cuiusquam opera scriptoris aemulari, (2) sed,
quod non piget confiteri, iamdudum me in peregri-
natione diuturna aerumnosi otii maerore marcescen-
tem misericordia, ut confido, divina ad huiusmodi me
solacia affectanda pellexit, quae simul et bene sibi
consciae senectuti et religioso proposito convenirent
—ut, qui me scilicet totam vitam meam deo debere
meminissem, totius quoque vitae meae actus ipsius
devotos obsequiis exhiberem eiusdemque gratia con-
cessa mihi tempora recensendo eucharisticon ipsi
opusculum sub ephemeridis meae relatione contexe-
rem, (3) sciens profecto et benignae ipsius miseri-

<hr>

[1] P : Incerti auctoris Εὐχαριστικός, B[3, 4].

THE *THANKSGIVING* OF
ST. PAULINUS

THE PREFACE

I KNOW that among famous men there have
been some who, in right of their brilliant qualities
and to immortalise the eminence of their renown,
have handed down to posterity a memoir of their
doings compiled in their own words.   Since I am of
course as far removed from these in their outstanding
worth as in point of time, it is certainly no similar
reason and design which has induced me to put
together a little work almost identical in subject;
for I have neither any such brilliant achievements
whereby I might hope to snatch some little gleam
of fame, nor so great a confidence in my powers of
expression as lightly to dare to challenge the work
of any author.   But—I am not ashamed to avow it—
I, who in my lengthy pilgrimage have long languished
in the misery of care-fraught idleness, have been led
on, as I surely believe, by divine mercy to seek such
consolations as befitted alike a good conscience in
old age and a devout purpose ; I mean that I, who
indeed felt that I owed my whole life to God,
should show that my whole life's doings also have
been subject to his direction ; and that, by telling
over the seasons granted me by his same grace, I
should form a little work, a *Thanksgiving* to him, in
the guise of a narrative memoir.   For I know indeed
both that the care of his kindly mercy was about

cordiae circa me fuisse, quod indultis humano generi
temporariis voluptatibus etiam ipse prima mea aetate
non carui, et in hac quoque parte curam mihi provi-
dentiae ipsius profuisse, quod me adsiduis adversi-
tatibus moderanter exercens evidenter instruxit nec
inpensius me praesentem beatitudinem debere dili-
gere quam amittere posse me scirem, nec adversis
magnopere terreri, in quibus subvenire mihi posse
misericordias ipsius adprobassem.

(4) Proinde si quando hoc opusculum meum in
cuiusquam manus venerit, ex ipso libelli titulo prae-
notato evidenter debet advertere me hanc medita-
tiunculam meam, quam omnipotenti deo dedico, otio
meo potius quam alieno negotio praestitisse, magis-
que id meorum esse votorum, ut hoc qualecumque
obsequium meum acceptum deo sit, quam ut carmen
incultum ad notitiam perveniat doctiorum.   (5) At-
tamen si cui forsitan magis curioso tantum otii ab re
sua fuerit, ut laboriosum vitae meae ordinem velit
agnoscere, exoratum eum cupio ut, sive aliquid seu
forsitan nihil in gestis vel in versibus meis quod
possit probare reppererit, ea tamen ipsa quae ele-
gerit oblivioni potius inculcanda deleget quam
memoriae diiudicanda commendet.

ΕΥΧΑΡΙCTΙΚΟC Deo sub Ephemeridis meae
Textu.

Enarrare parans annorum lapsa meorum
tempora et in seriem deducere gesta dierum
ambigua exactos vitae quos sorte cucurri,

me, because in my early life I lacked not even the
fleeting pleasures natural to mankind; and that in
this part of it also the care of his providence has been
before me, because, while reasonably chastening me
with continual misfortunes, he has clearly taught me
that I ought neither to love too earnestly present
prosperity which I knew I might lose, nor to be
greatly dismayed by adversities wherein I had found
that his mercies could succour me.

Therefore, if ever this little work of mine should
come into the hands of any, from the very title
prefixed to the book he ought clearly to understand
that this my little musing, which I consecrate to
God Almighty, is a gift to my leisure, rather than to
another's pleasure; and that my prayer is rather that
this my service, such as it is, may be accepted by
God, than that my uncouth poem should win its way
to the attention of the learned.   Nevertheless, if
someone perchance more inquisitive than ordinary
should have so much leisure from his own affairs
as to seek to learn the toilsome progress of my life, I
wish to beg him—whether he find anything, or perhaps
nothing, in my doings or in my verses which he can
praise—yet to elect for the trampling of oblivion
those very features which he has selected, rather
than to commend them to the discernment of
posterity.

A Thanksgiving to God in the Form of my Memoirs

Now as I make ready to tell o'er the bygone
seasons of my years and to trace out the succession
of past days through which I have sped with

te, deus omnipotens, placidus mihi, deprecor, adsis
adspiransque operi placita tibi coepta secundes,　5
effectum scriptis tribuens votisque profectum,
ut tua te merear percurrere dona iuvante.
Omnia namque meae tibi debeo tempora vitae,
auram ex quo primum vitalis luminis hausi,
inter et adversas iactatus saepe procellas　10
instabilis mundi te protectore senescens
altera ab undecima annorum currente meorum
hebdomade sex aestivi flagrantia solis
solstitia et totidem brumae iam frigora vidi
te donante, deus, lapsi qui temporis annos　15
instaurando novas cursu revolubilis aevi.
Sit mihi fas igitur versu tua dona canentem
pangere et expressas verbis quoque pendere grates,
quas equidem et clausas scimus tibi corde patere,
ultro sed abrumpens tacitae penetralia mentis　20
fontem exundantis voti vox conscia prodit.
　Tu mihi lactanti vires in corpore inerti
ad toleranda viae pelagique incerta dedisti,
editus ut Pellis inter cunabula quondam
regis Alexandri prope moenia Thessalonices　25
patre gerente vices inlustris praefecturae,
orbis ad alterius discretas aequore terras
perveherer trepidis nutricum creditus ulnis,
ninguida perque iuga et sectas torrentibus Alpes

---

[1] Literally "success to my writings and fulfilment to my prayers"; but it is desirable to reproduce the play on *effectum . . . profectum.*

changeful fortunes, thee I implore, Almighty God,
favourably to be nigh me and, breathing on my
work, to prosper a design favoured by thee, in
granting me sustainment in my task, attainment in
my prayers,[1] that by thy aid I may be worthy to run
o'er the list of thy gifts.   For all the seasons of my
life I owe to thee ever since I drew in the breath of
enlivening light, and, though oft tossed amid the
storms of this inconstant world, under thy protection
I grow old and in the course of my twelfth hebdomad
of years have now seen six scorching solstices of the
summer sun and as many winters' frosts—this
through thy gift, O God, who renewest the years of
bygone time in repairing the course of the circling
Ages.[2]   Be it permitted me, therefore, singing to re-
cord thy gifts in verse, and in setting forth of words
also to pay thanks which, indeed, even when shut
within the heart, we know are open to thee, but the
fraught voice unbidden breaks through the barriers
of the silent mind and reveals a fount of out-gushing
prayer.

Thou in my infancy didst give my helpless frame
strength to endure the hazards of travel by land and
sea, that I—born at Pella, the nursery of King
Alexander of old, near Salonika's walls, where my
father was vicegerent [3] of the illustrious Prefect—
might be conveyed to the shores of another world,
cut off by sea, entrusted to my nurses' trembling
arms, and so across snowy ridges and torrent-riven
ranges, across the main and the waves of the

---

[2] The reference is to the cycle of ages: *cp.* Virgil, *Ecl.*
iv. 5.

[3] *i.e. Vicarius* (deputy of the Prefect) of Macedonia.   But
possibly the rendering may be merely "performed the
functions of the illustrious Prefect."

Oceanumque fretum Tyrrheni et gurgitis undas   30
moenia Sidoniae Carthaginis usque venirem,
ante suum nono quam menstrua luna recursu
luce novata orbem nostro compleret ab ortu.
Illic, ut didici, ter senis mensibus actis
sub genitore meo proconsule rursus ad aequor   35
expertasque vias revocor, visurus et orbis
inclita culminibus praeclarae moenia Romae ;
quae tamen haud etiam sensu agnoscenda tuentis
subiacuere mihi, sed post comperta relatu
adsiduo illorum quibus haec tam nota fuere,   40
propositum servans operis subdenda putavi.

Tandem autem exacto longarum fine viarum
maiorum in patriam tectisque advectus avitis
Burdigalam veni, cuius speciosa Garumna
moenibus Oceani refluas maris invehit undas   45
navigeram per portam, quae portum spatiosum
nunc etiam muris spatiosa includit in urbe.
Tunc et avus primum illic fit mihi cognitus, anni
eiusdem consul, nostra trieteride prima.
Quae postquam est expleta mihi firmavit et artus   50
invalidos crescens vigor et mens conscia sensus
adsuefacta usum didicit cognoscere rerum—
quidquid iam . . .[1] potui meminisse, necesse est
ipse fide propria de me agnoscenda retexam.

Sed quid ego ex nostris aliud puerilibus annis,   55
quos mihi libertas ludusque et laetior aetas
conciliare suis meritis potuisse videntur,

[1] A word is lost.

Tyrrhenian flood, might come to the far walls of
Sidonian Carthage, ere yet the monthly moon in
her ninth orbit since my birth filled her disk with
renewed light. There, as I have learned, when
thrice six months were passed under the proconsul-
ship of my father, I was called back again to the sea
and paths already tried, soon also to behold the famed
bulwarks of all-glorious Rome on the world's heights.[1]
All this which passed before me, though not even to
be comprehended by my sense of sight but later
learned through the careful report of those to whom
these matters were well known, I have deemed
worthy of mention in accordance with the purpose
of my work.

But at length, the end of my long journeying
reached, I was borne into the land of my forefathers
and to my grandfather's house, coming to Bordeaux
where beauteous Garonne draws Ocean's tidal waves
within the walls through a ship-traversed portal
which even now enfolds a roomy port within the
roomy city's barriers. Then also my grandfather,
consul in that same year, was there first known to
me in my first *triennium*. And after this period was
outgrown, and when waxing power strengthened my
feeble limbs and my mind, aware of its faculties,
learned through wont to know the properties of
things—so far as now . . . I can remember, I myself
with due truth must needs narrate what is to be
known concerning me.

But what else in my boyish years, which free-
dom, play, and blithesome youth seemed to have been
able to commend to me by their own virtues, shall I

---

[1] *i.e.* "on the heights which dominate the world." But
the expression is very obscure.

vel magis ipse libens recolam, vel dignius ausim
inserere huic nostro, quem versu cudo, libello
quam pietatis opus studiumque insigne parentum 60
permixtis semper docta exercere peritum
blanditiis gnaramque apto moderamine curam
insinuare mihi morum instrumenta bonorum
ingenioque rudi celerem conferre profectum—
ipsius alphabeti inter prope prima elementa 65
nosse cavere decem specialia signa amathiae
nec minus et vitia vitare ἀκοινονόητα?
Quarum iam dudum nullus vigeat licet usus
disciplinarum, vitiato scilicet aevo,
me Romana tamen, fateor, servata vetustas 70
plus iuvat atque seni propria est acceptior aetas.

    Nec sero exacto primi mox tempore lustri
dogmata Socratus et bellica plasmata Homeri
erroresque legens cognoscere cogor Ulixis.
Protinus et libros etiam transire Maronis 75
vix bene conperto iubeor sermone Latino,
conloquio Graiorum adsuefactus famulorum,
quos mihi iam longus ludorum iunxerat usus;
unde labor puero, fateor, fuit hic mihi maior,
eloquium librorum ignotae apprehendere linguae. 80

    Quae doctrina duplex sicut est potioribus apta
ingeniis geminoque ornat splendore peritos,
sic sterilis nimium nostri, ut modo sentio, cordis
exilem facile exhausit divisio venam.
Quod nunc invito quoque me haec mea pagina prodit, 85
inconsulta quidem, quam sponte expono legendam,
sed mihi non rebus, quantum confido, pudenda,
quarum notitiam scriptis contexere conor:
namque ita me sollers castorum cura parentum
a puero instituit, laedi ne quando sinistro 90

more gladly dwell upon or more fitly dare to set in
this little book which I fashion in verse, than affec-
tion's work and my parents' noble pains, skilled to
season learning with mingled enticements, and their
wise care, exercising due control, to instil into me the
means of good living and on my untrained mind to
bestow speedy development—almost along with my
first steps in the alphabet itself to learn to shun the
ten special marks of ignorance and equally to avoid
vices anathematised? And albeit this discipline has
long since fallen out of use through the corruption,
doubtless, of the age, yet, I declare, the antique
Roman fashion I observed delights me more, and the
life natural to an old man is more tolerable therefor.

Full early, when the days of my first *lustrum*
were well-nigh spent, I was made to con and learn
the doctrines of Socrates, Homer's warlike fantasies,
and Ulysses' wanderings. And forthwith I was
bidden to traverse Maro's works as well, ere I well
understood the Latin tongue, used as I was to the
converse of Greek servants with whom long pursuit
of play had made me intimate; whereby, I affirm,
this was too heavy a task for me, a boy, to grasp the
eloquence of works in an unknown tongue.

This double learning, as it is suited to more
powerful minds and decks those skilled in it with
a two-fold radiance, so its wide range soon drained
dry the vein of my mind—too barren, as I now
understand. So much now even despite me this
my page reveals—a page ill-judged, indeed, which
I unasked set forth to be read, yet, as I hope, not
disgracing me in the matters whereof I seek to form
a written record; for so my chaste parents careful
taught me from my boyhood, lest some day the

cuiusquam sermone mea se fama timeret.
Quae licet obtineat proprium bene parta decorem,
hac potiore tamen tum me decorasset honore,
consona si nostris primo sub tempore votis
hac in parte etiam mansissent vota parentum,   95
perpetuo ut puerum servarent me tibi, Christe,
rectius hanc curam pro me pietatis habentes,
carnis ut inlecebris breviter praesentibus expers
aeternos caperem venturo in tempore fructus.
Sed quoniam nunc iam magis hoc me credere fas est 100
conduxisse mihi, quod te voluisse probasti,
omnipotens aeterne deus, qui cuncta gubernas,
culpato renovando mihi vitalia dona,
hoc nunc maiores pro me tibi debeo grates,
maiorum quanto errorum cognosco reatum.   105
Namque et, incautus quidquid culpabile gessi
inlicitumque vagus per lubrica tempora vitae,
te indulgente mihi totum scio posse remitti
ex quo me reprobans lapsum ad tua iura refugi,
et, si ulla unquam potui peccata cavere,   110
quae mihi maiorem parerent commissa reatum,
hoc quoque me indeptum divino munere novi.

  Sed redeo ad seriem decursaque illius aevi
tempora, quo studiis intentus litteraturae
ultro libens aliquem iam me mihi ipse videbar 115
votivum inpensi operis sentire profectum,
Argolico pariter Latioque instante magistro,
cepissemque etiam forsan fructum quoque dignum,
ni subito incumbens quarterna acerba meorum
conatus placitos studiorum destituisset   120
vix impleta aevi quinta trieteride nostri.
Consternata autem pro me pietate parentum,

malignant tongue of any man might endanger my
repute. And though this repute, well earned, still
keeps the lustre due to it, yet with this higher
grace would it then have adorned me, if with my
hopes in early life my parents' hopes had continued
to agree in this respect, namely, that forever they
should keep me as thy child, O Christ, more rightly
making this the aim of their love for me—that by
brief sacrifice of the present joys of the flesh I
might win endless reward in the world to come.
But—since I now am bound to believe that this has
more profited me which thou, O God, almighty,
everlasting, hast shown to have been thy will by
renewing to me, though sinful, thy gifts of life—so
much the greater thanks I now owe thee on my behalf,
as I perceive the greater guilt of my transgressions.
For both I know that—whatever deed blameworthy
or act unlawful I have unwarily committed, straying
through life's treacherous seasons—thou in thy
mercy canst wholly forgive, ever since scorning my
fallen self I fled back to thy obedience ; and, if ever
I have been able to shun any sins which, committed,
would bring me greater guilt, this too I feel that I
have gained through Heaven's bounty.

But I return to my course and to the seasons I
passed through at the time when, wrapt in study
and in learning, I gladly fancied to myself that
already I felt some of the desired outcome of my
pains lavished under the constant care of Greek and
Latin tutors both, and I should also have gained,
perchance, a meet return, had not a sharp quartan
fever, suddenly falling upon me, defrauded my
willing efforts in learning, when the fifth triad of
my life was scarce completed. But when my
parents' love for me was stricken with alarm at this

quippe quibus potior visa est curatio nostri
corporis invalidi quam doctae instructio linguae,
primitus hoc medicis suadentibus, ut mihi iugis   125
laetitia atque animo grata omnia perspicerentur ;
quae pater in tantum studuit per se ipse parare,
deposito ut nuper venandi attentius usu —
causa equidem sola studiorum quippe meorum,
neve his officeret, sibi me ad sua ludicra iungens, 130
neu sine me placitis umquam solus frueretur —
me propter rursus cura maiore resumens
eiusdem ludi cuncta instrumenta novaret,
ex quibus optatam possem captare salutem.
Quae protracta diu longi per tempora morbi   135
invexere mihi iugem iam deinde legendi
desidiam, officeret durans quae postea sano
succedente novo mundi fallacis amore
et tenero nimium affectu cedente parentum,
sufficeret quibus ex nostra gaudere salute.   140
　　Qua ratione auctus noster quoque crevit et error,
firmatus facile ad iuvenalia vota sequenda,
ut mihi pulcher equus falerisque ornatior esset,
strator procerus, velox canis et speciosus
accipiter, Romana et nuper ab urbe petita   145
aurata instrueret nostrum sphaera concita ludum,
cultior utque mihi vestis foret et nova saepe
quaeque Arabi muris leni fragraret odore.
Nec minus et vegetus veloci currere vectus
semper equo gaudens quotiens evasero casus   150
abruptos, recolens—Christi me munere fas est
credere servatum, quod tum nescisse dolendum est,
scilicet inlecebris urgentibus undique mundi.

—seeing they deemed more urgent the recovery of my enfeebled body than the training of my tongue in eloquence, and as physicians from the first advised that continual gaiety and amusement should be devised for me—my father was so eager by his own efforts to secure this end that, though of late he had laid by his wont of hunting zealously ('twas indeed for my studies' sake alone, that he might not hinder them by making me the companion of his pastimes, nor without me ever enjoy his delight alone), on my account he returned to it with greater interest, renewing all means this sport affords, in hope that thereby I might woo health. These pursuits, long continued during the slow period of my sickness, caused in me a distaste for study, thenceforward chronic, which persisting afterwards in time of health, harmed me when love of the false world made way and the too pliant fondness of my parents gave way, charmed with delight at my recovery.

Wherefore, as my growth, so my waywardness increased, readily settling down to the pursuit of youthful desires—as to have a fine horse bedecked with special trappings, a tall groom, a swift hound, a shapely hawk, a tinselled ball, fresh brought from Rome, to serve me in my games of pitching, to wear the height of fashion, and to have each latest novelty perfumed with sweet-smelling myrrh of Araby. Likewise when I recall how, grown robust, I ever loved to gallop riding a racing steed, and how many a headlong fall I escaped, 'tis right I should believe I was preserved by Christ's mercy; and pity 'tis that then I knew it not by reason of the world's thronging enticements.

Quas inter fluitans interque et vota parentum
iugiter in nostram tendentia posteritatem,   155
iam prope sero calens aevi pro tempore nostri
in nova prorupi iuvenalis gaudia luxus,
quae facile ante puer rebar me posse cavere.
Attamen in quantum lasciva licentia cauto
stricta coherceri potuit moderamine freni,   160
congererem graviora meis ne crimina culpis,
hac mea castigans lege incentiva repressi ;
invitam ne quando ullam iurisve alieni
adpeterem carumque memor servare pudorem
cedere et ingenuis oblatis sponte caverem,   165
contentus domus inlecebris famulantibus uti,
quippe reus culpae potius quam criminis esse
praeponens famaeque timens incurrere damna.
Sed neque hoc etiam mea inter gesta silebo,
unum me nosse ex me illo in tempore natum,   170
visum autem neque illum tum, quia est cito functus,
nec quemquam, fuerit spurius post qui meus, umquam
cum mihi lascivae inlecebris sociata iuventae
libertas gravius quisset dominando nocere,
ni tibi, Christe, mei iam tunc quoque cura fuisset.   175
    Talis vita mihi a ter senis circiter annis
usque duo durans impleta decennia mansit
donec me invitum, fateor, pia cura parentum
coge et invectum blanda suetudine ritum
deserere atque novum compelleret esse maritum   180
coniugis, antiquo potius cuius domus esset
nomine magnifica, quam quae possessa placere

As I was wavering betwixt such interests and my parents' wishes which were set constantly upon the renewal of their line through me, at length, late for my time of life, I felt new fires and broke out into the pleasures of youthful wantonness which, as a boy, I used to think I could easily avoid. Howbeit, so far as wilful wantonness could be curbed and bridled with prudent restraint, lest I should heap heavier offences on my faults, I checked my passions with this chastening rule : that I should never seek an unwilling victim, nor transgress another's rights, and, heedful to keep unstained my cherished reputation, should beware of yielding to free-born loves though voluntarily offered, but be satisfied with servile amours in my own home ; for I preferred to be guilty of a fault rather than of an offence,[1] fearing to suffer loss of my good name. Yet even this also among my doings I will confess : one son I know was born to me at that time—though neither he then (since he soon died), nor any bastard of mine afterwards, was ever seen by me—when freedom, allied with lusty youth's allurements, might by gaining mastery have more gravely harmed me, hadst not thou, O Christ, even then had care for me.

Such was the life I led from about my eighteenth year, and so continued until my second decade's close. when my parent's anxious care forced me, unwillingly, I admit, to give up this state, grown easy through soft custom, and drove me by way of change to mate with a wife, whose property was rather glorious for its ancient name than for the present a portion potent to please, because of the sore

[1] *Culpa* is a transgression of moral, *crimen* of statutory, law.

ad praesens posset nimiis obnoxia curis,
dudum desidia domini neglecta senili,
parva cui neptis functo genitore superstes   185
successit, taedisque meis quae postea cessit.
Sed semel inpositum statuens tolerare laborem,
suffragante animi studiis fervore iuventae
vix paucis domus indeptae exercere diebus
gaudia contentus, malesuada otia curis   190
mutare insolitis, cito meque meosque coegi,
quos potui exemplo proprii invitando laboris,
quosdam autem invitos domini adstringendo rigore.
Atque ita suscepti status actibus inpiger instans
protinus et culturam agris adhibere refectis,   195
et fessis celerem properavi inpendere curam
vinetis conperta mihi ratione novandis
et, quod praecipue plerisque videtur amarum,
ultro libens primus fiscalia debita certo
tempore persolvens, propere mihi fida paravi   200
otia privatae post inpendenda quieti.
Quae et mihi cara nimis semper fuit ingenioque
congrua prima meo mediocria desideranti,
proxima deliciis et ab ambitione remota,
ut mihi compta domus spatiosis aedibus esset   205
et diversa anni per tempora iugiter apta,
mensa opulenta nitens, plures iuvenesque ministri
inque usus varios grata et numerosa supellex
argentumque magis pretio quam pondere praestans
et diversae artis cito iussa explere periti   210

---

[1] *i.e.* the house was to be equipped with summer and
winter quarters—the latter heated by hypocausts such as

anxiety it involved, as long uncared for through the
lethargy of its aged lord, to whom, surviving her
own father's death, a young grandchild succeeded—
she who afterwards acceded to wedlock with me.
But once I was resolved to bear the toil laid upon
me, youth's zeal seconding my mind's desire, in
but few days I was content to enjoy the pleasures
of the estate thus gained, and soon forced both
myself and my thralls to exchange seductive idleness
for unwonted toils—inciting such as I could by the
example of my own labour, but compelling some
against their will with a master's sternness. And so,
tirelessly bent upon the pursuits of the condition I
had adopted, forthwith I hastened to bring fallowed
lands under tillage, and promptly to lavish pains in re-
newing the exhausted vineyards in the manner I had
learned, and also—though to many a one this seems
especially vexatious—by voluntarily paying down out-
right my taxes at the appointed time, I rapidly
earned for myself an assured leisure to lavish after-
wards upon my own relaxation. This was ever too
much prized by me, and though at first it was
conformable with my nature which then sought
but moderate satisfaction, later it became luxurious
and estranged from high purpose, only concerned
that my house should be equipped with spacious
apartments and at all times suited to meet the
varying seasons of the year,[1] my table lavish and
attractive, my servants many and those young,
the furniture abundant and agreeable for various
purposes, plate more preeminent in price than
poundage, workmen of divers crafts trained promptly

may be seen in the existing remains of the more important
Roman houses.

artifices stabula et iumentis plena refectis,
tunc et carpentis evectio tuta decoris.
Nec tamen his ipsis attentior amplificandis,
quam conservandis studiosior et neque census
augendi cupidus nimis aut ambitor honorum,   215
sed potius, fateor, sectator deliciarum,
si qua tamen minimo pretio expensaque parari
et salvo famae possent constare decore,
ne nota luxuriae studium macularet honestum.
Quae mihi cuncta tamen grata acceptaque fruenti 220
cara magis pietas superabat magna parentum,
obstringens sibi me nexu dominantis amoris,
maiore ut parte anni ipsis praesentia nostra
serviret, paribus perdurans consona votis
communemque parans per mutua gaudia fructum. 225

    Cuius vitae utinam nobis prolixior usus
concessus largo mansisset munere Christi,
persistente simul priscae quoque tempore pacis!
Multimodis quisset nostrae prodesse iuventae
consulti patris adsidua conlatio verbi   230
exemplisque bonis studiorum instructio crescens.
Sed transacta aevi post trina decennia nostri
successit duplicis non felix cura laboris,
publica quippe simul clade in commune dolenda
hostibus infusis Romani in viscera regni   235
privata cum sorte patris de funere functi :
ultima namque eius finitae tempora vitae
temporibus ruptae pacis prope iuncta fuere.

to fulfil my behests, my stables filled with well-conditioned beasts and, withal, stately carriages to convey me safe abroad. And yet I was not so much bent on increasing these same things as zealous in preserving them, neither too eager to increase my wealth nor a seeker for distinctions, but rather—I admit—a follower of luxury, though only when it could be attained at trifling cost and outlay and without loss of fair repute that the brand of prodigality should not disgrace a blameless pursuit. But while I found all these things sweet and pleasant to enjoy, my great affection for my parents, dearer still, outweighed them, so binding me to them with the stronger bands of overmastering love that for the most part of the year my visits put me at their service—visits which passed their length accordant with our prayers,[1] winning through mutual joys a general gain.

Of this life would that the enjoyment granted by Christ's rich bounty had continued longer for us, the former times of peace enduring likewise! In many ways could my youth have profited by frequent application of my father's spoken counsel and by the growth in my training won from his good example! But after the third decade of my life was passed, there followed hopeless sorrow caused by a double burden—a general grief at public calamity, when foes burst into the vitals of the Roman realm, together with personal misfortune in the end and death of my father; for the last days which closed his life were almost continuous with the days

---

[1] *i.e.* these visits, though long, passed without any friction arising to disturb the relations between Paulinus and his parents.

PAULINUS PELLÆUS

At mihi damna domus populantem inlata per hostem,
per se magna licet, multo leviora fuere   240
defuncti patris immodico conlata dolori,
per quem cara mihi et patria et domus ipsa fiebat:
tamque etenim fido tradentes mutua nobis
officia affectu conserto viximus aevo,
vinceret aequaevos nostra ut concordia amicos.   245
Hoc igitur mihi subtracto inter prima iuventae
tempora tam caro socio et monitore fideli,
ilico me indocilis fratris discordia acerba
excepit, validum genitoris testamentum
solvere conantis specialia commoda matris   250
inpugnandi animo, cuius mihi cura tuendae
hoc quoque maior erat, quo iustior, et pietatis
non minor affectus studium firmabat honestum.
Insuper adversis me pluribus exagitandum
laeva facultatum prorumpens fama meorum   255
exposuit blandas inter vanae ambitionis
inlecebras gravibus coniuncta et damna periclis.
Quae meminisse licet pigeat transactaque dudum
oblivione sua malim sopita silere,
invitant adversa tamen per nostra tuorum   260
cognita donorum solacia, Christe, bonorum
emensis indepta malis tua munera fando
prodere et in lucem proferre recondita corde.
Namque et quanta mihi per te conlata potentum
gratia praestiterit, facile experiendo probavi,   265
saepe prius claro procerum conlatus honori
ignorans, proprio quam praeditus ipse potirer,

when peace was broken.   But for me the havoc
wrought on my home by the ravage of the enemy,
though great in itself, was much lighter when
compared with boundless grief for my departed
father, who made both my country and my
home itself dear to me. For, indeed, by rendering
kindness to each other in genuine affection, we so
knit in one our uneven ages, that in our agreement
we surpassed friends of even ages. He, then, so
dear a comrade and trusty counsellor, was with-
drawn from me in the early season of my youth ; and
straightway succeeded bitter disagreement caused
by my wilful brother, who sought to overthrow our
father's valid will, desiring to annul the special
benefits therein granted to my mother ; and to safe-
guard her caused me concern the greater as it was
natural, my just endeavours being strengthened by
the yet greater impulse of affection. Besides, luck-
less rumour of my means being spread abroad exposed
me to be tossed by yet more misfortunes amid the
enticing lures of empty ambition and its forfeits
close-linked with sore dangers. And though their
memory irks me, and I would fain leave these
passages of long ago silently buried in their due
oblivion, yet the comfort of thy good gifts
realized through my misfortunes, call upon me,
O Christ, to reveal them and to bring them forth to
light from the depths of my heart, in declaring thy
bounty gained after full measure of ills. For I soon
learned through experience both what advantage the
favour of the powerful, bestowed on me through
thee, afforded, when ofttimes I was accredited
unconsciously with my ancestor's bright distinctions,
ere yet I myself acquired such attributes of my own;

quantum et e contra vi impugnante maligna
ipsa patronarum mihi ambitiosa meorum
obfuerint studia et nostri evidenter honores.   270
  Ac mihi ante omnes specialiter, altera cuius
pars orientis erat patria, in qua scilicet ortus
possessorque etiam non ultimus esse videbar,
iniecere manum mala, sed mihi debita dudum,
quod me et invitum protracto errore tenerent   275
agminis ipsa mei primum molitio pigra,
dissona et interdum carorum vota meorum,
saepius et propriis certans mens obvia votis,
ambigui eventus quotiens formido recurrens
tardabat coepto sorte obsistente paratus;   280
allicerent et contra animum suetudo quietis,
otia nota, domus specialia commoda plura,
omnibus heu! nimium blandis magnisque refertae
deliciis cunctisque bonis in tempore duro,
hospite tunc etiam Gothico quae sola careret;   285
quod post eventu cessit non sero sinistro,
nullo ut quippe domum speciali iure tuente
cederet in praedam populo permissa abeunti:
nam quosdam scimus summa humanitate Gothorum
hospitibus studuisse suis prodesse tuendis.   290
  Sed mihi ad sortem praefatae condicionis
addita maioris nova est quoque causa laboris,
ut me, conquirens solacia vana, tyrannus

---

[1] Priscus Attalus was an Ionian and originally a Pagan.
He was a Senator and Praefect of the city at the second
siege of Rome.   He was set up as a puppet Emperor by the
Goths, but deposed in 410 A.D.   He remained in the company
of Ataulf the Goth, at whose wedding with Placidia he per-

and on the other hand what hindrance in the assaults of ill-will my patrons' own ambitious aims and my own distinctions surely presented.

And on me particularly above all, who had a second country in the East—where indeed I was born and was also held to be an owner of great consequence—did misfortunes lay hold, yet such as were long my due; because, albeit reluctant, I was kept absent on a journey prolonged, first by the mere sluggish effort of my train, sometimes also by the conflicting wishes of my dear ones, and too often by the struggle of their resolves with my own wishes whenever their returning dread of an uncertain issue delayed by some perverse chance preparations already begun; and on the other hand because my nature was enticed by my habits of ease, my wonted repose, the many special comforts of my home—too full, alas! with all great and pleasant luxuries and every blessing in those rough days, and which alone at that time lacked a Gothic guest. This circumstance was followed not long afterwards by a disastrous result, namely that, since no particular authority protected it, my house was given up to be pillaged by the retiring horde; for I know that certain of the Goths most generously strove to serve their hosts by protecting them.

But on me, besides my lot in the condition just described, a fresh cause of greater trouble was also imposed; namely that in his general groping after empty consolations, the tyrant Attalus[1] bur-

formed as a musician. During the revolt of Jovinus he was again set up as a rival Emperor, but was soon abandoned, and in 416 A.D. was banished by Honorius to Lipari. On Attalus see Gibbon (ed. Bury), iii. 318 ff.

Attalus absentem casso oneraret honoris
nomine, privatae comitivam largitionis   295
dans mihi, quam sciret nullo subsistere censu
iamque suo ipse etiam desisset fidere regno,
solis quippe Gothis fretus male iam sibi notis,
quos ad praesidium vitae praesentis habere,
non etiam imperii poterat, per se nihil ipse   300
aut opibus propriis aut ullo milite nixus.
Unde ego non partes infirmi omnino tyranni,
sed Gothicam fateor pacem me esse secutum,
quae tunc ipsorum consensu optata Gothorum
paulo post aliis cessit mercede redempta   305
nec penitenda manet, cum iam in re publica nostra
cernamus plures Gothico florere favore,
tristia quaeque tamen perpessis antea multis,
pars ego magna fui quorum, privatus et ipse
cunctis quippe bonis propriis patriaeque superstes. 310
Namque profecturi regis praecepto Atiulfi
nostra ex urbe Gothi, fuerant qui in pace recepti,
non aliter nobis quam belli iure subactis
aspera quaeque omni urbe inrogavere cremata :
in qua me inventum comitem tum principis eius, 315
imperio cuius sociatos non sibi norant,
nudavere bonis simul omnibus et genetricem
iuxta meam mecum, communi sorte subactos,
uno hoc se nobis credentes parcere captis,
quod nos immunes poena paterentur abire,   320

---

[1] Alaric's brother-in-law, who brought reinforcements of
Goths and Huns to aid Alaric in 409 A.D. In 410 he became
King of the Visigoths on the death of Alaric. Later he

dened me in my absence with an empty title of
distinction, making me Count of Private Largesses,
although he knew that this office was sustained by
no revenue, and even himself had now ceased to
believe in his own royalty, dependent as he was
upon the Goths alone of whom already he had had
bitter experience, finding with them protection at
the moment of his life but not of his authority,
while of himself he was supported neither by re-
sources of his own nor by any soldiery. Wherefore
'twas by no means the cause of that tottering tyrant,
but, I declare, peace with the Goths that I pursued
—peace which, at that time desired by the general
consent of the Goths themselves, was soon after
granted to others and, though purchased at a price,
remains unregretted, since already in our state we
see full many prospering through Gothic favour,
though many first endured the full range of suffering,
not least of whom was I, seeing that I was stripped
of all my goods and outlived my fatherland. For when
about to depart from our city at the command of
their king Ataulf,[1] the Goths, though they had
been received peaceably, imposed the harshest treat-
ment on us, as though subdued by right of war, by
burning the whole city. There finding me—then a
Count of that Prince, whose allies they did not
recognise as their own—they stripped me of all my
goods, and next my mother also, both of us over-
taken by the same lot, for this one grace considering
that they were showing us, their prisoners, mercy—
that they suffered us to depart without injury;

married Placidia, sister of Honorius, and was murdered at
Barcelona (see Gibbon, *ed.* Bury, iii. 313, 318 ff.). The
name Ataulf survives in the modern Adolf.

cunctarumque tamen comitum simul et famularum,
eventum fuerant nostrum quaecumque secutae,
inlaeso penitus nullo adtemptante pudore,
me graviore tamen relevato suspicione
munere divino, iuges cui debeo grates,   325
filia ut ante mea per me sociata marito
excedens patria communi clade careret.

   Nec postrema tamen tolerati meta laboris
ista fuit nostri, quem diximus.   Ilico namque
exactos laribus patriis tectisque crematis   330
obsidio hostilis vicina excepit in urbe
Vasatis, patria maiorum et ipsa meorum,
et gravior multo circumfusa hostilitate
factio servilis paucorum mixta furori
insano iuvenum [nequam[1]] licet ingenuorum,   335
armata in caedem specialem nobilitatis.
Quam tu, iuste deus, insonti a sanguine avertens
ilico paucorum sedasti morte reorum
instantemque mihi specialem percussorem
me ignorante alio iussisti ultore perire,   340
suetus quippe novis tibi me obstringere donis,
pro quis me scirem grates debere perennes.

   Sed mihi tam subiti concusso sorte pericli,
quo me intra urbem percelli posse viderem,
subrepsit, fateor, nimium trepido novus error,   345
ut me praesidio regis dudum mihi cari,
cuius nos populus longa obsidione premebat,

----

[1] Suppl. *Brandes.*

howbeit, of all the companions and handmaidens who had followed our fortunes none suffered any wrong at all done to her honour, nor was any assault offered, yet I was spared more serious anxiety by the divine goodness, to which I owe constant thanks, because my daughter, previously wedded by me to a husband, was spared the general calamity by her absence from our country.

But not even this was the extreme limit of the sufferings we endured, as I have said : for when we were driven from our ancestral home and our house burned, straightway siege by the enemy overtook us in the neighbouring city of Bazas, which also was my forefathers' native place,[1] and, far more dangerous than the beleaguering foe, a conspiracy of slaves supported by the senseless frenzy of some few youths, abandoned though of free estate, and armed specially for the slaughter of the gentry. From this danger thou, O righteous God, didst shield the innocent blood, quelling it forthwith by the death of some few guilty ones, and didst ordain that the special assassin threatening me should without my knowledge perish by another's avenging hand, even as thou hast been wont to bind me to thee with fresh gifts for which I might feel I owed thee endless thanks.

But in my alarm at the hap of so sudden a danger by which I saw I might be stricken down within the city, there entered into me—too fearful, I admit—a new error of judgment, leading me to hope that under the protection of the king,[2] long since my friend, whose people were afflicting us with

---

[1] *cp.* Ausonius, *Epicedion* l. 4 (Vol. I. pp. 42 f.), where Julius Ausonius (Paulinus' great-grandfather) declares that Bazas was his native place.　　[2] *i.e.* Ataulf.

urbe a obsessa sperarem abscedere posse
agmine carorum magno comitante meorum,
hac tamen hos nostros spe sollicitante paratus,   350
quod scirem imperio gentis cogente Gothorum
invitum regem populis incumbere nostris.
Explorandi igitur studio digressus ab urbe
ad regem intrepidus nullo obsistente tetendi,
laetior ante tamen, primo quam affarer amicum   355
alloquio, gratumque magis fore quem mihi rebar.
Perscrutato autem, ut potui, interius viri voto
praesidium se posse mihi praestare negavit
extra urbem posito, nec tutum iam sibi prodens,
ut visum remeare aliter pateretur ad urbem,   360
ipse nisi mecum mox susciperetur in urbe,
gnarus quippe Gothos rursum mihi dira minari
seque ab ipsorum cupiens absolvere iure.
Obstipui, fateor, pavefactus condicione
proposita et nimio indicti terrore pericli,   365
sed miserante deo, afflictis qui semper ubique
imploratus adest, paulo post mente resumpta
ipse licet trepidus, sed adhuc nutantis amici
consilium audacter studui pro me ipse fovere,
ardua dissuadens, quaé scirem omnino neganda,   370
praestanda quae autem, quam mox temptanda
        perurgens.
    Quae non sero probans vir prudens ipse secutus,
ilico consultis per se primatibus urbis
rem coeptam adcelerans una sub nocte peregit
auxiliante deo, cuius iam munus habebat,   375

the long siege, I might be able to escape from the besieged city together with the large train of my dear ones : and yet this hope induced this attempt of mine, because I knew that 'twas by the constraining will of the Gothic host that the king reluctantly oppressed our folk. So, purposing to investigate, I set out from the city and hastened to the king, no man withstanding me, yet with greater cheer before I addressed my first words to the friend who, I thought, would be more favourable to me. But when I had closely examined as best I might the inwardness of the man's intent, he declared he could not afford me protection if dwelling outside the city, avowing that it was no longer safe for him, having once seen me, to suffer me to return to the city on other terms than that he himself should presently be admitted with me into the city—for he knew that the Goths again meant me mischief, and he himself desired to break free from their influence. I was dumbfounded, I admit, with alarm at the terms proposed and with exceeding fear at the danger threatened, but by the mercy of God who always and everywhere is with them who beseech his aid, I presently regained my faculties and, albeit quaking, boldly set myself to foster in my interest the design of my still wavering friend, discouraging difficult conditions which I knew must be utterly rejected, but strongly pressing for instant attempt to secure the attainable.

These the far-sighted man speedily approved and adopted. Straightway, when he had for himself conferred with the leaders of the city, he so hastened on the business in hand as to complete it in a single night through the help of God, whose

quo nobis populoque suo succurrere posset.
Concurrit pariter cunctis ab sedibus omnis
turba Alanarum armatis sociata maritis.
Prima uxor regis Romanis traditur obses,
adiuncto pariter regis caro quoque nato,   380
reddor et ipse meis pactae inter foedera pacis,
communi tamquam Gothico salutatus ab hoste,
vallanturque urbis pomeria milite Alano,
acceptaque dataque fide certare parato
pro nobis, nuper quos ipse obsederat hostis.   385
Mira urbis facies cuius magna undique muros
turba indiscreti sexus circumdat inermis
subiecta exterius ; muris haerentia nostris
agmina barbarica plaustris vallantur et armis.
Qua se truncatam parte agminis haud mediocri [1] 390
circumiecta videns populantum turba Gothorum,
ilico diffidens tuto se posse morari
hospite intestino subito in sua viscera verso,
nil temptare ausa ulterius properanter abire
sponte sua legit.   Cuius non sero secuti   395
exemplum et nostri, quos diximus, auxiliares
discessere, fidem pacis servare parati
Romanis, quoque ipsos sors oblata tulisset.
Atque ita res [ingens [2]] temere a me coepta benigno
auxilio domini eventu est expleta secundo,   400
erroremque meum deus in nova gaudia vertit
multorum pariter mecum obsidione levata,

[1] Suggested by *Brandes* : mediocris, *BP.*
[2] Suppl. *Brandes.*

bounty he now enjoyed, thereby to help us and his
own people. The whole throng of Alan women
flocks together from all their abodes in company
with their warrior lords.[1] First the king's wife is
delivered to the Romans as a hostage, the king's
favourite son also accompanying her, while I myself
am restored to my friends by one of the articles of
peace, as though I had been rescued from our
common enemy the Goths: the city's boundaries are
fenced round with a bulwark of Alan soldiery pre-
pared for pledges given and received to fight for us
whom they, lately our enemies, had besieged.
Strange was the aspect of the city, whose unmanned
walls were compassed on every side with a great
throng of men and women mixed who lay without;
while, clinging to our walls, barbarian hosts were
fenced in with waggons and armed men. But when
they saw themselves thus shorn of no slight portion
of their host, the encircling hordes of ravaging
Goths, straightway feeling they could not safely
tarry now that their bosom friends were turned to
mortal enemies, ventured no further effort, but chose
of their own accord to retire hurriedly. And not long
after our allies also, above named, followed their
example and departed, though prepared to maintain
loyally the peace made with the Romans wherever
the chance which befell might have carried them.
Thus did a great business, rashly commenced by me,
result in a happy issue through the Lord's kindly
aid, and God turned my misjudgment into fresh
joys in the deliverance of many from the siege

[1] The army besieging Bazas was partly of Goths and
partly of Alans. The latter, headed by Ataulf, went over
to the Roman side and prepared to defend the city against
the Goths.

adcrescunt quae cuncta mihi simul ad referendas,
Christe, tibi grates, quas inpos solvere verbis
parte rependo aliqua semper debere professus.   405
    Sit tamen ista satis super his me esse profatum,
inter barbaricas longo quae tempore gentes
expositus gessi.   Quorum mihi plurima saepe
adversa experto rursum suasere moranti
linquendas patriae sedes quantocius esse—   410
quod fecisse prius fuerat magis utile nobis—
illa ut contento peteremus litora cursu,
pars ubi magna mihi etiamnunc salva manebat
materni census, complures sparsa per urbes
Argivas atque Epiri veterisque novaeque ;   415
per quas non minima numerosis farta colonis
praedia diffusa nec multum dissociata
quamvis profusis dominis nimiumque remissis
praebere expensas potuissent exuberantes.
Sed nec sero mea est proventus vota secutus,   420
ut vel migrare exoptata hinc ad loca possem,
vel mihi pars aliqua ex rebus superesset avitis
inter barbaricas hostili iure rapinas
Romanumque nefas, contra omnia iura licenter
in mea grassatum diverso tempore damna.   425
A quo se exuere admisso nec nomina possunt
cara mihi, maior nostri est quae causa doloris,
cum mihi damna rei damnis cumulentur amoris,
quem scio me fidum primis debere propinquis,
quamlibet offensum, nec fas non reddere duco.   430
Sed bene si sapio, gratanda haec nunc mihi sors est,
quae tibi conplacuit, multo potiora parante
iam te, Christe, mihi, quam cum securior ipse

along with me—all which things increase my debt of thanks to thee, O Christ; which knowing not how to discharge, I repay in some measure in words by declaring my continual indebtedness.

But let it suffice that I have said so much on what I did during the long period when I was exposed amid barbarous peoples. Through them I suffered so numerous reverses as again convinced me, lingering still, that I should leave my country with all speed possible (and to have done so earlier had been more profitable for me), to make my way directly to that land where a large part of my mother's property still remained intact, scattered among full many states of Greece and Epirus the Old and New; for there the extensive farms, well-manned by numerous serfs, though scattered, were not widely separated and even for a prodigal or a careless lord might have furnished means abundant. But not even at this stage did success follow my hope, either to be able to depart hence to the land I longed for, or to recover some part of my grandfather's property dispersed partly through the ravages of barbarians acting by the laws of war and partly through the iniquity of Romans, proceeding wantonly and in defiance of all laws to my hurt at various times. Of this guilt even persons dear to me cannot rid themselves; and 'tis the chief cause of my pain, since upon hurt to my substance is heaped hurt to that affection which I feel I owe inviolate, however slighted, to my nearest kin, and which I deem it sinful not to render. But if I am truly wise, I should now rejoice in this lot of mine which thou, O Christ, didst approve, since thou dost prepare for me far better things now than when,

placatum rebar nostris adsistere votis,
cum mihi laeta domus magnis floreret abundans 435
deliciis, nec pompa minor polleret honoris
instructa obsequiis et turbis fulta clientum.
Quae peritura cito illo me in tempore amasse
nunc piget et tandem sensu meliore senescens
utiliter subtracta mihi cognosco fuisse, 440
amissis opibus terrenis atque caducis
perpetuo potius mansura ut quaerere nossem—
sero quidem, sed nil umquam, deus, est tibi serum,
qui sine fine manens miserandi ponere finem
nescis et ignaris solis succurrere nosti 445
praeveniendo prior multorum vota precantum
et supra quam petimus bona nobis prospiciendo
ambiguisque etiam, quid pro se quisque precetur,
plura petita negas, magis apta his dare paratus,
qui sapiunt tua dona suis praeponere votis. 450
Namque et me moresque meos quanto prior ipso
me melius nosses, in me prodendo probasti,
quem maiora meis audentem viribus ante
prospiciens melius per te mihi consuluisti
conatus inhibendo meos nimis alta petentes, 455
auderem ut monachi perfecto vivere ritu,
cum mihi plena domus caris affectibus esset,
qui sibi servari consuetam indicere curam
posse viderentur, filii, mater socrus, uxor

more free from care, I fancied that thy approval
furthered my hopes; when my house was gay and
prosperous in the great abundance of its luxury;
and when the pageantry of my rank flourished no
less in its setting of deferential crowds and throngs
of supporting clients. That in those days I loved
such things, quickly doomed to perish, I now regret,
and with perception improving with old age I recog-
nise at last that to my profit they were withdrawn
from me, that by the loss of earthly and failing
riches I might learn to seek rather those which will
endure for ever. 'Tis late, indeed, but nought, O
God, is ever late with thee who, continuing without
end, knowest not how to make an end of pity,
and knowest how to aid those who unaided
know not how, by anticipating the prayers of
many ere they ask, and by providing good things
for us beyond what we seek—and who to the mis-
guided [1] also, whatso each one prays for himself,
dost refuse full many a request, though ready to
grant things more expedient to those wise enough
to prefer thy gifts to their own wishes. For how
much better than I myself thou didst know me and
my character thou didst prove in preventing me
when, foreseeing that I was venturing on a task
beyond my strength, thou of thyself didst take
better measure for me by thwarting my designs
which aimed too high in venturing to live after the
perfect pattern of a monk, though my home was full
of dear relatives who seemed to have the right to
claim for themselves continuance of my wonted
care—sons, mother, wife's mother, wife, with

---

[1] *i.e.* those who pray for what they themselves desire, but
which is not for their ultimate good.

cum grege non minimo famularum quippe suarum, 460
quem totum pariter peregrinae exponere terrae
nec ratio aut pietas mens aut religiosa sinebat.
Sed tua magna manus divina et provida virtus
consilio sanctorum cuncta operando peregit,
suadentum mihi tum morem servare vetustum, 465
quem semel invectum maiorum traditione
nunc etiam servans ecclesia nostra teneret;
confessusque igitur, penitenda quae mihi noram,
proposita studui constrictus vivere lege,
non digno fortasse pians commissa labore, 470
sed rectam servare fidem non inscius ipse,
errorum discendo vias per dogmata prava,
quae reprobans sociata aliis nunc respuo culpis.
Post autem, exacta iam ter trieteride quinta,
rite recurrente statuto tempore Pascha 475
ad tua, Christe Deus, altaria sacra reversus
te miserante tua gaudens sacramenta recepi
ante hos ter decies super et bis [1] quattuor annos—
salvo tunc etiam propriae domus ordine, nuper
qui fuerat, linqui et quam iam non posse probarem 480
nec retinere tamen peregrino iugiter esset
possibile adstricto iam censu; quominus autem
rem propriam expeterem, cuius meritumque situmque
anteriore loco iam me exposuisse recordor,
obstabat flecti ad communia commoda coniunx 485
indocilis nimioque metu navigare recusans,
quam nec invitam trahere usquam fas mihi rebar
parque nefas esset subtractis linquere natis.

[1] *Barth* (accepted by Brandes) : his, *BP*.

the considerable company of their attendants : for
to expose all these together to the strangeness
of a foreign land neither reason, nor affection, nor
religious feeling would allow.   But thy mighty
hand divine and foreseeing power directed all things
through the counsel of the saints, who then urged
me to follow the ancient custom which, once intro-
duced by the tradition of our forefathers, our
Church still retained and held.   So when I had con-
fessed such deeds as I knew needed repentance, I
set myself to live under the discipline of a set rule—
not, as it chanced, atoning for my sins by any meet
penance, but, though of myself not without know-
ledge to keep the right faith, by learning the paths
of error through corrupt doctrines,[1] which now I
reject and repudiate along with my other faults.
But afterwards, when now I had passed thrice five
triennia, and Easter duly came round at its appointed
season, to thy holy altar, Christ my God, I returned,
and through thy mercy joyfully received thy Sacra-
ment—thrice ten and twice four years ago.   Then
also still unbroken were the ranks of my own family
which I now found I could not leave and yet could
not continually maintain, now that my foreign in-
come was curtailed.   But from seeking out my own
property—whose value and position, I recall, was set
forth by me in a previous passage—I was hindered
by my wife who stubbornly refused to yield for our
general good, refusing from undue fear to make the
voyage ; and I held it right for me not to tear her
away anywhere against her will, and no less wrong
to leave her, tearing her children from her.

---

[1] Paulinus passed a season in performing some form of
penance.   How he came to lapse into " corrupt doctrine "
(possibly Arianism) is not clear.

Atque ita frustratus spe iam meliore quietis
in rebus propriis post plura adversa fruendae   490
perpetuum exilium diversa sorte dierum
exigo, iam dudum cunctis affectibus expers,
primo socru ac matre, dehinc et coniuge functa,
quae mihi cum fuerit rectis contraria votis
officiente metu, fuit et defuncta dolori,   495
tum subtracta, meae potuisset cum magis esse
apta senectuti iunctae ad solamina vitae;
quae mihi iam derant natis abeuntibus a me,
non equidem paribus studiis nec tempore eodem,
succensis pariter sed libertatis amore,   500
quam sibi maiorem contingere posse putabant
Burdigalae, Gothico quamquam consorte colono.
Quod licet invito me illos voluisse dolerem,
sic compensandum tamen hoc ipsum mihi rebar,
commoda ut absentis praesentum cura iuvaret,   505
fructus quippe rei nostrae, quicumque fuissent,
sponte sua mecum paulatim participando.
Sed cito praereptus iuvenis iam presbyter unus
morte repentina luctum mihi liquit acerbum,
summa autem rerum, tenuit quascumque, mearum   510
tota erepta mihi multis fuit una rapina.
Insuper ipse etiam, velut ad solacia nostra
qui superest, actu simul eventuque sinistro
inter amicitias regis versatus et iras
destituit prope cuncta pari mea commoda sorte.   515

Thus disappointed in my brightening hopes of enjoying repose on my own property after so many misfortunes, I now spend my days in perpetual exile with varying fortunes, long since deprived of all my dear ones. For first my wife's mother and my mother died; then my wife also, who, when she lived, thwarted my natural hopes through the hindrance of her fears, and in her death caused me grief in being reft from me at a time when her life, if continuous with mine, might have been more serviceable in affording my old age consolations which now it lacked, as my sons left me. These went, not with like aims, indeed, nor at the same time; but both alike were fired with the desire for freedom which they thought they could find in greater measure at Bordeaux, albeit in company with Gothic settlers. And though I grieved that their desires thus ran counter to my own, yet I thought that this same thing would so be made up to me that their care while present in Bordeaux would advance the interests of their absent father, namely, by gradually sharing with me of their own will the income of our property, such as it might be.[1] But soon was one — a youth, yet already a priest — hurried off untimely by a sudden death, leaving me bitter sorrow; while all such of my possessions as he held were wholly torn from me by the single act of many robbers. Moreover, he also, who was left as though to console me, ill-starred alike in his course and its consequence, experienced both the king's friendship and his enmity, and after losing almost all my goods came to a like end.

[1] *i.e.* he hoped that his sons living in Bordeaux might be able to recover some of the wreck of his property. Paulinus himself seems to have feared to reside in the city.

Atque ita subtracta spe omni solaciorum,
quae mihi per nostros rebar contingere posse,
cunctaque sero probans a te magis esse petenda,
quae cupimus, deus alme, subest cui summa potestas,
Massiliae demum paulisper consistere legi,   520
urbe quidem in qua plures sancti essent mihi cari,
parva autem census substantia familiaris
nec spes magna novis subitura ex fructibus esset,
non ager instructus propriis cultoribus ullus,
non vineta—quibus solis urbs utitur ipsa   525
omne ad praesidium vitae aliunde parandum—
sed tantum domus urbana vicinus et hortus
atque ad perfugium secreti parvus agellus,
non sine vite quidem vel pomis, sed sine terra
digna coli ; verum exigui iactura laboris   530
suasit et in vacuum culturae inpendere curam
vix plena exesi per iugera quattuor agri
et fundare domum summa in crepidine saxi,
ne quid de spatio terrae minuisse viderer.
Porro autem expensas, vitae quas posceret usus,   535
conductis studui ex agris sperare paratas,
donec plena magis servis mansit domus et dum
maiores melior vires mihi praebuit aetas.
At postquam in peius pariter mutavit utraque
condicio instabilis semper generaliter aevi,   540
paulatim, fateor, curis evictus et annis
exul inops caelebs [caris] facile in nova versus
consilia et varia multum ratione vacillans,
Burdigalam revocare gradum conducere duxi.
Nec tamen effectus nostra est incepta secutus,   545
utilitas cum vota sibi coniuncta iuvaret ;

When thus all hope of that solace, which I thought I might gain through my family, was withdrawn, finding, though late, that all things we desire are rather to be sought of thee, O bounteous God, with whom all power rests, I chose at length to settle awhile at Marseilles, a city where indeed were many saints dear to me, but only a small property, part of my family estate. Here no fresh revenues were like to give rise to great hopes—no tilth tended by appointed labourers, no vineyards (on which alone that city relies to procure from elsewhere every necessary of life), but, as a refuge for my loneliness, only a house in the city with a garden near, and a small plot, not destitute of vines, indeed, and fruit-trees, but without land worth tillage. Yet the outlay of a little toil induced me to lavish pains in tilling the vacant part—scarce four full acres—of my exhausted land, and to build a house upon the crest of the rock, lest I should seem to have reduced the extent of soil available. Further, for the outlay which the needs of life demand, I made it my hope to earn them by renting land, so long as my house remained well stocked with slaves, and while my more active years furnished me with undiminished strength. But afterwards, when my fortunes in a world generally ever variable changed for the worse in both these respects, by degrees, I admit, I was broken down by troubles and by age : so as a wanderer, poor, bereaved of my loved ones, I readily inclined to new designs, and, greatly wavering betwixt various purposes, thought it profitable to return to Bordeaux. Yet my efforts did not attain success ; though expediency seconded my prayers allied with it.

quod mihi firmandae fidei, quantum puto, causa
a te provisum fas est me credere, Christe,
ut, praestare mihi quantum tua gratia posset,
prolixo paulatim usu experiendo probarem,　　　　550
plurima subtracto cum per dispendia censu
perdurare mihi speciem domus et renovatas
saepius expensas te prospiciente viderem.
Pro qua sorte quidem vitae scio me tibi grates
immodicas debere, deus, pro me tamen ipse　　　　555
nescio, si salvo possim gaudere pudore—
sive quod ipse adhuc propriae specie domus utens,
seu quod divitibus contentus cedere natis
omnia quae possunt etiamnunc nostra videri,
expensis patior me sustentari alienis—　　　　560
ni mihi nostra fides quae nil proprium docet esse,
subveniat, tam tuto aliena ut nostra putemus,
quam nos nostra aliis debemus participanda.

Nec tamen hoc ipso vitae me in ordine passus
ambiguum nutare diu, velociter ultro　　　　565
solari es dignatus, deus, nostramque senectam
invalidam variis diverso tempore morbis
iugiter adsuetus blandis palpare medellis,
nunc quoque sic ipsi iuvenascere posse dedisti,
ut, cum iam penitus fructus de rebus avitis　　　　570
sperare ulterius nullos me posse probasses,
cunctaque ipsa etiam, quae iam tenuatus habere
Massiliae potui, amissa iam proprietate
conscripta adstrictus sub condicione tenerem,

---

[1] *i.e.* the house was only his by courtesy.
[2] Yet his sons (ll. 498 ff.) had died previously. Possibly
these are younger sons ignored in the earlier passage.

346

This I may lawfully believe to have been ordained by thee, O Christ, for the strengthening of my faith, as I suppose, that by prolonged experience I might gradually find out how far thy favour could avail me, when, though deprived of means through countless losses, I still saw the semblance[1] of a house always remained to me, and my means ofttimes replenished by thy providence. For this lot, indeed, I know I owe thee boundless thanks, O God ; yet on my own account I know not whether I can rejoice with full self-respect—because, whether in occupying a house in semblance still my own, or in contentedly resigning to my wealthy sons[2] all that can still be thought of as my own, I suffer myself to be supported at others' charges[3]—did not our faith come to my aid, teaching that nothing is our own ; so that we may as surely consider others' goods to be ours, as we are bound to share our own with others.

Yet in this same state of life thou didst not suffer me long to drowse in doubt, but unasked, O God, didst speedily deign to comfort me ; and— ever wont to soothe with gentle remedies my old age weakened at various times with divers sicknesses—now also thou didst enable it to grow young again. For when thou hadst shown I could no longer hope for further profit from my grand-father's property ; and when all that also which in my poverty I was able to hold at Marseilles was retained by me under the terms of a written contract, the freehold now being lost--thou didst raise up for

---

[3] The use of the present tense here suggests that ll. 564 ff. (in which he tells of his improved fortunes) were subsequently added.

emptorem mihi ignotum de gente Gothorum 575
excires, nostri quondam qui iuris agellum
mercari cupiens pretium transmitteret ultro,
haut equidem iustum, verumtamen accipienti
votivum, fateor, possem quo scilicet una
et veteres lapsi census fulcire ruinas 580
et vitare nova cari mihi damna pudoris.
   Quo me donatum praestanti munere gaudens
ecce novas, deus omnipotens, tibi debeo grates,
exuperent quae paene alias cumulentque priores,
quas contestatus tota haec mea pagina praesens 585
continet; et quamquam spatiis prolixior amplis
evagata diu claudi se iam prope poscat,
nostra tamen iugis devotio ponere finem
nescit ad explenda tibi debita munia, Christe,
hoc unum ipse bonum statuens, hoc esse tenendum 590
conscius, hoc toto cupiens adquirere corde,
omnibus usque locis et tempore iugiter omni
te praefando loqui, te [et¹] meminisse silendo.
quo circa et totum tibi me, deus optime, debens
cunctaque quae mea sunt, opus hoc abs te, deus,
   orsus 595
nunc quoque concludens tibi desino teque precatus
saepius attente nunc multo inpensius oro,
ut—quia vita in hac, qua nunc ego dego, senili
ipsa morte magis plura [haut ¹] agnosco timenda,
nec mihi, quid potius cupiam, discernere promptum
   est— 600
quamcumque in partem tua iam sententia vergit,
da, precor, intrepidam contra omnia tristia mentem
constantemque tuae virtutis munere praesta,
ut, qui iam dudum placitis tibi vivo dicatus
legibus et sponsam conor captare salutem, 605

¹ Suppl. *Brandes.*

348

me a purchaser among the Goths who desired to
acquire the small farm, once wholly mine, and of his
own accord sent me a sum, not indeed equitable, yet
nevertheless a godsend, I admit, for me to receive,
since thereby I could at once support the tottering
remnants of my shattered fortune and escape fresh
hurt to my cherished self-respect.

Rejoicing in my enrichment with this exceeding
gift, to thee, Almighty God, I owe fresh thanks,
such as may almost overwhelm and bury all those
preceding, whereof each page of mine holds record.
And although my constant devotion, grown too
lengthy, has o'erspread its wide limits this while
past, and almost calls upon itself to halt; yet it
knows not how to make an end of dwelling on the
gifts I owe to thee, O Christ. This I make my only
good, this I feel must be held fast, this with my
whole heart I long to secure—in all places every-
where and at all times continually, in utterance to
tell of thee, and in silence to remember thee.
Wherefore—owing all myself to thee, O God most
excellent, and all things that are mine—as I began
this work from thee, so in finishing it I end to
thee; and while I have often prayed thee earnestly,
now much more fervently I beseech thee—seeing
that in this decrepit age which I now spend I see
nought more to be feared but death itself, and
cannot readily descry what further I can desire—
whichever way thy will inclines,[1] grant me, I pray,
a heart unflinching in the face of any sorrow, and
make it steadfast by the gift of thy power; that I
who long have lived obedient to the laws approved

---

[1] *i.e.* whether sorrows are or are not to be my lot.

nec vicina magis pro condicione senectae
tempora plus metuam mortis, cui subiacet omnis
aetas, ambiguae nec me discrimine [1] vitae
suspectum exagitent varii formidine casus,
vitari quos posse, deus, te praesule fido,   6
sed, quaecumque manet nostrum sors ultima finem
mitiget hanc spes, Christe, tui conspectus et omnem
discutiat dubium fiducia certa pavorem,
me, vel in hoc proprio mortali corpore dum sum,
esse tuum, cuius sunt omnia, vel resolutum
corporis in quacumque tui me parte futurum.

[1] *Brandes* : discrimina, *B*[1], *P.*

of thee, and seek to win thy promise of salvation,
may not too greatly dread the hour of death—now
nearer by reason of my advanced age, though every
season of life is subject to him.   And at the crisis of
my changeful life may no idle chances—for these, I
trust, may be avoided under thy leadership, O God
—distress me with misdoubtful fears ; but whatever
lot awaits me at my end let hope of beholding thee,
O Christ, assuage it, and let all fearful doubts be
dispelled by the sure confidence that alike while I
am in this mortal body I am thine, since all is
thine, and that when released from it I shall be in
some part of thy body.

INDEX

[NOTE.—Fictitious names are distinguished by an asterisk (*). The abbreviations *Aus.*, *Mt.*, *R.* stand for *Ausonius, Mountain, River*.]

353

INDEX

INDEX

INDEX

357

INDEX

Geryones, I. 201, **369**; II. 43, 55
Gestidius, II. 149
Getae, I. 51, 301
Getic Mars, II. 171
Glabrio, Acilius (grammarian), I. 135, 137
Gladiatorial Shows at Funerals, I. 363
*Glaucias, II. 193
Glaucus, Legend of, I. 245
*Glycera, II. 181
God, I. 15 ff., 365, 369; II. 109, 127, 129, 267, 307 ff. (*passim*)
Gorgons, The, I. 369
Gortyn, I. 247
Goths, Gothic, I. 51, 301; II. 171, 173, 297; pillage Bordeaux, 327, 329, 333, 335, 343, 349
Gracchus, the Elder, II. 257
Graces, The, I. 361; II. 89
Gradivus, I. 51
Gratian (Emperor), taught by Aus., I. ix, xi; dedication of *Epigrams* to, xxxviii; 5, 39, 41; II. 79, 81; as poet-warrior, 169, 171, 219 ff. (*passim*)
Grayling in the Moselle, I. 231
Greece, II. 285, 337 and *passim*.
Greek Rules for drinking, I. 355; — credit, II. 21, 97; — fables, II. 267; — invasion of Rome, 285; —tutors, 315
Gregorius Proculus, I. xxxv, 207, 349, 351
Griphus, The, I. x, xxviii, xxxiv, 353 ff.
Gudgeon in the Moselle, I. 235
Gunes (hero), I. 147

Hades, I. 167
Hadrian, I. 343
Haemus, I. 283
Hamadryad Nymphs, I. 175, 299
Hannibal, Relations with Capua, I. 275; death of, 301; II. 117
Hare, The (constellation), II. 283
Harmonia, I. 211
Harmonius (grammarian), II. 45
Harpies, The, I. 369
Hebromagus (estate of Paulinus of Nola), II. 91, 95, 99, 109
Hecate, I. 361; II. 71
Hector, I. 149, 151, 153

Hecuba, I. 155
Helen, I. 141; origin of, 361; II. 195
Helicon, II. 45
Heliogabalus (Emperor), I. xix, 347
Helle, I. 247
Helvius: *see* Pertinax
Herculanus, Pomponius Maximus (nephew of Aus., grammarian), I. 81, 117
Hercules, taught by Atlas, I. 5; birthday of, 199; 363; II. 201
Herculeus (*sc.* Maximian), Baths of, at Milan, I. 273
Hermaphroditus, II. 199, 213
Hermes Trismegistus, I. 357
*Hermione, II. 211
Herodotus, I. 129; Works of, in library of Aus., II. 31
Herrick, Debt to poem *de Rosis*, II. 271, 281 and note
Hesiod, I. 173, 203 (note); II. 37
Hesperides, Apples of, I. 201
Hesperius (s. of Aus.), I. ix, xix, xxxv, xxxvi, 75, 331, 349; II. 61, 67, 71, 91, 295, 296
Hesperus, I. 239
Hiberus (R. Ebro), II. 141
Hippocratas, I. 303
Hippocrene, II. 45, 91
Hippolytus, Fate of, I. 165; = Virbius, 373; significance of his name, II. 181
Hipponax of Ephesus, II. 283 note
Hippothöus (Trojan War hero), I. 153
Hispalis: *see* Seville
Homer, I. 131, 143; work of Zenodotus and Aristarchus on, 311; II. 43; his scattered verses collected by Zenodotus (*sic*), 45 and note; read in schools, 77; 171, 231; used in schools, 296, 313
Horace, imitated by Aus., I. xxix, 15; 131, 217, 355; read in schools, II. 77
Huns, I. 51; II. 171
Hyacinthus, I. 209
Hyades, II. 43
Hybla, Bees of, II. 115
*Hylas, II. 209, 211
Hylas and the Nymphs, II. 211
Hyperion, I. 241

359

INDEX

INDEX

INDEX

INDEX

INDEX

365

INDEX

366

INDEX

Tribunes, derivation of the title, I. 367

Trinity, The, analogous with the Three Emperors, I. 37; 369

Triptolemus, II. 99

Tritonia (Athene), II. 169

Troilus, I. 151

Trojan War, the, Heroes of, I. 141; length of, II. 55

Tropics, The two, I. 53

Tros, son of Dardanus, I. 301

Trout, I. 231

Troy, I. 149, 151, 153, 155; II. 181

Tully: *see* Cicero

Tuscan Sea, The, II. 141, 311

Twins, The (constellation), I. 201; II. 283

Tydeus, II. 253

Tyndareus, reputed father of Castor, Pollux, and Helen, I. 143; II. 195

Tyrian fabrics, II. 189

Tyrrhenian: *see* Tuscan

Ulysses, I. 121, 131, 143, 147; II. 35, 107; bow of, 107, 231, 313

Urania, II. 281

Urbica, Pomponia (relative by marriage of Aus.), I. 95

Urbicus (grammarian), I. 131

Ursinus (a provincial), II. 47

Ursulus (grammarian), II. 41, 45

Vacuna, II. 53

Valens (Emperor), II. 173, 175; death of, 243

Valentinian I. (Emperor), I. x, 371; II. 173, 261

Valentinian II. (Emperor), I. xi; b rth of, xvii; II. 173

Valentinus, I. 79

Vallebana (unknown), II. 199

Varro (M. Terentius), I. 129, 357; II. 45

Vasconia (Basque country), II. 117, 139

Veneria, Julia, aunt of Aus., I. 93

Venetia, II. 269

Venus (planet), I. 175, 183; (goddess), 205, 213, 215, 241, 291, 299, 381, 393; II. 49, 167, 169, 187,

189; represented as armed at Sparta, 193, 195, 279

Venus' Haven (Port Vendres), II. 15

Veria Liceria, I. 79

Verona, I. 63

Vespasian (Emperor), I. 333, 335, 339; II. 261

Vesta, I. 361; II. 257

Vestal Virgins, II. 55

Vesuvius, I. 241

Victoria, II. 169

Victorinus (one of the "Thirty Tyrants"), I. viii, 65

Victorius (grammarian), I. 133

Vienne (Vienna), I. 63, 277; II. 105

Vincum (Bingen), I. 225

Virbius (= Hippolytus), I. 373

Virgil, I. 131, 133, 149, 207, 209, 267; *Catalepta* of, 307; *Bucolics* of, 309, 371, 387, 393; II. 7; birthday of, 71; read in schools, 77, 121, 296, 299, 313

Virgin, The (constellation), II. 283

Visontio (Besançon), II. 237

Vitellius (Emperor), I. 333, 335, 339

Vivisci (Bituriges, dwelling about Bordeaux), I. 259

Vonones (Parthian King), II. 83

Vossianus, Codex, I. xxxvii.

Vulcan, Festival of, 197, 251; 355, 393

Wain, The (constellation), I. 203

Water-Snake, The (constellation), II. 283

Whale, The (constellation), II. 283

Word of God, The, I. 17, 23, 37

Wordsworth, Wm., *Laodameia* of, I. 211 note

Xenophon, *Cyropaedia* of, II. 257

Xerxes, I. 247, 285

Zaleucus (the Locrian Lawgiver), I. 133

Zenodotus (Homeric critic), I. 119, 311; "collects" the scattered remains of Homer, II. 45

Zodiac, Signs of the, II. 283

*Zoilus, II. 209

Zoilus of Trèves, I. 207

367

Printed in Great Britain by
Richard Clay (The Chaucer Press), Ltd.,
Bungay, Suffolk

THE LOEB CLASSICAL LIBRARY

VOLUMES ALREADY PUBLISHED

Latin Authors

AMMIANUS MARCELLINUS. Translated by J. C. Rolfe. 3 Vols.

APULEIUS: THE GOLDEN ASS (METAMORPHOSES). W. Adlington (1566). Revised by S. Gaselee.

ST. AUGUSTINE: CITY OF GOD. 7 Vols. Vol. I. G. E. McCracken. Vols. II and VII. W. M. Green. Vol. III. D. Wiesen. Vol. IV. P. Levine. Vol. V. E. M. Sanford and W. M. Green. Vol. VI. W. C. Greene.

ST. AUGUSTINE, CONFESSIONS OF. W. Watts (1631). 2 Vols.

ST. AUGUSTINE, SELECT LETTERS. J. H. Baxter.

AUSONIUS. H. G. Evelyn White. 2 Vols.

BEDE. J. E. King. 2 Vols.

BOETHIUS: TRACTS and DE CONSOLATIONE PHILOSOPHIAE. Rev. H. F. Stewart and E. K. Rand. Revised by S. J. Tester.

CAESAR: ALEXANDRIAN, AFRICAN and SPANISH WARS. A. G. Way.

CAESAR: CIVIL WARS. A. G. Peskett.

CAESAR: GALLIC WAR. H. J. Edwards.

CATO: DE RE RUSTICA. VARRO: DE RE RUSTICA. H. B. Ash and W. D. Hooper.

CATULLUS. F. W. Cornish. TIBULLUS. J. D. Postgate. PERVIGILIUM VENERIS. J. W. Mackail.

CELSUS: DE MEDICINA. W. G. Spencer. 3 Vols.

CICERO: BRUTUS and ORATOR. G. L. Hendrickson and H. M. Hubbell.

[CICERO]: AD HERENNIUM. H. Caplan.

CICERO: DE ORATORE, etc. 2 Vols. Vol. I. DE ORATORE, Books I and II. E. W. Sutton and H. Rackham. Vol. II. DE ORATORE, Book III. DE FATO; PARADOXA STOICORUM; DE PARTITIONE ORATORIA. H. Rackham.

CICERO: DE FINIBUS. H. Rackham.

CICERO: DE INVENTIONE, etc. H. M. Hubbell.

CICERO: DE NATURA DEORUM and ACADEMICA. H. Rackham.

CICERO: DE OFFICIIS. Walter Miller.

CICERO: DE REPUBLICA and DE LEGIBUS. Clinton W. Keyes.

2

MINUCIUS FELIX. Cf. TERTULLIAN.

NEPOS CORNELIUS. J. C. Rolfe.

OVID: THE ART OF LOVE and OTHER POEMS. J. H. Mosley. Revised by G. P. Goold.

OVID: FASTI. Sir James G. Frazer

OVID: HEROIDES and AMORES. Grant Showerman. Revised by G. P. Goold

OVID: METAMORPHOSES. F. J. Miller. 2 Vols. Revised by G. P. Goold.

OVID: TRISTIA and EX PONTO. A. L. Wheeler.

PERSIUS. Cf. JUVENAL.

PERVIGILIUM VENERIS. Cf. CATULLUS.

PETRONIUS. M. Heseltine. SENECA: APOCOLOCYNTOSIS. W. H. D. Rouse. Revised by E. H. Warmington.

PHAEDRUS and BABRIUS (Greek). B. E. Perry.

PLAUTUS. Paul Nixon. 5 Vols.

PLINY: LETTERS, PANEGYRICUS. Betty Radice. 2 Vols.

PLINY: NATURAL HISTORY. 10 Vols. Vols. I–V and IX. H. Rackham. VI.–VIII. W. H. S. Jones. X. D. E. Eichholz.

PROPERTIUS. H. E. Butler.

PRUDENTIUS. H. J. Thomson. 2 Vols.

QUINTILIAN. H. E. Butler. 4 Vols.

REMAINS OF OLD LATIN. E. H. Warmington. 4 Vols. Vol. I. (ENNIUS AND CAECILIUS) Vol. II. (LIVIUS, NAEVIUS PACUVIUS, ACCIUS) Vol. III. (LUCILIUS and LAWS OF XII TABLES) Vol. IV. (ARCHAIC INSCRIPTIONS)

RES GESTAE DIVI AUGUSTI. Cf. VELLEIUS PATERCULUS.

SALLUST. J. C. Rolfe.

SCRIPTORES HISTORIAE AUGUSTAE. D. Magie. 3 Vols.

SENECA, THE ELDER: CONTROVERSIAE, SUASORIAE, M. Winterbottom. 2 Vols.

SENECA: APOCOLOCYNTOSIS. Cf. PETRONIUS.

SENECA: EPISTULAE MORALES. R. M. Gummere. 3 Vols.

SENECA: MORAL ESSAYS. J. W. Basore. 3 Vols.

SENECA: TRAGEDIES. F. J. Miller. 2 Vols.

SENECA: NATURALES QUAESTIONES. T. H. Corcoran. 2 Vols.

SIDONIUS: POEMS and LETTERS. W. B. Anderson. 2 Vols.

SILIUS ITALICUS. J. D. Duff. 2 Vols.

STATIUS. J. H. Mozley. 2 Vols.

SUETONIUS. J. C. Rolfe. 2 Vols.

TACITUS: DIALOGUS. Sir Wm. Peterson. AGRICOLA and GERMANIA. Maurice Hutton. Revised by M. Winterbottom, R. M. Ogilvie, E. H. Warmington.

TACITUS: HISTORIES and ANNALS. C. H. Moore and J. Jackson. 4 Vols.

TERENCE. John Sargeaunt. 2 Vols.

TERTULLIAN: APOLOGIA and DE SPECTACULIS. T. R. Glover. MINUCIUS FELIX. G. H. Rendall.

TIBULLUS. Cf. CATULLUS.

VALERIUS FLACCUS. J. H. Mozley.

VARRO: DE LINGUA LATINA. R. G. Kent. 2 Vols.

VELLEIUS PATERCULUS and RES GESTAE DIVI AUGUSTI. F. W. Shipley.

VIRGIL. H. R. Fairclough. 2 Vols.

VITRUVIUS: DE ARCHITECTURA. F. Granger. 2 Vols.

Greek Authors

ACHILLES TATIUS. S. Gaselee.

AELIAN: ON THE NATURE OF ANIMALS. A. F. Scholfield. 3 Vols.

AENEAS TACTICUS. ASCLEPIODOTUS and ONASANDER. The Illinois Greek Club.

AESCHINES. C. D. Adams.

AESCHYLUS. H. Weir Smyth. 2 Vols.

ALCIPHRON, AELIAN, PHILOSTRATUS: LETTERS. A. R. Benner and F. H. Fobes.

ANDOCIDES, ANTIPHON. Cf. MINOR ATTIC ORATORS.

APOLLODORUS. Sir James G. Frazer. 2 Vols.

APOLLONIUS RHODIUS. R. C. Seaton.

APOSTOLIC FATHERS. Kirsopp Lake. 2 Vols.

APPIAN: ROMAN HISTORY. Horace White. 4 Vols.

ARATUS. Cf. CALLIMACHUS.

ARISTIDES: ORATIONS. C. A. Behr. Vol. I.

ARISTOPHANES. Benjamin Bickley Rogers. 3 Vols. Verse trans.

ARISTOTLE: ART OF RHETORIC. J. H. Freese.

ARISTOTLE: ATHENIAN CONSTITUTION, EUDEMIAN ETHICS, VICES AND VIRTUES. H. Rackham.

ARISTOTLE: GENERATION OF ANIMALS. A. L. Peck.

ARISTOTLE: HISTORIA ANIMALIUM. A. L. Peck. Vols. I.–II.

ARISTOTLE: METAPHYSICS. H. Tredennick. 2 Vols.

ARISTOTLE: METEOROLOGICA. H. D. P. Lee.

ARISTOTLE: MINOR WORKS. W. S. Hett. On Colours, On Things Heard, On Physiognomies, On Plants, On Marvellous Things Heard, Mechanical Problems, On Indivisible Lines, On Situations and Names of Winds, On Melissus, Xenophanes, and Gorgias.

ARISTOTLE: NICOMACHEAN ETHICS. H. Rackham.

ARISTOTLE: OECONOMICA and MAGNA MORALIA. G. C. Armstrong (with METAPHYSICS, Vol. II).

ARISTOTLE: ON THE HEAVENS. W. K. C. Guthrie.

ARISTOTLE: ON THE SOUL, PARVA NATURALIA, ON BREATH. W. S. Hett.

ARISTOTLE: CATEGORIES, ON INTERPRETATION, PRIOR ANALYTICS. H. P. Cooke and H. Tredennick.

ARISTOTLE: POSTERIOR ANALYTICS, TOPICS. H. Tredennick and E. S. Forster.

ARISTOTLE: ON SOPHISTICAL REFUTATIONS.
On Coming to be and Passing Away, On the Cosmos. E. S. Forster and D. J. Furley.

ARISTOTLE: PARTS OF ANIMALS. A. L. Peck; MOTION AND PROGRESSION OF ANIMALS. E. S. Forster.

ARISTOTLE: PHYSICS. Rev. P. Wicksteed and F. M. Cornford. 2 Vols.

ARISTOTLE: POETICS and LONGINUS. W. Hamilton Fyfe; DEMETRIUS ON STYLE. W. Rhys Roberts.

ARISTOTLE: POLITICS. H. Rackham.

ARISTOTLE: PROBLEMS. W. S. Hett. 2 Vols.

ARISTOTLE: RHETORICA AD ALEXANDRUM (with PROBLEMS. Vol. II). H. Rackham.

ARRIAN: HISTORY OF ALEXANDER and INDICA. Rev. E. Iliffe Robson. 2 Vols. New version P. Brunt.

ATHENAEUS: DEIPNOSOPHISTAE. C. B. Gulick. 7 Vols.

BABRIUS AND PHAEDRUS (Latin). B. E. Perry.

ST. BASIL: LETTERS. R. J. Deferrari. 4 Vols.

CALLIMACHUS: FRAGMENTS. C. A. Trypanis. MUSAEUS: HERO AND LEANDER. T. Gelzer and C. Whitman.

CALLIMACHUS, Hymns and Epigrams, and LYCOPHRON. A. W. Mair; ARATUS. G. R. Mair.

CLEMENT OF ALEXANDRIA. Rev. G. W. Butterworth.

COLLUTHUS. Cf. OPPIAN.

DAPHNIS AND CHLOE. Thornley's Translation revised by J. M. Edmonds: and PARTHENIUS. S. Gaselee.

DEMOSTHENES I.: OLYNTHIACS, PHILIPPICS and MINOR ORATIONS I.–XVII. AND XX. J. H. Vince.

DEMOSTHENES II.: DE CORONA and DE FALSA LEGATIONE. C. A. Vince and J. H. Vince.

DEMOSTHENES III.: MEIDIAS, ANDROTION, ARISTOCRATES, TIMOCRATES and ARISTOGEITON I. and II. J. H. Vince.

DEMOSTHENES IV.–VI: PRIVATE ORATIONS and IN NEAERAM. A. T. Murray.

DEMOSTHENES VII: FUNERAL SPEECH, EROTIC ESSAY, EXORDIA and LETTERS. N. W. and N. J. DeWitt.

DIO CASSIUS: ROMAN HISTORY. E. Cary. 9 Vols.

Dio Chrysostom. J. W. Cohoon and H. Lamar Crosby. 5 Vols.

Diodorus Siculus. 12 Vols. Vols. I.–VI. C. H. Oldfather. Vol. VII. C. L. Sherman. Vol. VIII. C. B. Welles. Vols. IX. and X. R. M. Geer. Vol. XI. F. Walton. Vol. XII. F. Walton. General Index. R. M. Geer.

Diogenes Laertius. R. D. Hicks. 2 Vols. New Introduction by H. S. Long.

Dionysius of Halicarnassus: Roman Antiquities. Spelman's translation revised by E. Cary. 7 Vols.

Dionysius of Halicarnassus: Critical Essays. S. Usher. 2 Vols. Vol. I.

Epictetus. W. A. Oldfather. 2 Vols.

Euripides. A. S. Way. 4 Vols. Verse trans.

Eusebius: Ecclesiastical History. Kirsopp Lake and J. E. L. Oulton. 2 Vols.

Galen: On the Natural Faculties. A. J. Brock.

Greek Anthology. W. R. Paton. 5 Vols.

Greek Bucolic Poets (Theocritus, Bion, Moschus). J. M. Edmonds.

Greek Elegy and Iambus with the Anacreontea. J. M. Edmonds. 2 Vols.

Greek Lyric. D. A. Campbell. 4 Vols. Vol. I.

Greek Mathematical Works. Ivor Thomas. 2 Vols.

Herodes. Cf. Theophrastus: Characters.

Herodian. C. R. Whittaker. 2 Vols.

Herodotus. A. D. Godley. 4 Vols.

Hesiod and The Homeric Hymns. H. G. Evelyn White.

Hippocrates and the Fragments of Heracleitus. W. H. S. Jones and E. T. Withington. 4 Vols.

Homer: Iliad. A. T. Murray. 2 Vols.

Homer: Odyssey. A. T. Murray. 2 Vols.

Isaeus. E. W. Forster.

Isocrates. George Norlin and LaRue Van Hook. 3 Vols.

[St. John Damascene]: Barlaam and Ioasaph. Rev. G. R. Woodward, Harold Mattingly and D. M. Lang.

Josephus. 10 Vols. Vols. I.–IV. H. Thackeray. Vol. V. H. Thackeray and R. Marcus. Vols. VI.–VII. R. Marcus. Vol. VIII. R. Marcus and Allen Wikgren. Vols. IX.–X. L. H. Feldman.

Julian. Wilmer Cave Wright. 3 Vols.

Libanius. A. F. Norman. 3 Vols. Vols. I.–II.

Lucian. 8 Vols. Vols. I.–V. A. M. Harmon. Vol. VI. K. Kilburn. Vols. VII.–VIII. M. D. Macleod.

Lycophron. Cf. Callimachus.

LYRA GRAECA, J. M. Edmonds. 2 Vols.

LYSIAS. W. R. M. Lamb.

MANETHO. W. G. Waddell.

MARCUS AURELIUS. C. R. Haines.

MENANDER. W. G. Arnott. 3 Vols. Vol. I.

MINOR ATTIC ORATORS (ANTIPHON, ANDOCIDES, LYCURGUS, DEMADES, DINARCHUS, HYPERIDES). K. J. Maidment and J. O. Burtt. 2 Vols.

MUSAEUS: HERO AND LEANDER. Cf. CALLIMACHUS.

NONNOS: DIONYSIACA. W. H. D. Rouse. 3 Vols.

OPPIAN, COLLUTHUS, TRYPHIODORUS. A. W. Mair.

PAPYRI. NON-LITERARY SELECTIONS. A. S. Hunt and C. C. Edgar. 2 Vols. LITERARY SELECTIONS (Poetry). D. L. Page.

PARTHENIUS. Cf. DAPHNIS and CHLOE.

PAUSANIAS: DESCRIPTION OF GREECE. W. H. S. Jones. 4 Vols. and Companion Vol. arranged by R. E. Wycherley.

PHILO. 10 Vols. Vols. I.–V. F. H. Colson and Rev. G. H. Whitaker. Vols. VI.–IX. F. H. Colson. Vol. X. F. H. Colson and the Rev. J. W. Earp.

PHILO: two supplementary Vols. (*Translation only.*) Ralph Marcus.

PHILOSTRATUS: THE LIFE OF APOLLONIUS OF TYANA. F. C. Conybeare. 2 Vols.

PHILOSTRATUS: IMAGINES; CALLISTRATUS: DESCRIPTIONS. A. Fairbanks.

PHILOSTRATUS and EUNAPIUS: LIVES OF THE SOPHISTS. Wilmer Cave Wright.

PINDAR. Sir J. E. Sandys.

PLATO: CHARMIDES, ALCIBIADES, HIPPARCHUS, THE LOVERS, THEAGES, MINOS and EPINOMIS. W. R. M. Lamb.

PLATO: CRATYLUS, PARMENIDES, GREATER HIPPIAS, LESSER HIPPIAS. H. N. Fowler.

PLATO: EUTHYPHRO, APOLOGY, CRITO, PHAEDO, PHAEDRUS, H. N. Fowler.

PLATO: LACHES, PROTAGORAS, MENO, EUTHYDEMUS. W. R. M. Lamb.

PLATO: LAWS. Rev. R. G. Bury. 2 Vols.

PLATO: LYSIS, SYMPOSIUM, GORGIAS. W. R. M. Lamb.

PLATO: Republic. Paul Shorey. 2 Vols.

PLATO: STATESMAN, PHILEBUS. H. N. Fowler; ION. W. R. M. Lamb.

PLATO: THEAETETUS and SOPHIST. H. N. Fowler.

PLATO: TIMAEUS, CRITIAS, CLITOPHO, MENEXENUS, EPISTULAE. Rev. R. G. Bury.

PLOTINUS: A. H. Armstrong. 7 Vols. Vols. I.–V.

PLUTARCH: MORALIA. 16 Vols. Vols I.–V. F. C. Babbitt. Vol. VI. W. C. Helmbold. Vols. VII. and XIV. P. H. De Lacy and B. Einarson. Vol. VIII. P. A. Clement and H. B. Hoffleit. Vol. IX. E. L. Minar, Jr., F. H. Sandbach, W. C. Helmbold. Vol. X. H. N. Fowler. Vol. XI. L. Pearson and F. H. Sandbach. Vol. XII. H. Cherniss and W. C. Helmbold. Vol. XIII 1–2. H. Cherniss. Vol. XV. F. H. Sandbach.

PLUTARCH: THE PARALLEL LIVES. B. Perrin. 11 Vols.

POLYBIUS. W. R. Paton. 6 Vols.

PROCOPIUS. H. B. Dewing. 7 Vols.

PTOLEMY: TETRABIBLOS. F. E. Robbins.

QUINTUS SMYRNAEUS. A. S. Way. Verse trans.

SEXTUS EMPIRICUS. Rev. R. G. Bury. 4 Vols.

SOPHOCLES. F. Storr. 2 Vols. Verse trans.

STRABO: GEOGRAPHY. Horace L. Jones. 8 Vols.

THEOCRITUS. Cf. GREEK BUCOLIC POETS.

THEOPHRASTUS: CHARACTERS. J. M. Edmonds. HERODES, etc. A. D. Knox.

THEOPHRASTUS: ENQUIRY INTO PLANTS. Sir Arthur Hort, Bart. 2 Vols.

THEOPHRASTUS: DE CAUSIS PLANTARUM. G. K. K. Link and B. Einarson. 3 Vols. Vol. I.

THUCYDIDES. C. F. Smith. 4 Vols.

TRYPHIODORUS. Cf. OPPIAN.

XENOPHON: CYROPAEDIA. Walter Miller. 2 Vols.

XENOPHON: HELLENICA. C. L. Brownson. 2 Vols.

XENOPHON: ANABASIS. C. L. Brownson.

XENOPHON: MEMORABILIA AND OECONOMICUS. E. C. Marchant. SYMPOSIUM AND APOLOGY. O. J. Todd.

XENOPHON: SCRIPTA MINORA. E. C. Marchant. CONSTITUTION OF THE ATHENIANS. G. W. Bowersock.